HARBRACE
ESSENTIALS

WITH RESOURCES FOR MULTILINGUAL WRITERS

CHERYL GLENN
The Pennsylvania State University

LORETTA GRAY
Central Washington University

ralia • Brazil • Japan • Korea • Mexico • Singapore • Spain • United Kingdom • United States

Harbrace Essentials with Resources for Multilingual Writers
Cheryl Glenn, Loretta Gray

Senior Publisher: Lyn Uhl

Publisher: Monica Eckman

Acquiring Sponsoring Editor: Kate Derrick

Development Editor: Michell Phifer

Editorial Assistant: Marjorie Cross

Media Editor: Cara Douglass-Graff

Executive Marketing Manager: Stacey Purviance

Marketing Coordinator: Brittany Blais

Marketing Communications Manager: Linda Yip

Content Project Manager: Rosemary Winfield

Art Director: Marissa Falco

Manufacturing Buyer: Betsy Donaghey

Rights Acquisition Specialist: Alexandra Ricciardi

Production Service: Lifland et al., Bookmakers

Text and Cover Designer: Anne Bell Carter

Compositor: PreMediaGlobal

© 2013 Wadsworth, Cengage Learning

ALL RIGHTS RESERVED. No part of this work covered by the copyright herein may be reproduced, transmitted, stored, or used in any form or by any means graphic, electronic, or mechanical, including but not limited to photocopying, recording, scanning, digitizing, taping, Web distribution, information networks, or information storage and retrieval systems, except as permitted under Section 107 or 108 of the 1976 United States Copyright Act, without the prior written permission of the publisher.

> For product information and technology assistance, contact us at **Cengage Learning Customer & Sales Support, 1-800-354-9706**.
>
> For permission to use material from this text or product, submit all requests online at **www.cengage.com/permissions**.
> Further permissions questions can be emailed to **permissionrequest@cengage.com**.

Library of Congress Control Number: 2011943897

ISBN-13: 978-1-133-59078-1

ISBN-10: 1-133-59078-0

Wadsworth
20 Channel Center Street
Boston, MA 02210
USA

Cengage Learning is a leading provider of customized learning solutions with office locations around the globe, including Singapore, the United Kingdom, Australia, Mexico, Brazil and Japan. Locate your local office at **international.cengage.com/region**.

Cengage Learning products are represented in Canada by Nelson Education, Ltd.

For your course and learning solutions, visit **www.cengage.com**.

Purchase any of our products at your local college store or at our preferred online store **www.cengagebrain.com**.

Instructors: Please visit **login.cengage.com** and log in to access instructor-specific resources.

Printed in the United States of America
1 2 3 4 5 6 7 16 15 14 13 12

Contents

Preface xiii

PART 1 GRAMMAR

CHAPTER 1 — Sentence Essentials 2 — se
- **1a** Parts of speech 2
- **1b** Subjects and predicates 11
- **1c** Complements 12
- **1d** Phrases 14
- **1e** Clauses 20

CHAPTER 2 — Sentence Fragments 25 — frag
- **2a** Recognizing sentence fragments 25
- **2b** Phrases as sentence fragments 25
- **2c** Dependent clauses as sentence fragments 27

CHAPTER 3 — Comma Splices and Fused Sentences 29 — cs/fs
- **3a** Locating comma splices and fused sentences 29
- **3b** Revising comma splices and fused sentences 30
- **3c** Divided quotations 33

CHAPTER 4 — Verbs 34

- **4a** Verb forms 34
- **4b** Verb tenses 40
- **4c** Verb tense consistency 44
- **4d** Voice 47
- **4e** Mood 49
- **4f** Subject-verb agreement 51

CHAPTER 5 — Pronouns 57

- **5a** Recognizing pronouns 57
- **5b** Pronoun case 61
- **5c** Pronoun-antecedent agreement 66
- **5d** Clear pronoun reference 69
- **5e** Pronoun consistency 72
- **5f** Use of first-person and second-person pronouns 73

CHAPTER 6 — Modifiers 75

- **6a** Recognizing modifiers 75
- **6b** Comparatives and superlatives 79
- **6c** Double negatives 81
- **6d** Placement of modifiers 82
- **6e** Dangling modifiers 84

PART 2 EFFECTIVE SENTENCES

CHAPTER 7 — Sentence Unity 88

- **7a** Choosing and arranging details 88
- **7b** Revising mixed metaphors 89
- **7c** Revising mixed constructions 89
- **7d** Relating sentence parts 90

Contents

7e	Including necessary words 93	
7f	Completing comparisons 94	
7g	Completing intensifiers 95	

CHAPTER 8 — **Subordination and Coordination 97** — **sub/coor**

- **8a** Using subordination effectively 97
- **8b** Using coordination effectively 98
- **8c** Avoiding faulty or excessive subordination and coordination 100

CHAPTER 9 — **Parallelism 103** — **//**

- **9a** Recognizing parallel elements 103
- **9b** Repeating words and grammatical forms 104
- **9c** Linking two or more sentences 105
- **9d** Using correlative conjunctions 106

CHAPTER 10 — **Emphasis 108** — **emp**

- **10a** Placing words for emphasis 108
- **10b** Using cumulative and periodic sentences 108
- **10c** Ordering ideas from least to most important 109
- **10d** Repeating important words 109
- **10e** Inverting word order 110
- **10f** Using an occasional short sentence 111

CHAPTER 11 — **Variety 113** — **var**

- **11a** Revising sentence length and form 113
- **11b** Varying sentence openings 115
- **11c** Using questions, exclamations, and commands 116

Contents

PART 3 EFFECTIVE LANGUAGE

CHAPTER 12 Good Usage 120 usg
- **12a** Clear style 120
- **12b** Appropriate word choice 121
- **12c** Inclusive language 122

CHAPTER 13 Precise Word Choice 127 wc
- **13a** Accurate and precise word choice 127
- **13b** Clichés and euphemisms 129
- **13c** Idioms and collocations 130
- **13d** Clear definitions 131

CHAPTER 14 Conciseness 133 con
- **14a** Eliminating wordiness and other redundancies 133
- **14b** Using elliptical constructions 135

PART 4 PUNCTUATION

CHAPTER 15 The Comma 138 ,
- **15a** Before a coordinating conjunction linking independent clauses 138
- **15b** After an introductory word or word group 139
- **15c** Separating elements in a series 141
- **15d** With nonessential elements 142
- **15e** With geographical names and items in dates and addresses 145
- **15f** With direct quotations 146
- **15g** Unnecessary or misplaced commas 147

Contents

CHAPTER 16	**The Semicolon and the Colon** 149	
16a	The semicolon 149	;
16b	The colon 151	:

CHAPTER 17	**The Apostrophe** 154	ʼ
17a	Indicating ownership and other relationships 154	
17b	Marking omissions of letters or numbers 158	
17c	Forming certain plurals 158	

CHAPTER 18	**Quotation Marks** 160	" "
18a	Direct quotations 160	
18b	Titles of short works 162	
18c	With other punctuation marks 163	

CHAPTER 19	**The Period and Other Punctuation Marks** 166	
19a	The period 166	.
19b	The question mark 167	?
19c	The exclamation point 167	!
19d	The dash 168	—
19e	Parentheses 169	( )
19f	Square brackets 170	[ ]
19g	Ellipsis points 171	. . .
19h	The slash 173	/

PART 5   MECHANICS

CHAPTER 20	**Spelling, the Spell Checker, and Hyphenation** 176	sp
20a	Spelling and pronunciation 176	

20b	Words that sound alike 177	
20c	Prefixes and suffixes 178	
20d	Confusion of *ei* and *ie* 180	
20e	Hyphens 181	

CHAPTER 21 — **Capitals 183** — *cap*

21a	Proper names 183
21b	Titles and subtitles 184
21c	Beginning a sentence 185
21d	Computer keys, menu items, and icon names 187

CHAPTER 22 — **Italics 188** — *ital*

22a	Titles of works published or produced separately 188
22b	Other uses of italics 189
22c	Words not italicized 190

CHAPTER 23 — **Abbreviations, Acronyms, and Numbers 191** — *ab/ac/n*

23a	Abbreviations with names 191
23b	Addresses in correspondence 192
23c	Acceptable abbreviations in academic and professional writing 192
23d	Acronyms 193
23e	General uses of numbers 194
23f	Special uses of numbers 195

PART 6 WRITING

CHAPTER 24 — **Writing and Reading Rhetorically 198** — *rhet*

24a	Understanding the rhetorical situation 198

Contents

24b	Addressing exigence with a specific purpose 200	
24c	Considering audience 201	
24d	Writing and reading a message within a context 203	

CHAPTER 25 — **Planning and Drafting Essays 204** — pln/dft

25a	Stages of the writing process 204
25b	Focusing a topic into a clearly stated thesis 205
25c	Creating an outline 206
25d	Drafting well-developed paragraphs 207

CHAPTER 26 — **Revising and Editing Essays 209** — rev/ed

26a	Revising for unity and coherence 209
26b	Editing and proofreading 212
26c	Sample final draft 213

CHAPTER 27 — **Using Visuals 217** — vis

27a	Using graphics 217
27b	Using pictures 218

CHAPTER 28 — **Writing Arguments 221** — arg

28a	Determining the purpose of your argument 221
28b	Considering differing viewpoints 222
28c	Distinguishing between fact and opinion 223
28d	Taking a position or making a claim 223
28e	Providing evidence for an effective argument 224

28f	Using the rhetorical appeals to ground your argument 226	
28g	Arranging an effective argument 227	
28h	Sample argument 228	

CHAPTER 29 — Writing in Business 236 — bus

29a	Business letters 237	
29b	Business memos 240	
29c	Résumés 242	
29d	Letters of application 245	

PART 7 — RESEARCH

CHAPTER 30 — Finding Sources in Print, Online, and in the Field 248 — find

30a	Research and the rhetorical situation 248	
30b	Finding books 250	
30c	Finding articles 252	
30d	Finding online sources 253	
30e	Field research 255	

CHAPTER 31 — Evaluating Print and Online Sources 259 — eval

31a	Credibility of authors 259	
31b	Credibility of publishers 261	
31c	Online sources 262	
31d	Relevance and timeliness 262	

CHAPTER 32 — Using Sources Effectively and Responsibly 264 — src

32a	The rhetorical situation and the research paper 264	

32b	Organizing notes 265	
32c	Working bibliography and annotated bibliography 267	
32d	Integrating sources 268	
32e	Avoiding plagiarism 274	
32f	Responding to sources 276	

PART 8 DOCUMENTATION

CHAPTER 33 — MLA Documentation 280 — mla
- **33a** MLA-style in-text citations 280
- **33b** MLA list of works cited 290
- **33c** Sample MLA-style paper 323

CHAPTER 34 — APA Documentation 337 — apa
- **34a** APA-style in-text citations 337
- **34b** APA-style reference list 340
- **34c** Sample APA-style paper 355

CHAPTER 35 — CMS Documentation 366 — cms
- **35a** CMS note and bibliographic forms 366
- **35b** Sample CMS-style paper 379

CHAPTER 36 — CSE Documentation 384 — cse
- **36a** CSE citation-sequence, name-year, and citation-name systems 384
- **36b** Sample CSE-style paper 392

PART 9 ADVICE for MULTILINGUAL WRITERS

CHAPTER 37 — Determiners, Nouns, and Adjectives 398   det/n/adj
- **37a** Determiners and proper nouns 398
- **37b** Determiners and count nouns 399
- **37c** Determiners and noncount nouns 400
- **37d** Determiners and adjectives 403
- **37e** Shifting from nonspecific to specific references 404

CHAPTER 38 — Verbs and Verb Forms 406   v/vf
- **38a** Verb tenses 406
- **38b** Auxiliary verbs 414
- **38c** Prepositional verbs and phrasal verbs 417
- **38d** Participles used as adjectives 419

CHAPTER 39 — Word Order 420   wo
- **39a** Ordering adjectives 420
- **39b** Placing adverbs of frequency 420
- **39c** Placing adverbs and direct objects 421
- **39d** Ordering words within clauses 421

Glossary of Usage 425   gu

Credits 441

Index 443

Preface

Welcome to *Harbrace Essentials with Resources for Multilingual Writers*. Whether you are a high school student, a college student, or a professional, you will find in this book the practical information and strategies you need to make your writing voice heard. If you are like many of our students and colleagues, you want a portable handbook that provides answers to all your questions about writing—a small book you can carry with you in your purse, briefcase, or backpack. We have therefore created a concise handbook that includes only essential topics and provides the information you need at your fingertips.

What are the essentials? When we ask this question of students and composition instructors, they tell us they want information on grammar, style, punctuation, and mechanics, as well as strategies for writing paragraphs and essays, conducting research, and documenting sources. This response is reflected in the contents of this handbook:

Part 1 Grammar

Part 2 Effective Sentences

Part 3 Effective Language

Part 4 Punctuation

Part 5 Mechanics

Part 6 Writing

Part 7 Research

Part 8 Documentation

Part 9 Advice for Multilingual Writers

You will find samples of student writing throughout *Harbrace Essentials with Resources for Multilingual Writers*. Full papers are presented and discussed in chapters 26, 28, 33, and 34. It is our hope that wherever you are in the writing process, you will be able to access the information you need quickly and easily.

Here are a few suggestions for using this book efficiently:

- **Brief Table of Contents.** If you have a topic in mind, such as writing an argument or using commas correctly, check the contents list inside the front cover of this book.

- **Index.** You can also find information quickly by consulting the index at the back of the book. There you will find not only chapter and section numbers but page numbers as well.

- **MLA, APA, CMS, and CSE Directories.** If you have a specific question about citing a source you have used or listing the source in a bibliography, use one of these style-specific directories. The MLA section is marked by a tab for quick access.

- **Resources for Multilingual Writers.** If English is not your primary language, you will find the topics covered in chapters 37, 38, and 39 of special interest. These chapters cover grammar topics that pose challenges for many multilingual writers. Chapter 37, "Determiners, Nouns, and Adjectives," can help you decide when (and when not) to use determiners (such as articles) before nouns and adjectives. Chapter 38, "Verbs and Verb Forms," provides detailed information on verb tenses, modal auxiliaries, phrasal and prepositional verbs, and participles used as adjectives. Chapter 39, "Word Order," focuses on the ordering of adverbs and adjectives as well as on word order in embedded questions and in adjectival clauses. To help you find information when you need it, these chapters highlight important facts that you can refer to easily as you write or revise your writing.

- **Revision Symbols.** Inside the back cover of the book is a list of revision symbols. If you are taking a writing course and receive feedback that includes these symbols, you can look at this list to find the sections of the book where pertinent guidelines or strategies are discussed.

- **Glossary of Usage.** This glossary includes definitions of words that are commonly confused or misused (such as *accept* and *except*). It is organized like a dictionary, so you just look up a word whose usage you are uncertain about and find not only common meanings for the word but sample sentences as well.

We believe that *Harbrace Essentials with Resources for Multilingual Writers* will help you answer any question you have about writing. However, if you have suggestions for improving the next edition or if we can assist you in any way, don't hesitate to write to us c/o Cengage Learning, English Editorial, 20 Channel Center Street, Boston, MA 02210.

Cheryl Glenn
Loretta Gray
December 2011

Teaching and Learning Resources

Enhanced InSite™ for *Harbrace Essentials with Resources for Multilingual Writers*

Printed Access Card (1 semester): 978-1-133-59522-9
Instant Access Code (1 semester): 978-1-133-59526-7
Printed Access Card (2 semesters): 978-1-133-59529-8
Instant Access Code (2 semesters): 978-1-133-59530-4

From a single, easy-to-navigate site, you and your students can manage the flow of papers online, check for originality, and conduct peer reviews. Students can access a multimedia eBook with text-specific workbook, private tutoring options, and resources for writers that include anti-plagiarism tutorials and downloadable grammar podcasts. **Enhanced InSite™** provides the tools and resources you and your students need *plus* the training and support you want. Learn more at **www.cengage.com/insite**. *(Access card/code is required)*

Interactive eBook

Printed Access Card: 978-1-133-59517-5
Instant Access Code: 978-1-133-59515-1

Harbrace Essentials with Resources for Multilingual Writers is available as a multimedia eBook! Now students can do all of their reading online or use the eBook as a handy reference while they're completing other coursework. The eBook includes the full text of the print version with interactive exercises, an integrated text-specific workbook, user-friendly navigation, search, and highlighting tools, and links to videos that enhance the handbook content. *(Access card/code is required)*

Online College Workbook

A great companion to the handbook, the **Online College Workbook** covers grammar, punctuation, usage, style, and writing. Also included are exercises with clear examples and explanations that supplement the exercises found in the handbook. The workbook is available as part of the **Interactive**

eBook (see above) or as a password-protected, downloadable PDF for instructors at the companion Website. The **Answer Key** is in the **Online Instructor's Resource Manual.**

Online Instructor's Resource Manual
ISBN: 978-1-133-59398-0
Available for easy download at the companion Website, the password-protected **Online Instructor's Resource Manual** is designed to provide maximum flexibility in planning and customizing a course. Materials include a variety of pedagogical questions (and possible solutions) to use when teaching a course with this handbook, sample syllabi with possible assignments for a semester-long course and for a quarter-long course, sample in-class collaborative learning activities, technology-oriented activities, and critical thinking and writing activities.

Companion Website for *Harbrace Essentials with Resources for Multilingual Writers*
www.cengage.com/english/glenn
ISBN: 978-1-133-59399-7
This open-access site contains an extensive library of interactive exercises and animations that cover grammar, diction, mechanics, punctuation, and research and writing concepts. It also includes a complete library of student papers and a section on avoiding plagiarism.

Additional Resources

Merriam-Webster's Collegiate® Dictionary, **11th Edition**
Casebound: 978-0-8777-9809-5   *Not available separately*

Merriam-Webster's Dictionary, **2nd Edition**
Paperbound: 978-0-8777-9930-6   *Not available separately*

Merriam-Webster's Dictionary/Thesaurus
Paperbound: 978-0-8777-9851-4   *Not available separately*

Acknowledgments

We would like to thank our colleagues who reviewed this handbook during the course of its development. Their astute comments and thoughtful suggestions helped shape this first edition.

Susan Achziger, *Community College of Aurora*; William Allegrezza, *Indiana University Northwest*; Chris Allen and Kristin Gardner, *Piedmont Technical College*; Andrew Andermatt, *Clinton Community College*; Heidi Anderson and Susan Perala-Dewey, *University of Minnesota Duluth*; Martha Bachman, *Camden County College*; Ned Bachus and Joseph Kenyon, *Community College of Philadelphia*; Anne Balay, *Indiana University Northwest*; Joy Barta, *California State University–San Bernardino*; Ann Bliss, *University of California–Merced*; Christel Broady, *Georgetown College*; Susan Butterworth and Timothy Quigley, *Salem State College*; Anthony Cavaluzzi, *Adirondack Community College*; Cindy Cochran, *Illinois College*; Anita Cook, *Bridgewater College*; Patricia Cullinan, *Truckee Meadows Community College*; Susan Dalton, *Alamance Community College*; Joshua Dickinson, *Jefferson Community College*; Clark Draney, *College of Southern Idaho*; Jeannine Edwards, *University of Memphis*; Tahmineh Entessar, *Webster University*; Daniela Falco and Patricia Taylor, *University of Connecticut*; Eugene Flinn and Patricia Flinn, *New Jersey City University*; Jennifer Garcia, *Ventura College*; Susan Garrett, *Goucher College*; Marivel Gonzales-Hernandez and Sara Kaplan, *Del Mar College*; Carl Herzig, *St. Ambrose University*; Monica Hogan, *Johnson County Community College*; Martha Holder, *Wytheville Community College*; Michelle Holt, *University of Montana–Helena*; Nancy Hull, *Calvin College*; Brian Jackson and Brett McInelly, *Brigham Young University*; Geri Jacobs, *Jackson Community College*; Peter Jacoby, *San Diego Mesa College*; Joseph Justice, *South Plains College*; Christy Kinnion, *Wake Technical Community College*; Edis Kittrell,

Montana State University–Bozeman; Patti Kurtz, *Minot State University*; Angela Laflen, *Marist College*; Jeanette Lukowski, *Bemidji State University*; Kara Lybarger-Monson, *Moorpark College*; Christopher Manley, *University of Notre Dame*; Kevin McKelvey, *University of Indianapolis*; Timothy Messick, *Mohawk Valley Community College*; Kevin Miller, *Emerson College*; Robert Mellin, *Purdue University–North Central*; Edwin Miner, *Utah Valley University*; Lyle Morgan, *Pittsburg State University*; Susana Morris, *Auburn University*; David Mulry, *Schreiner University*; Joanna Murray, *Heald College*; Dana Nkana, *Illinois Central College*; Karen O'Donnell, *Finger Lakes Community College*; Dave Page, *Inver Hills Community College*; Callie Palmer, *Linn Benton Community College*; Twila Papay, *Rollins College*; Marjorie Pitts, *Ohio Northern University*; Bridget Pool, *Northern Virginia Community College*; Cheryl Renee, *Brevard Community College*; Jennifer Richardson, *State University of New York–Potsdam*; Heather Rodgers, *Saint Charles Community College*; Anne Schmit, *North Platte Community College*; Stacy Waddoups, *Utah Valley University*; Mary Williams, *Midland College*; Robert Williams, *Grossmont College*; and Paul Wise, *University of Toledo*.

GRAMMAR

CHAPTER 1
Sentence Essentials 2

- 1a Parts of speech 2
- 1b Subjects and predicates 11
- 1c Complements 12
- 1d Phrases 14
- 1e Clauses 20

CHAPTER 2
Sentence Fragments 25

- 2a Recognizing sentence fragments 25
- 2b Phrases as sentence fragments 25
- 2c Dependent clauses as sentence fragments 27

CHAPTER 3
Comma Splices and Fused Sentences 29

- 3a Locating comma splices and fused sentences 29
- 3b Revising comma splices and fused sentences 30
- 3c Divided quotations 33

CHAPTER 4
Verbs 34

- 4a Verb forms 34
- 4b Verb tenses 40
- 4c Verb tense consistency 44
- 4d Voice 47
- 4e Mood 49
- 4f Subject-verb agreement 51

CHAPTER 5
Pronouns 57

- 5a Recognizing pronouns 57
- 5b Pronoun case 61
- 5c Pronoun-antecedent agreement 66
- 5d Clear pronoun reference 69
- 5e Pronoun consistency 72
- 5f Use of first-person and second-person pronouns 73

CHAPTER 6
Modifiers 75

- 6a Recognizing modifiers 75
- 6b Comparatives and superlatives 79
- 6c Double negatives 81
- 6d Placement of modifiers 82
- 6e Dangling modifiers 85

Sentence Essentials

The second you decide to write, you are making a decision. You will make many more before you lift your hands from the keyboard and say, "Finished." Whether you are choosing a word, connecting thoughts, or crafting an essay, you will find it easier to make decisions if you have a clear purpose in mind. The purposeful use of language is called **rhetoric.** Throughout this book, you will be encouraged to *think rhetorically*—to consider how to achieve your purpose with a given audience and within a specific context. This chapter covers concepts of grammar that will help you write clear, convincing sentences.

1a Parts of speech

When you look up a word in the dictionary, you will often find it followed by one or more of these labels: *adj., adv., conj., interj., n., prep., pron.,* and *v.* (or *vb.*). These are the abbreviations for the traditional eight parts of speech: *adjective, adverb, conjunction, interjection, noun, preposition, pronoun,* and *verb*.

(1) Verbs

Verbs that indicate action (*walk, drive, study*) are called **action verbs.** Verbs that express being or experiencing are called **linking verbs;** they include *be, seem,* and *become* and the sensory verbs *look, taste, smell, feel,* and *sound*. Both action verbs and linking verbs are frequently accompanied by **auxiliary** or **helping verbs** that add shades of meaning, such as information about time (*will* study this afternoon), ability (*can* study), or obligation (*must* study).

THINKING RHETORICALLY

VERBS

Decide which of the following sentences evokes a clearer image:

The team captain **was** absolutely ecstatic.

Grinning broadly, the team captain **shot** both her arms into the air.

You probably chose the sentence with the action verb *shot* rather than the sentence with *was*. Most writers avoid using the verb *be* in any of its forms (*am, is, are, was, were,* or *been*) when their goal is vibrant imagery. Instead, they use vivid action verbs.

(2) Nouns

Nouns usually name people, places, things, and ideas. **Proper nouns** are specific names: *Bill Gates, Redmond, Microsoft Corporation*. **Common nouns** refer to any member of a class or category: *person, city, company.* There are three types of common nouns.

- **Count nouns** refer to people, places, things, and ideas that can be counted. They have singular and plural forms: *boy, boys; park, parks; car, cars; concept, concepts.*
- **Noncount nouns** refer to things or ideas that cannot be counted: *furniture, information.*
- **Collective nouns** are nouns that can be either singular or plural, depending on the context: *The **committee** published its report* [singular]. *The **committee** disagree about their duties* [plural].

THINKING RHETORICALLY

NOUNS

Nouns like *entertainment* and *nutrition* that refer to concepts are called **abstract nouns.** In contrast, nouns like *guitar* and *apple* that refer to things perceivable by the senses are called **concrete nouns.** When your rhetorical situation calls for the use of abstractions, balance them with tangible details conveyed through concrete nouns.

(3) Pronouns

Most pronouns (*it, he, she, they,* and many others) replace antecedents—nouns that have already been mentioned.

Dan thinks **he** will have the report done by Friday.

An antecedent may also be a noun and the words modifying it.

My parents bought the cheap, decrepit house because they thought **it** had charm.

The pronouns in the preceding examples are **personal pronouns.** For a discussion of other types of pronouns, see chapter 5.

(4) Adjectives

Adjectives most commonly modify nouns: *spicy* food, *special* price. Sometimes they modify pronouns: *blue* ones, anyone *thin*. Adjectives usually answer one of these questions: Which one? What kind of . . . ? How many? What color or size or shape (and so on)? Although adjectives usually precede the nouns they modify, they occasionally follow them: *enough* time, time *enough*. Adjectives may also follow linking verbs such as *be, seem,* and *become*:

The moon is **full** tonight.   He seems **shy.**

Articles are a subclass of adjectives because, like adjectives, they are used before nouns. There are three articles: *a, an,* and *the*. The article *a* is used before a consonant sound (**a** yard, **a** university, **a** VIP); *an* is used before a vowel sound (**an** apple, **an** hour, **an** NFL team).

MULTILINGUAL WRITERS

ARTICLE USAGE

English has two types of articles: indefinite and definite. The **indefinite articles** *a* and *an* indicate that a singular noun is used in a general way.

- Use an indefinite article when you introduce a singular noun for the first time.

  Pluto is **a** dwarf planet.

- When you are defining a word, use an indefinite article.

  A planet is a celestial body orbiting a star such as our sun.

The **definite article,** *the,* is used before a noun that has already been introduced or when a reference is obvious.

- Once a noun has been introduced, use the definite article to refer to it a second time.

  Scientists distinguish between planets and dwarf planets. One of **the** dwarf planets in our solar system is Pluto.

- Subsequent mention does not always include exact repetition of a noun. However, the noun chosen must be close in meaning to a word already introduced.

  Scientists are not sure how to classify some celestial bodies. **The** classification of Pluto proved to be controversial.

- Use the definite article before a noun that everyone in the audience considers unique, such as *moon, universe,* and *sky.*

  The moon is full tonight.

(5) Adverbs

Adverbs most frequently modify verbs. They provide information about time, manner, place, and frequency, thus answering one of these questions: When? How? Where? How often?

The conference <u>starts</u> **tomorrow.** [time]

I **rapidly** <u>calculated</u> the cost. [manner]

We <u>met</u> **here.** [place]

They **often** <u>work</u> late on Thursdays. [frequency]

Adverbs that modify verbs can often move from one position in a sentence to another.

He **carefully** removed the radio collar.

He removed the radio collar **carefully.**

Adverbs also modify adjectives and other adverbs by intensifying or otherwise qualifying the meanings of those words.

I was **extremely** <u>curious</u>. [modifying an adjective]

The team played **surprisingly** <u>well</u>. [modifying an adverb]

THINKING RHETORICALLY

ADVERBS

What do the adverbs add to the following sentences?

The scientist **delicately** places the slide under the microscope.
"You're late," he whispered **vehemently.**
She is **wistfully** hopeful.

Adverbs can help you portray an action, indicate how someone is speaking, and add detail to a description.

(6) Prepositions

A **preposition** is a word that combines with a noun and any of its modifiers to provide additional detail—often answering one of these questions: Where? When?

> <u>**In** the early afternoon</u>, we walked <u>**through** our old neighborhood</u>. [answers the questions *When?* and *Where?*]

A preposition may also combine with a pronoun.

> We walked **through** it.

A grammar rule that has caused much controversy over the years is the one that advises against ending a sentence with a preposition. Most professional writers now follow this rule only when they adopt a formal tone. If their rhetorical situation calls for an informal tone, they will not hesitate to place a preposition at the end of a sentence.

> He found friends **on** whom he could depend. [formal]
>
> He found friends he could depend **on**. [informal]

SOME COMMON PREPOSITIONS				
about	behind	for	of	to
above	between	from	on	toward
after	by	in	out	under
as	despite	into	past	until
at	during	like	since	up
before	except	near	through	with

Phrasal prepositions consist of more than one word.

Except for the last day, it was a wonderful trip.

SOME COMMON PHRASAL PREPOSITIONS

according to	due to	in spite of
as for	except for	instead of
because of	in addition to	with regard to

(7) Conjunctions

Conjunctions are connectors; they fall into four categories: coordinating, correlative, subordinating, and adverbial. A **coordinating conjunction** connects similar words or groups of words; that is, it generally links a word to a word, a phrase to a phrase, or a clause to a clause. There are seven coordinating conjunctions. Use the made-up word *fanboys* to help you remember them.

F	A	N	B	O	Y	S
for	and	nor	but	or	yet	so

tired **yet** excited [*Yet* joins two words and signals contrast.]

in the boat **or** on the pier [*Or* joins two phrases and marks them as alternatives.]

We did not share a language, **but** somehow we communicated. [*But* joins two independent clauses and signals contrast.]

In the example sentence above, *but* links two independent clauses and thus is preceded by a comma. A coordinating conjunction such as *but* may also link independent clauses that stand alone as sentences.

The momentum in the direction of globalization seems too powerful to buck, the economic logic unmatchable. **But** in a region where jobs are draining away, and where an ethic of self-reliance remains a dim, vestigial, but honored memory, it seems at least an outside possibility.   —BILL MCKIBBEN, "Small World"

A **correlative conjunction** (or **correlative**) consists of two parts. The most common correlatives are *both . . . and, either . . . or, neither . . . nor,* and *not only . . . but also.*

Not only did they run ten miles, **but** they **also** swam twenty laps. [*Not only . . . but also* joins two independent clauses and signals addition.]

Generally, a correlative conjunction links similar structures. The following sentence has been revised because the correlative conjunction was linking a phrase to a clause.

Not only ~~saving~~ *did he save* the lives of the accident victims, **but** he **also** prevented many spinal injuries.

A **subordinating conjunction** introduces a dependent clause. It also carries a specific meaning; for example, it may indicate cause, concession, condition, purpose, or time. A dependent clause that begins a sentence is followed by a comma.

Unless the project receives funding, the research will stop. [*Unless* signals a condition.]

She studied Spanish **when** she worked in Costa Rica. [*When* signals time.]

SUBORDINATING CONJUNCTIONS

after	before	once	unless
although	even if	since	until
as if	even though	so that	when
as though	if	than	whether
because	in that	though	while

Adverbial conjunctions—such as *however, nevertheless, then,* and *therefore*—link independent clauses. These conjunctions, also called **conjunctive adverbs,** signal relationships such as cause, condition, and contrast. Adverbial conjunctions are set off by commas. An independent clause preceding an adverbial conjunction may end in a semicolon or a period.

The senator thought the plan was reasonable; **however,** the voters did not.

The senator thought the plan was reasonable. **However,** the voters did not.

The senator thought the plan was reasonable. The voters, **however,** did not.

The senator thought the plan was reasonable. The voters did not, **however.**

ADVERBIAL CONJUNCTIONS

also	indeed	moreover	still
finally	instead	nevertheless	then
furthermore	likewise	nonetheless	therefore
however	meanwhile	otherwise	thus

(8) Interjections

Interjections most commonly express an emotion such as surprise or dread. Interjections that come before a sentence end in a period or an exclamation point.

Oh. Now I understand.

Wow! Your design is astounding.

Interjections that begin or interrupt a sentence are set off by commas.

Hey, what are you doing?

The solution, **alas,** was not as simple as I had hoped it would be.

EXERCISE 1

Identify the part of speech for each word in the sentences below.

1. The hike to Lake Ann was short but quite challenging.
2. Neither Lee nor I expected trouble; nonetheless, we packed gear for emergencies.
3. After we unpacked at our campsite, we swam slowly across the lake.

1b Subjects and predicates

A sentence consists of two parts:

SUBJECT + PREDICATE

The **subject** is generally someone or something that either performs an action or is described. The **predicate** expresses the action initiated by the subject or gives information about the subject.

The <u>landlord</u> + <u>renovated</u> the apartment.
[The subject performs an action; the predicate expresses the action.]

<u>They</u> + <u>had sounded</u> reasonable.
[The subject is described; the predicate gives information about the subject.]

The central components of the subject and the predicate are often called the **simple subject** (the main noun or pronoun) and the **simple predicate** (the main verb and any auxiliary verbs). They are underlined in the examples above.

Compound subjects and **compound predicates** include a connecting word (conjunction) such as *and, or,* or *but*.

The Republicans **and** the Democrats are debating this issue. [compound subject]

The candidate stated his views on abortion **but** did not discuss stem-cell research. [compound predicate]

1c Complements

Complements are parts of the predicate required by the verb to make a sentence complete. A complement is generally a pronoun, a noun, or a noun with modifiers.

The chair of the committee introduced
- **her.** [pronoun]
- **Sylvia Holbrook.** [noun]
- **the new member.** [noun with modifiers]

There are four different complements: direct objects, indirect objects, subject complements, and object complements.

The **direct object** either receives the action of the verb or shows the result of the action.

I. M. Pei designed **the East Building of the National Gallery.**

Steve McQueen invented **the bucket seat** in 1960.

Indirect objects typically name the person(s) receiving or benefiting from the action indicated by the verb. Verbs that often take indirect objects include *buy, give, lend, sell, send,* and *write*.

The supervisor gave **the new employees** computers.

[*To whom* were the computers given?]

She wrote **them** recommendation letters.

[*For whom* were the recommendation letters written?]

The **subject complement** follows a linking verb. The most common linking verb is *be* (*am, is, are, was, were, been*). Other linking verbs are *become, seem,* and *appear* and the sensory verbs *feel, look, smell, sound,* and *taste*. A subject complement can be a pronoun, a noun, or a noun with modifiers. It can also be an adjective.

The winner was
- **you.** [pronoun]
- **Harry Solano.** [noun]
- **the <u>person</u> with the highest score.** [noun with modifiers]
- **ecstatic.** [adjective]

The **object complement** helps complete the meaning of a verb such as *call, elect, make, name,* or *paint*. The object complement can be a noun or an adjective, along with any modifiers.

Reporters called the rookie **the best <u>player</u>.** [noun with modifiers]

The strike left the fans **somewhat <u>disappointed</u>.** [adjective with modifier]

EXERCISE 2

Identify the subject and the predicate in each sentence. Then, looking at just the predicate, identify the type of complement the sentence contains.

1. Octopuses and their relatives have been living in our oceans for millions of years.
2. They can change color or shape.
3. These shape-changers are often frightening.
4. The blue-ringed octopus can give an unsuspecting diver an unpleasant surprise.
5. Researchers consider the poison of the blue-ringed octopus one of the deadliest in the world.

1d Phrases

A **phrase** is a sequence of grammatically related words without a subject, a predicate, or both. A phrase is categorized according to its most important word.

(1) Noun phrases

A noun phrase consists of a main noun and its modifiers. It can serve as a subject or as a complement. It can also be the object of a preposition such as *in, of, on, at,* or *to*.

The heavy frost killed **many fruit trees.** [subject and direct object]

My cousin is **an organic farmer.** [subject and subject complement]

His farm is in **eastern Oregon.** [subject and object of the preposition *in*]

MULTILINGUAL WRITERS

NUMBER AGREEMENT IN NOUN PHRASES

Some words must agree in number with the nouns they precede. The words *a, an, this,* and *that* are used before singular nouns; *some, few, these, those,* and *many* are used before plural nouns:

an/that opportunity [singular noun]
some/few/those opportunities [plural noun]

The words *less* and *much* precede nouns representing abstract concepts or masses that cannot be counted (noncount nouns):

less freedom, **much** water [noncount nouns]

(2) Verb phrases

A verb is essential to the predicate of a sentence. It generally expresses action or a state of being. Besides a main verb, a verb phrase includes one or more **auxiliary verbs,** sometimes called *helping verbs,* such as *be, have, do, will,* and *should.*

The passengers **have deplaned.** [auxiliary verb + main verb]

(3) Verbal phrases

A **verbal phrase** differs from a verb phrase in that the verb form in a verbal phrase serves as a noun or a modifier rather than as a verb.

He was **reading** the story aloud. [*Reading* is part of the verb phrase *was reading.*]

Reading is fundamental to academic success. [*Reading* serves as a noun. COMPARE: **It** is fundamental to academic success.]

The student **reading** aloud is an education major. [*Reading aloud* modifies *the student.*]

Verbal phrases are divided into three types: gerund phrases, participial phrases, and infinitive phrases.

Gerund phrases include a verb form ending in *-ing*. A gerund phrase serves as a noun, usually functioning as the subject or object in a sentence.

Writing a bestseller was her only goal. [subject]

My neighbor enjoys **writing about distant places.** [object]

Because gerund phrases act as nouns, pronouns can replace them.

That was her only goal.   My neighbor enjoys **it.**

THINKING RHETORICALLY

GERUNDS

What is the difference between the following sentences?

> They bundle products together, which often results in higher consumer costs.
>
> Bundling products together often results in higher consumer costs.

In the first sentence, the actor, *they,* is the focus. In the second sentence, the action of the gerund phrase, *bundling products together,* is the focus. As you revise, ask yourself whether you want to emphasize actors or actions.

Participial phrases include either a present participle (a verb form ending in *-ing*) or a past participle (a verb form ending in *-ed* for regular verbs or another form for irregular verbs). Participial phrases function as modifiers.

Fearing a drought, the farmers used less irrigation water.

All the farmers in the area, **plagued by drought,** used less irrigation water.

Farmers conserved water, **fearing a drought in late summer.**

Remember that gerund and participial phrases differ in function. A gerund phrase functions as a noun; a participial phrase functions as a modifier.

Working together can spur creativity. [gerund phrase]

Working together, the students designed their own software. [participial phrase]

A present participle (*-ing* form) cannot function alone as the main verb in a sentence. It must be accompanied by a form of *be* (*am, is, are, was,* or *were*).

They ^are **thinking** about the future.

> ### THINKING RHETORICALLY
> #### PARTICIPIAL PHRASES
>
> If some of your sentences sound monotonous or choppy, try combining them by using participial phrases.
>
> > Fans crowded along the city streets. They were celebrating their team's first state championship.
> >
> > REVISED
> >
> > **Crowded along the city streets,** fans celebrated their team's first state championship.

Infinitive phrases serve as nouns or as modifiers. The form of the infinitive is distinct—the infinitive marker *to* followed by the base form of the verb.

The company intends **to hire twenty new employees.** [noun]

We discussed his plan **to use a new packing process.** [modifier of the noun *plan*]

To attract customers, the company changed its advertising strategy. [modifier of the verb *changed*]

Some instructors advise against putting words between the infinitive marker *to* and the base form of the verb.

^Under the circumstances, the The jury was unable to, ~~under the circumstances,~~ convict the defendant.

This is good advice to remember if the intervening words create a cumbersome sentence. However, most writers today recognize that a single word splitting an infinitive can provide emphasis.

He did not expect to actually publish his work.

MULTILINGUAL WRITERS

VERBS FOLLOWED BY GERUNDS AND/OR INFINITIVES

Some verbs in English can be followed by a gerund, some can be followed by an infinitive, and some can be followed by either.

Verbs Followed by a Gerund

admit consider dislike finish avoid deny enjoy

Example: She **enjoys playing** the piano.

Verbs Followed by an Infinitive

agree decide deserve hope need plan promise seem

Example: She **promised to play** the piano for us.

Verbs Followed by Either a Gerund or an Infinitive

begin continue like prefer remember stop try

Examples: She **likes to play** the piano. She **likes playing** the piano.

Although either a gerund phrase or an infinitive phrase can follow these verbs, the resulting sentences may differ in meaning.

We **stopped discussing** the plan. [The discussion has ended.]

We **stopped to discuss** the plan. [The discussion has not yet started.]

(4) Prepositional phrases

Prepositional phrases provide information about time, place, cause, manner, and so on. They can also answer one of these questions: Which one? What kind of . . . ?

> **With great feeling,** Martin Luther King expressed his dream **of freedom.**
> [*With great feeling* describes the way the speech was delivered, and *of freedom* specifies the kind of dream.]
>
> King delivered his most famous speech **at a demonstration in Washington, DC.**
> [Both *at a demonstration* and *in Washington, DC* provide information about place.]

A **prepositional phrase** consists of a **preposition** (a word such as *at, of,* or *in*) and a pronoun, noun, or noun phrase (called the **object of the preposition**). A prepositional phrase modifies another element in the sentence.

> Everyone **in class** went to the play. [modifier of the pronoun *everyone*]
>
> Some students met the professor **after the play.** [modifier of the verb *met*]

(5) Appositives

An **appositive** is most often a noun or a noun phrase that refers to the same person, place, thing, or idea as a preceding noun or noun phrase but in different words. When the appositive simply specifies the referent, no commas are used.

> Cormac McCarthy's novel ***The Road*** won a Pulitzer Prize.
> [The appositive specifies which of McCarthy's books won the award.]

When the appositive provides extra details, commas set it off.

> *The Road*, **a novel by Cormac McCarthy,** won a Pulitzer Prize.
> [The appositive provides an extra detail about the book.]

(6) Absolute phrases

An **absolute phrase** is usually a noun phrase modified by a prepositional phrase or a participial phrase.

Her guitar in the front seat, she pulled away from the curb.

More vaccine having arrived, the staff scheduled its distribution.

The first absolute phrase provides details; the second expresses cause.

EXERCISE 3

Label the underlined phrases in the following sentences as noun, verb, prepositional, verbal, appositive, or absolute phrases. For verbal phrases, specify the type: gerund, participial, or infinitive. When a long phrase includes a short phrase, identify just the long phrase.

1. <u>Dedicated to the collection and diffusion of knowledge</u>, the Smithsonian comprises <u>over a dozen museums</u>.

2. People come <u>from every state</u> <u>to visit the museums</u>.

3. Scientists and scholars <u>visiting a Smithsonian museum</u> can use its <u>outstanding facilities</u>.

4. <u>Receiving a Smithsonian fellowship</u> is <u>the dream</u> <u>of many students</u>.

5. The Smithsonian owes <u>its existence</u> <u>to James Smithson</u>, <u>a scientist from Great Britain</u>.

6. <u>His bequest firmly rooted in the Enlightenment ideals of democracy and education</u>, James Smithson left the citizens <u>of the United States</u> <u>an unsurpassable legacy</u>.

1e Clauses

(1) Independent clauses

A **clause** is a group of related words that contains a subject and a predicate. An **independent clause,** sometimes called a *main clause,* has the same grammatical structure as a simple sentence: both contain a subject and a predicate.

The students earned high grades. [S: The students | pred: earned high grades]

An independent clause can stand alone as a complete sentence. Other clauses can be added to independent clauses to form longer, more detailed sentences.

(2) Dependent clauses

A **dependent clause** also has a subject and a predicate. However, it cannot stand alone as a complete sentence because of the word introducing it—usually a relative pronoun or a subordinating conjunction.

The athlete **who placed first** grew up in Argentina. [relative pronoun]

She received the gold medal **because she performed flawlessly**. [subordinating conjunction]

Noun clauses are dependent clauses that serve as subjects or objects. They are introduced by *if, that,* or a *wh-* word such as *why, what,* or *when*. Notice the similarity in usage between noun phrases and noun clauses.

What the witness said may not be true. [subject]

We do not understand **why they did it**. [direct object]

When no misunderstanding would result, the word *that* can be omitted from the beginning of a clause.

The scientist said **she was moving to Australia.** [*that* omitted]

However, *that* should always be retained when there are two noun clauses.

The scientist said **that she was moving to Australia** and **that her research team was planning to accompany her.** [*that* retained in both noun clauses]

An **adjectival clause,** or **relative clause,** follows a pronoun, noun, or noun phrase and answers one of these questions: Which one? What kind of . . . ? Such clauses, which nearly always follow the words they modify, usually begin with a **relative pronoun** (*who, whom, that, which,* or *whose*) but sometimes start with a **relative adverb** (*when, where,* or *why*).

Nobody likes news reports **that pry into someone's private life.** [answers the question *What kind of news reports?*]

Students **who have good study habits** begin their research early. [answers the question *Which students?*]

A relative pronoun can be omitted as long as the meaning of the sentence is still clear.

Mother Teresa was someone **the whole world admired.** [*Whom,* the direct object of the clause, has been omitted: the whole world admired *whom*.]

She was someone **who cared more about serving than being served.** [*Who* cannot be omitted because it is the subject of the clause.]

An **adverbial clause** usually answers one of the following questions: Where? When? Why? How? How frequently? In what manner? Adverbial clauses are introduced by subordinating conjunctions such as *because, although,* and *when.*

When the need arises, the company hires new writers. [answers the question *How frequently does the company hire new writers?*]

She acted **as though she cared only about herself.** [answers the question *How did she act?*]

THINKING RHETORICALLY

ADVERBIAL CLAUSES

In an adverbial clause that refers to time or establishes a fact, both the subject and any form of the verb *be* can be omitted. Using such **elliptical clauses** will make your writing more concise.

Though tired, they continued to study for the exam.

[COMPARE: **Though they were tired,** they continued to study for the exam.]

Be sure that the omitted subject of an elliptical clause is the same as the subject of the independent clause. Otherwise, revise either the adverbial clause or the main clause.

While [I was] reviewing your report, a few questions occurred to me.

OR

While reviewing your report, a few questions [I thought of] ~~occurred to me~~.

EXERCISE 4

1. Identify the dependent clauses in the following paragraph.
2. Identify the underlined words as coordinating, correlative, subordinating, or adverbial conjunctions.

¹<u>If</u> you live by the sword, you might die by the sword. ²<u>However,</u> <u>if</u> you make your living by swallowing swords, you will not necessarily die by swallowing swords. ³At least, this is the conclusion Brian Witcombe and Dan Meyer reached <u>after</u> they surveyed forty-six professional sword swallowers. ⁴(Brian Witcombe is a radiologist, <u>and</u> Dan Meyer is a famous sword swallower.) ⁵Some of those surveyed mentioned <u>that</u> they had experienced <u>either</u> "sword throats" <u>or</u> chest pains, <u>and</u> others who let their swords drop to their stomachs described perforation of their innards, <u>but</u> the researchers could find no listing of a sword-swallowing mortality in the medical studies they reviewed. ⁶The researchers did not inquire into the reasons for swallowing swords in the first place.

TECH SAVVY

Using a Grammar Checker

Most word-processing programs have features that help writers identify grammar errors as well as problems with usage and style, but these grammar checkers have significant limitations. A grammar checker will usually identify

- fused sentences, sometimes called run-on sentences (chapter 3),
- wordy or overly long sentences (chapter 14), and
- missing apostrophes in contractions (17b).

However, a grammar checker can easily miss

- sentence fragments (chapter 2),
- dangling or misplaced modifiers (chapter 6),
- problems with pronoun-antecedent agreement (5c),
- errors in subject-verb agreement (4f), and
- misused or missing commas (chapter 15).

Because these omissions can weaken your credibility as a writer, you should never rely solely on a grammar checker to find them. Furthermore, grammar checkers can mark as wrong words or phrases that you have chosen deliberately to suit your rhetorical situation (chapter 24).

Used carefully, a grammar checker can be a helpful tool, but keep the following advice in mind:

- Use a grammar checker only in addition to your own editing and proofreading.
- Always evaluate any sentences flagged by a grammar checker to determine whether there is, in fact, a problem.
- Adjust the settings on your grammar checker to look for specific types of errors. If you are using Microsoft Word, select Tools; then select either Spelling and Grammar or Options to customize your settings.
- Carefully review the revisions proposed by a grammar checker before accepting them. Sometimes the proposed revisions create new errors.

2 Sentence Fragments

As its name suggests, a **sentence fragment** is only a piece of a sentence; it is not complete.

2a Recognizing sentence fragments

A sentence is considered a fragment when it is incomplete in one of three ways.

- It is missing a subject *or* a verb.

    I stared at the blank screen. **Wondering where to begin.** [no subject]

    Alternative medical treatment may include hypnosis. **The placement of a patient into a sleeplike state.** [no verb]

- It is missing both a subject *and* a verb.

    They slept soundly. **Despite the noise from the party upstairs.**

- It is a dependent clause.

    Ultimate Frisbee is a popular sport. **Because it can be played almost anywhere.**

2b Phrases as sentence fragments

A phrase is a group of words without a subject and/or predicate. When punctuated as a sentence (that is, with a period, a question mark, or an exclamation point), it becomes a fragment. You can revise such a fragment by attaching it to a related sentence, usually the one preceding it.

Verbal phrase as a fragment

Early humans valued color~~.~~, creating ~~Creating~~ permanent colors with natural pigments.

Prepositional phrase as a fragment

For years, the Scottish have dyed sweaters with soot~~.~~, originally ~~Originally~~ from the chimneys of peat-burning stoves.

Appositive phrase as a fragment

During the Renaissance, one of the most highly valued pigments was ultramarine~~.~~—an ~~An~~ extract from lapis lazuli.

Absolute phrase as a fragment

The deciduous trees of New England are known for their brilliant autumn color~~.~~, sugar ~~Sugar~~ maples dazzling tourists with their orange and red leaves.

Instead of attaching a fragment to the preceding sentence, you can recast the fragment as a complete sentence.

Fragment	Humans painted themselves for a variety of purposes. **To attract a mate, to hide themselves from game or predators, or to signal aggression.**
Revision	Humans used color for a variety of purposes. For example, they painted themselves to attract a mate, to hide themselves from game or predators, or to signal aggression.

2c Dependent clauses as sentence fragments

A dependent clause is a group of words with both a subject and a predicate, but because it begins with a subordinating conjunction or a relative pronoun, it cannot stand alone as a sentence. To revise such a fragment, attach it to a related sentence, usually the sentence preceding it.

The iceberg was no surprise. ~~Because~~ because the *Titanic*'s wireless operators had received reports of ice in the area.

More than two thousand people were aboard the *Titanic*. ~~Which~~ , which was the largest ocean liner in 1912.

You can also recast the fragment as a complete sentence by removing the subordinating conjunction or relative pronoun and supplying any missing elements.

The iceberg was no surprise. The *Titanic*'s wireless operators had received reports of ice in the area.

More than two thousand people were aboard the *Titanic*. In 1912, this ocean liner was the world's largest.

THINKING RHETORICALLY

FRAGMENTS

When used judiciously, fragments—like short sentences—emphasize ideas or add surprise. However, fragments are generally permitted only when the rhetorical situation allows the use of a casual tone.

May. When the earth's Northern Hemisphere awakens from winter's sleep and all of nature bristles with the energies of new life. My work has kept me indoors for months now. I'm not sure I'll ever get used to it.

—KEN CAREY, *Flat Rock Journal: A Day in the Ozark Mountains*

EXERCISE 1

Locate and revise the fragments in the following paragraph.

¹Folklore from around the world contains references to wild men in the woods. ²Such as the Greek satyrs, the Russian *leshiy*, and the Yetis of the Himalayas. ³In North America, many people, including normally skeptical citizens and scientists, are fascinated by stories of Sasquatch. ⁴A name originating in the Salish word *saskehavas*. ⁵Another name commonly used is Big Foot. ⁶An allusion to the size of the footprints reportedly belonging to a giant apelike creature. ⁷That smells bad. ⁸Most sightings of Sasquatch occur in the Pacific Northwest. ⁹From northern California to central Alaska. ¹⁰Although reports have come from almost every state. ¹¹During the settlement of the United States, stories of hairy ape-men were told by Native Americans. ¹²And later on by trappers. ¹³Teddy Roosevelt recorded one such story.

Comma Splices and Fused Sentences

A **comma splice,** or **comma fault,** refers to the incorrect use of a comma between two independent clauses.

Most stockholders favored the merger,_but_ the management did not.

A **fused sentence,** or **run-on sentence,** consists of two independent clauses run together without any punctuation at all.

The first section of the proposal was approved_; however,_ the budget will have to be resubmitted.

To revise a comma splice or a fused sentence, include appropriate punctuation and any necessary connecting words.

3a Locating comma splices and fused sentences

You can find comma splices and fused sentences by remembering that they commonly occur in certain contexts.

- With transitional words and phrases such as *however, therefore,* and *for example*

    Comma splice: The director is unable to meet you this week,_;_ however_,_ next week she has time on Tuesday.

- When an explanation or an example is given in the second sentence

  Fused sentence: The cultural center has a new collection of spear points~. Many~ ~~many~~ of them were donated by a retired anthropologist.

- When a positive clause follows a negative clause, or vice versa

  Comma splice: A World Cup victory is not just an everyday sporting event~. It~ ~~, it~~ is a national celebration.

- When the subject of the second clause is a pronoun whose antecedent is in the preceding clause

  Fused sentence: Lake Baikal is located in southern Russia~. It~ ~~it~~ is 394 miles long.

3b Revising comma splices and fused sentences

If you find comma splices or fused sentences in your writing, try one of the following methods to revise them.

(1) Linking independent clauses with a comma and a coordinating conjunction

By linking clauses with a comma and a coordinating conjunction (such as *and* or *but*), you signal the relationship between the clauses (addition or contrast, for example).

Fused sentence: Joseph completed the first experiment~, and~ he will complete the other by Friday.

Comma splice: Some diplomats applauded the treaty,~ but~ others opposed it vehemently.

(2) Linking independent clauses with a semicolon or a colon or separating them with a period

When you link independent clauses with a semicolon, the semicolon usually indicates addition or contrast. When you link clauses with a colon, the second clause serves as an explanation or an elaboration of the first. A period indicates that each clause is a complete sentence, distinct from surrounding sentences.

Comma splice: Our division's reports are posted on our Web page, hard copies are available by request.

Revision 1: Our division's reports are posted on our Web page; hard copies are available by request.

Revision 2: Our division's reports are posted on our Web page. Hard copies are available by request.

Fused sentence: His choice was difficult he would either lose his job or betray his ethical principles.

(3) Recasting an independent clause as a dependent clause or as a phrase

A dependent clause includes a subordinating conjunction such as *although* or *because,* which indicates how the dependent and independent clauses are related (in a cause-and-effect relationship, for example). A prepositional phrase includes a preposition such as *in, on,* or *because of* that may also signal a relationship directly. Verbal, appositive, and absolute phrases suggest relationships less directly because they do not include connecting words.

Comma splice: The wind had blown down trees and power lines, the whole city was without electricity for several hours.

Revision 1: Because the wind had blown down power lines, the whole city was without electricity for several hours. [dependent clause]

Revision 2: Because of the downed power lines, the whole city was without electricity for several hours. [prepositional phrase]

Revision 3: The wind having blown down power lines, the whole city was without electricity for several hours. [absolute phrase]

(4) Integrating one clause into the other

When you integrate clauses, you will generally retain the important details but omit or change some words.

Fused sentence: The proposal covers all but one point it does not describe how the project will be assessed.

Revision: The proposal covers all the points except assessment procedures.

(5) Using transitional words or phrases to link independent clauses

Another way to revise fused sentences and comma splices is to use transitional words and phrases such as *however*, *on the contrary*, and *in the meantime*.

Fused sentence: Sexual harassment is not just an issue for women . After all, men can be sexually harassed too.

Comma splice: The word *status* refers to relative position within a group; however, it is often used to indicate only positions of prestige.

EXERCISE 1

Revise each comma splice or fused sentence in the following paragraph. Some sentences may not need revision.

[1] In the introduction to his book of true stories, *I Thought My Father Was God*, Paul Auster describes how he was able to collect these accounts of real and sometimes raw experience. [2] In October 1999, Auster, in collaboration with National Public Radio, began the *National Story Project*, during an interview on the radio program *Weekend All Things Considered*, he invited listeners to send in their stories about unusual events—"true stories that sounded like fiction." [3] In just one year, over four thousand stories were submitted Auster read every one of them.

[4]"Of the four thousand stories I have read, most have been compelling enough to hold me until the last word," Auster affirms, "most have been written with simple, straightforward conviction, and most have done honor to the people who sent them in." [5]Some of the stories Auster collected can now be read in his anthology choosing stories for the collection was difficult, though. [6]"For every story about a dream or an animal or a missing object," explains Auster, "there were dozens of others that were submitted, dozens of others that could have been chosen."

3c Divided quotations

When dividing quotations with attributive tags such as *he said* or *she asked,* use a period between independent clauses.

Comma splice: "Beauty brings copies of itself into being," states Elaine Scarry. "It makes us draw it, take photographs of it, or describe it to other people."

Both parts of the quotation are complete sentences, so the attributive tag is attached to the first, and the sentence is punctuated with a period.

4 Verbs

Choosing verbs to convey your message precisely is the first step toward writing clear sentences.

4a Verb forms

Regular verbs have four forms: a base form, an *-s* form (third-person singular in the present tense), an *-ing* form (present participle), and an *-ed* form (past participle).

VERB FORMS OF REGULAR VERBS

Base Form	-s Form (Present Tense, Third Person, Singular)	-ing Form (Present Participle)	-ed Form (Past Form or Past Participle)
work	works	working	worked
watch	watches	watching	watched
apply	applies	applying	applied
stop	stops	stopping	stopped

CAUTION

When verbs are followed by words with similar sounds, you may find their endings (*-s* or *-ed*) difficult to hear. In addition, these verb endings may seem unfamiliar because your dialect does not have them. Nonetheless, you should use *-s* and *-ed* when you write for an audience that expects you to include these endings.

She ~~seem~~ *seems* satisfied with the report.

We were ~~suppose~~ *supposed* to receive the results yesterday.

Irregular verbs have from three to eight forms. Most irregular verbs, such as *write,* have forms similar to some of those for regular verbs: base form (*write*), *-s* form (*writes*), and *-ing* form (*writing*). However, the past form (*wrote*) and the past participle (*written*) vary from the regular forms. The following list includes the base form, the past-tense form, and the past participle for irregular verbs.

VERB FORMS OF IRREGULAR VERBS

Base Form	Past Form	Past Participle
arise	arose	arisen
awake	awaked, awoke	awaked, awoken
be	was/were	been
begin	began	begun
break	broke	broken
bring	brought	brought
buy	bought	bought
choose	chose	chosen
come	came	come
dive	dived, dove	dived
do	did	done
dream	dreamed, dreamt	dreamed, dreamt
drink	drank	drunk
drive	drove	driven
eat	ate	eaten
forget	forgot	forgotten
forgive	forgave	forgiven
get	got	gotten, got

(Continued on page 36)

(Continued from page 35)

Base Form	Past Form	Past Participle
give	gave	given
go	went	gone
hang (suspend)	hung	hung
hang (execute)	hanged	hanged
keep	kept	kept
know	knew	known
lay (to place)	laid	laid
lead	led	led
lie (to recline)	lay	lain
lose	lost	lost
pay	paid	paid
rise	rose	risen
say	said	said
see	saw	seen
set	set	set
sink	sank	sunk
sit	sat	sat
speak	spoke	spoken
stand	stood	stood
steal	stole	stolen
swim	swam	swum
take	took	taken
tell	told	told
throw	threw	thrown
wear	wore	worn
write	wrote	written

MULTILINGUAL WRITERS

OMISSION OF FORMS OF *BE* IN OTHER LANGUAGES

Forms of the verb *be* can be omitted in some languages. In English, however, they are necessary.

    Sentence without an auxiliary verb: The population _^growing. *(is)*

    Sentence without a linking verb: It _^quite large. *(is)*

A **prepositional verb** is a frequently occurring combination of a verb and a preposition. *Rely on, think about, look like,* and *ask for* are all prepositional verbs. A **phrasal verb** is a combination of a verb and a particle such as *up, out,* or *on.* A **particle** resembles an adverb or a preposition, but it is so closely associated with a verb that together they form a unit of meaning. *Carry out, go on, make up, take on,* and *turn out* are common phrasal verbs. Notice that these five phrasal verbs have meanings that can be expressed in one word: *do, continue, form, accept,* and *attend.*

MULTILINGUAL WRITERS

PHRASAL VERBS

Definitions of phrasal verbs are often not obvious—for example, *find out* means "to discover." To learn more about phrasal verbs, see 38c.

The **auxiliary verbs** *be, do,* and *have* combine with main verbs, both regular and irregular.

    be   *am, is, are, was, were surprised*
             am, is, are, was, were writing

do *does, do, did call*
doesn't, don't, didn't spend

have *has, have, had prepared*
has, have, had read

Another type of auxiliary verb is called a **modal auxiliary**. There are nine modal auxiliaries: *can, could, may, might, must, shall, should, will,* and *would*. The following box provides examples of common meanings conveyed by modal auxiliaries.

COMMON MEANINGS OF MODAL AUXILIARIES

Meaning	Modal Auxiliary +	Main Verb	Example
Ability	can, could	afford	They *can afford* to buy a small house.
Certainty	will	leave	We *will leave* tomorrow.
Obligation	must	return	You *must return* the books soon.
Advice	should	talk	He *should talk* with his counselor.
Permission	may	use	You *may* use the computers in the library.

CAUTION

When a modal auxiliary occurs with the auxiliary *have* (*must have forgotten, should have known*), *have* frequently sounds like the word *of*. When you proofread, be sure that modal auxiliaries are not followed by *of*.

They **could** ~~of~~ *have* **taken** another route.

Writers generally do not combine modal auxiliaries unless they want to portray a regional dialect.

We **might** ~~could~~ *be able to* plan the meeting for after the holidays.

MULTILINGUAL WRITERS

PHRASAL MODALS

Some modal auxiliary verbs consist of two or three words. These verbs are called **phrasal modals**; their meanings are often similar to those of single-word modals. For example, *have to* shares with *must* the sense of obligation.

> The researchers **have to** report their findings on Friday.
>
> The researchers **must** report their findings on Friday.

Although there is similarity between one-word modals and phrasal modals, there are also differences, which are especially evident when the verbs are negated.

> The researchers **do not have to** report their findings on Friday. [They can report the findings if they want to, but they are not required to.]
>
> The researchers **must not** report their findings on Friday. [They have no choice about not reporting the findings.]

EXERCISE 1

Revise the following sentences. Explain any changes you make.

1. Any expedition into the wilderness suffer its share of mishaps.
2. The Lewis and Clark Expedition began in May 1804 and end in September 1806.
3. Fate must of smiled on Meriwether Lewis and William Clark, for there were no fatalities under their leadership.
4. Lewis and Clark lead the expedition from St. Louis to the Pacific Ocean and back.
5. By 1805, the Corps of Discovery, as the expedition was call, included thirty-three members.
6. The Corps might of lost all maps and specimens had Sacajawea, a Native American woman, not fish them from the Missouri River.

4b Verb tenses

Providing information about time, verb tenses are labeled as present, past, or future and as simple, progressive, perfect, or perfect progressive. (Multilingual writers can find a detailed discussion of verb tenses in 38a.)

VERB TENSES			
	Present	**Past**	**Future**
Simple	walk, walks	walked	will walk
Progressive	am, is, are walking	was, were walking	will be walking
Perfect	has, have walked	had walked	will have walked
Perfect progressive	has, have been walking	had been walking	will have been walking

(1) Simple tenses

Simple present I, you, we, they *work*
 he, she, it *works*

Simple past *worked* (only one form)

Future *will work* (only one form)

The **simple present tense** is used to indicate a current state, a habitual action, or a general truth.

We **are** ready. [current state]

Dana **uses** common sense. [habitual action]

The sun **rises** in the east. [general truth]

It is also commonly used to add a sense of immediacy to historical actions and to discuss literary and artistic works.

> In 1939, Hitler's armies **attack** Poland. [historical present]
>
> Joseph Conrad **writes** about what he sees in the human heart. [literary present]

On occasion, the simple present tense is used to refer to future time.

> The festival **begins** next month.

The **simple past tense** refers to completed past actions or events.

> He **traveled** to the Philippines. [past action]
>
> The accident **occurred** several weeks ago. [past event]

The **simple future tense** refers to future actions or states.

> I **will call** you after work today. [future action]
>
> The video **will be** ready by Friday. [future state]

(2) Progressive tenses

Present progressive	I *am working*
	he, she, it *is working*
	you, we, they *are working*
Past progressive	I, he, she, it *was working*
	you, we, they *were working*
Future progressive	*will be working* (only one form)

The **present progressive tense** signals an activity in progress or a temporary situation.

> The doctor **is attending** a conference. [activity in progress]
>
> We **are living** in a yurt right now. [temporary situation]

The present progressive tense can also refer to a future event when it occurs with an expression indicating time.

> They **are leaving** for Alaska next week. [*Next week* indicates a time in the future.]

The **past progressive tense** signals an action or event that occurred in the past and was repeated or ongoing.

> The new member **was** constantly **interrupting** the discussion. [repeated past action]
>
> We **were eating** dinner when we heard the news. [ongoing past action]

The **future progressive tense** refers to actions that will occur over some period of time in the future.

> She **will be giving** her report at the end of the meeting. [future action]

MULTILINGUAL WRITERS

VERBS NOT USED IN THE PROGRESSIVE FORM

Some verbs that do not express actions but rather mental states, emotions, conditions, or relationships are not used in the progressive form. These verbs include *believe, belong, contain, cost, know, own, prefer,* and *want.*

> The book ~~is containing~~ contains many Central American folktales.

(3) Perfect tenses

Present perfect	I, you, we, they *have worked*
	he, she, it *has worked*
Past perfect	*had worked* (only one form)
Future perfect	*will have worked* (only one form)

The **present perfect tense** signals a time prior to the present. It can refer to a situation originating in the past but continuing into the present. It can also refer to a past action that has current relevance.

> They **have lived** in New Zealand for twenty years. [situation originating in the past and still continuing]
>
> I **have read** that book already, but I could certainly read it again. [past action that is completed but currently relevant]

The **past perfect tense** refers to an action completed at a time in the past prior to another past time or past action.

> Before 1990, he **had worked** in a shoe factory. [past action prior to a given time in the past]
>
> I **had studied** geology before I transferred to this school. [past action prior to another past action]

The **future perfect tense** refers to an action that is to be completed prior to a future time.

> By this time next year, I **will have finished** medical school.

(4) Perfect progressive tenses

Present perfect progressive	I, you, we, they *have been working*
	he, she, it *has been working*
Past perfect progressive	*had been working* (only one form)
Future perfect progressive	*will have been working* (only one form)

The **present perfect progressive tense** signals that an action, state, or event originating in the past is ongoing or incomplete.

> I **have been feeling** tired for a week. [ongoing state]
>
> We **have been organizing** the conference since April. [incomplete action]

The **past perfect progressive tense** refers to a situation or an action occurring over a period of time in the past and prior to another past action or time.

> She **had been living** so frugally all year that she saved enough money for a new car. [past situation prior to another action in the past]

The **future perfect progressive tense** refers to an action that is occurring in the present and will continue to occur for a specific amount of time.

> In one more month, I **will have been working** on this project for five years.

4c Verb tense consistency

By using verb tenses consistently, you help your readers understand when the actions or events you are describing took place. Every verb tense can be discussed in terms of time frame and aspect. *Time frame* refers to whether the tense is present, past, or future. *Aspect* refers to whether it is simple, progressive, perfect, or perfect progressive. (See the chart on page 40.) Consistency in the time frame of verbs, though not necessarily in their aspect, ensures that sentences reporting a sequence of events link together logically. In the following paragraph, notice that the time frame remains in the past, but the aspect may be either simple, perfect, or progressive.

In the summer of 1983, I **had** just **finished** [past perfect] my third year of architecture school and **had** [simple past] to find a six-month internship.

I **had grown** up and **gone** through my entire education in the [past perfect (compound predicate)] Midwest, but I **had been** to New York City once on a class field [past perfect] trip and I **thought** it **seemed** like a pretty good place to live. [simple past, simple past] So, armed with little more than an inflated ego and my school portfolio, I **was** off to Manhattan, oblivious to the bad economy and the fact [simple past] that the city **was overflowing** with young architects. [past progressive]

—PAUL K. HUMISTON, "Small World"

If you do need to shift to another time frame, you can use a time marker:

now, then, today, yesterday

in two years, during the 1920s

after you finish, before we left

For example, in the following paragraph, the time frame shifts back and forth between present and past. The time markers are bracketed.

These woods **are** not wild; indeed, they **were** not wild [in Thoreau's day]. [Today], the beach and trails of Walden Pond State Reservation **draw** about 500,000 visitors a year. Few of them **hunt** ants, however.

Underfoot and under the leaf litter there **is** [simple present] a world as wild as it **was** [simple past] [before human beings **came** [simple past] to this part of North America].
—JAMES GORMAN, "Finding a Wild, Fearsome World Beneath Every Fallen Leaf"

On occasion, a shift in time is indicated implicitly—that is, without an explicit time marker. A writer may change tenses, without including time markers, (1) to explain or support a general statement with information about the past, (2) to compare and contrast two different time periods, or (3) to comment on a topic. In the following pair of sentences, the second sentence provides evidence from the past to support the claim in the first sentence.

> Thomas Jefferson, author of the Declaration of Independence, **is** considered one of our country's most brilliant citizens. His achievements **were** many, as **were** his interests.

EXERCISE 2

Revise the following paragraph so that it contains no unnecessary shifts in verb tense.

> I **had** already **been walking** for a half hour in the semidarkness of Amsterdam's early-morning streets when I **came** to a red light. I **am** in a hurry to get to the train station and no cars **were** out yet, so I **cross** over the cobblestones, passing a man waiting for the light to change. I never **look** back when he **scolds** me for breaking the law. I **had** a train to catch. I **was** going to Widnau, in Switzerland, to see Aunt Marie. I **have** not **seen** her since I **was** in second grade.

4d Voice

Voice indicates the relationship between a verb and its subject. When a verb is in the **active voice,** the subject is generally a person or thing performing an action. When a verb is in the **passive voice,** the subject is usually the *receiver* of the action.

Jen Wilson **wrote** the essay. [active voice]

The essay **was written** by Jen Wilson. [passive voice]

Notice that the actor, Jen Wilson, appears in a prepositional phrase beginning with *by* in the passive sentence. Some sentences, however, do not include a *by* phrase because the actor is unknown or unimportant.

Jen Wilson's essay **was published** in the student newspaper.

The best way to decide whether a sentence is in the passive voice is to examine its verb phrase.

(1) Verbs in the passive voice

The verb phrase in a sentence written in the passive voice consists of a form of the auxiliary verb *be* (*am, is, are, was, were, been*) and a past participle. Depending on the verb tense, other auxiliaries such as *have* and *will* may appear as well. The following sentences include common forms of *call* in the passive voice:

Simple present	The meeting *is called* to order.
Simple past	The recruits *were called* to duty.
Present progressive	The council *is being called* to act on the proposal.
Past perfect	Ms. Jones *had been called* to jury duty twice last year, but she was glad to serve again.

If a verb phrase does not include both a form of the auxiliary verb *be* and a past participle, it is in the active voice.

(2) Choosing between the active and passive voice

To use the active voice for emphasizing an actor and an action, first make the actor the subject of the sentence; then choose verbs that will help your readers see what the actor is doing.

A group of students **planned** the graduation ceremony.

Use the passive voice when you want to stress the recipient of the action, rather than the actor, or when the actor's identity is unimportant or unknown.

Tuition increases **were discussed** at the board meeting.

Writers of scientific prose often use the passive voice to highlight the experiment rather than the experimenter. The following is an excerpt from a lab report by student Heather Jensen:

> First, the slides **were placed** on a compound microscope under low power, a 40× magnification level. The end of the root tip **was located**; then the cells immediately behind the root cap **were examined**.

EXERCISE 3

Identify the voice in each sentence as active or passive.

1. In a *National Geographic* report, Tom O'Neill describes the discovery of ancient art in Guatemala.
2. Archaeologist William Saturno recently discovered the oldest known Maya mural.
3. The mural was found in a tunnel used by looters.
4. The tunnel was actually a small room attached to a pyramid.
5. The mural was dated to about 150 years before the beginning of the Maya Classic period.

4e Mood

The **mood** of a verb expresses the writer's attitude toward the factuality of what is being expressed. The **indicative mood** is used for statements and questions regarding fact or opinion. The **imperative mood** is used to give commands or directions. The **subjunctive mood** is used to state requirements, make requests, and express wishes.

Indicative	We will be on time.
Imperative	Be on time!
Subjunctive	The director insists that we be on time.

The subjunctive mood is also used to signal hypothetical situations (situations that are not real or not currently true—for example, *If I were president, . . .*).

Verb forms in the subjunctive mood serve a variety of functions. The **present subjunctive** is the base form of the verb. It is used to express necessity.

> The doctor recommended that he **go** on a diet. [active voice]
>
> We demanded that you **be reimbursed**. [passive voice]

The **past subjunctive** has the same form as the simple past (for example, *had, offered, found,* or *wrote*). However, the past subjunctive form of *be* is *were*, regardless of person or number. This form is used to present hypothetical situations.

> If they **offered** me the job, I would take it. [active voice]
>
> Even if he **were promoted**, he would not change his mind. [passive voice]

The **perfect subjunctive** verb has the same form as the past perfect tense: *had* + past participle. The perfect subjunctive signals that a statement is not factual.

I wish I **had known** about the scholarship competition. [active voice]

If she **had been awarded** the scholarship, she would have quit her part-time job. [passive voice]

The following guidelines should help you avoid pitfalls when using the subjunctive.

TIPS FOR USING THE SUBJUNCTIVE

- In clauses beginning with *as if* and *as though*, use the past subjunctive or the perfect subjunctive:

    He acts as if he ~~was~~ *were* the owner.

    She looked at me as though she *had* **heard** this story before.

- In nonfactual dependent clauses beginning with *if*, use the past subjunctive or the perfect subjunctive. Avoid using *would have* in the *if* clause.

    If I ~~was~~ *were* rich, I would buy a yacht.

    If the driver ~~would have~~ *had* **checked** his rearview mirror, the accident would not have happened.

- In dependent clauses following verbs that express wishes, requirements, or requests, use the past subjunctive or the perfect subjunctive.

    I wish I ~~was~~ *were* taller.

    My brother wishes he *had* **studied** harder years ago.

EXERCISE 4

Use subjunctive verb forms to revise the following sentences.

1. The planners of Apollo 13 acted as if the number 13 was a lucky number.
2. Superstitious people think that if NASA changed the number of the mission, the astronauts would have had a safer journey.
3. They also believe that if the lunar landing would have been scheduled for a day other than Friday the Thirteenth, the crew would not have encountered any problems.
4. The crew used the lunar module as though it was a lifeboat.
5. If NASA ever plans a space mission on Friday the Thirteenth again, the public would object.

4f Subject-verb agreement

To say that a verb *agrees* with a subject means that the form of the verb (*-s* form or base form) is appropriate for the subject. For example, if the subject refers to one person or thing (*an athlete, a computer*), the *-s* form of the verb (*runs*) is appropriate. If the subject refers to more than one person or thing (*athletes, computers*), the base form of the verb (*run*) is appropriate. Notice in the following examples that the singular third-person subjects in the first line take a singular verb (*-s* form) and all the other subjects take the base form.

He, she, it, Joe, a student	has, looks, writes
I, you, we, they, the Browns, the students	have, look, write

The verb *be* has three different present-tense forms and two different past-tense forms:

I	am/was
He, she, it, Joe, a student	is/was
You, we, they, the Browns, the students	are/were

(1) Words between the subject and the verb

When phrases such as the following occur between the subject and the verb, they do not affect the number of the subject or the form of the verb:

| along with | in addition to | not to mention |
| as well as | including | together with |

Her **salary,** together with tips, **is** just enough to live on.

Tips, together with her salary, **are** just enough to live on.

(2) Subjects joined by *and*

A compound subject (two nouns joined by *and*) that refers to a single person or thing takes a singular verb.

The **founder and president** of the art association **was** elected to the board of the museum.

(3) Subjects joined by *or* or *nor*

When singular subjects are linked by *or, either . . . or,* or *neither . . . nor,* the verb is singular as well.

The **provost or** the **dean** usually **presides** at the meeting.

Either his **accountant or** his **lawyer has** the will.

If the linked subjects differ in number, the verb agrees with the subject closer to the verb.

Neither the basket nor the **apples were** expensive. [plural]

Neither the apples nor the **basket was** expensive. [singular]

(4) Inverted order

In most sentences, the subject precedes the verb.

The large **cities** of the Northeast **were** the hardest hit by the winter storms.

The subject and verb can sometimes be inverted for emphasis; however, they must still agree.

The hardest hit by the winter storms **were** the large **cities** of the Northeast. [V, S]

When *there* begins a sentence, the subject and verb are always inverted; the verb still agrees with the subject, which follows it.

There **are** several **cities** in need of federal aid. [V, S]

(5) Clauses with relative pronouns

In an adjectival (relative) clause, the subject is generally a relative pronoun (*that, who,* or *which*). To determine whether the relative pronoun is singular or plural, you must find its antecedent (the word or words it refers to). When the antecedent is singular, the relative pronoun is singular; when the antecedent is plural, the relative pronoun is plural. In essence, the verb in the adjectival clause agrees with the antecedent.

The person <u>who</u> reviews proposals is out of town this week. [sing ant, sing v]

The director met with the **students <u>who</u> are** studying abroad next quarter. [pl ant, pl v]

The Starion is one of the new **models <u>that</u> include** a DVD player as standard equipment. [pl ant, pl v]

(6) Indefinite pronouns

The indefinite pronouns *each, either, everybody, everyone,* and *anyone* are considered singular and so require singular verb forms.

Either of them **is willing** to lead the discussion.

Everybody in our apartment building **has** a parking place.

All, any, some, none, half, and *most* can be either singular or plural, depending on whether they refer to a unit or quantity (singular) or to individuals (plural).

My sister collects antique **jewelry; some** of it **is** quite valuable. *(sing ant, sing v)*

My sister collects comic **books; some are** quite valuable. *(pl ant, pl v)*

When an indefinite pronoun is followed by a prepositional phrase beginning with the preposition *of,* the verb agrees in number with the object of the preposition.

None of **those are** spoiled. *(pl obj, pl v)*

None of the **food is** spoiled. *(sing obj, sing v)*

(7) Collective nouns and measurement words

Collective nouns and measurement words require singular verbs when they refer to groups or units. They require plural verbs when they refer to individuals or parts.

Singular (regarded as a group or unit)	**Plural (regarded as individuals or parts)**
The **majority rules.**	The **majority** of us **are** in favor.
Ten million gallons of oil **is** more than enough.	**Ten million gallons** of oil **were spilled.**

(8) Words ending in -s

Titles of works that are plural in form (for example, *Star Wars* and *Dombey and Son*) are treated as singular because they refer to a single book, movie, recording, or other work.

Julie & Julia **is** one of the films she discussed in her paper.

Some nouns ending in *-s* are singular: *linguistics, news,* and *Niagara Falls*.

The **news is** encouraging.

Nouns such as *athletics, politics,* and *electronics* can be either singular or plural, depending on their meanings.

Statistics is an interesting subject. [singular]
Statistics are often misleading. [plural]

(9) Subjects and subject complements

Some sentences may have a singular subject and a plural subject complement, or vice versa. In either case, the verb agrees with the subject.

Her primary **concern is** rising health-care **costs**.
Croissants are the bakery's **specialty**.

THINKING RHETORICALLY

AGREEMENT OF RELATED SINGULAR AND PLURAL NOUNS

When a sentence has two or more nouns that are related, use either the singular form or the plural form consistently.

The **student** raised her **hand**.   The **students** raised their **hands**.

Occasionally, you may have to use a singular noun to retain an idiomatic expression or to avoid ambiguity.

They kept their **word**.

(10) Subjects beginning with *what*

When *what* may be understood as "the thing that," the verb in the main clause is singular.

> What we need **is** a new policy. [*The thing that* we need is a new policy.]

If *what* is understood as "the things that," the verb in the main clause is plural.

> What we need **are** new guidelines. [*The things that* we need are new guidelines.]

EXERCISE 5

Choose the correct form of the verb in parentheses.

1. There (is/are) at least two good reasons for changing motor oil: risk of contamination and danger of additive depletion.
2. Reasons for not changing the oil (include/includes) the cost to the driver and the inconvenience of the chore.
3. What I want to know (is/are) the number of miles I can drive before changing my oil.
4. But my brother says three thousand miles (is/are) not long enough.
5. Each of the car manuals I consulted (recommends/recommend) five-thousand-mile intervals.
6. Neither the automakers nor the oil station attendants (know/knows) how I drive, however.

5 Pronouns

When you use pronouns effectively, you add clarity and coherence to your writing.

5a Recognizing pronouns

A **pronoun** is commonly defined as a word used in place of a noun that has already been mentioned—its antecedent.

John said **he** would guide the trip.

Most pronouns refer to nouns, but some modify nouns.

This man is our guide.

Pronouns are categorized as personal, reflexive/intensive, relative, interrogative, demonstrative, or indefinite.

(1) Personal pronouns

Personal pronouns are like nouns: they refer to people, places, things, ideas, and so on.

Singular   I, me, you, he, him, she, her, it
Plural   we, us, you, they, them

(2) Possessive pronouns

Possessive pronouns are personal pronouns that indicate ownership and similar relationships.

Singular   my, mine, your, yours, his, her, hers, its
Plural   our, ours, your, yours, their, theirs

Avoid confusing possessive forms with common contractions: *it's (it is), they're (they are),* and *who's (who is).*

(3) Reflexive/intensive pronouns

Reflexive pronouns direct the action back to the subject (*I saw myself*); intensive pronouns are used for emphasis (*I myself questioned the judge*).

Singular   myself, yourself, himself, herself, itself
Plural   ourselves, yourselves, themselves

Avoid using a reflexive pronoun as a subject.

Ms. Palmquist and ~~myself~~ I discussed our concern with the senator.

Hisself, themself, and *theirselves* are inappropriate in college or professional writing. Instead, use *himself* and *themselves.*

(4) Relative pronouns

An adjectival clause (or relative clause) ordinarily begins with a relative pronoun: *who, whom, which, that,* or *whose.* To provide a link between this type of dependent clause and the main clause, the relative pronoun corresponds to a word or words in the main clause called the **antecedent.**

The students talked to **a reporter** (ant) **who** (rel pro) had just returned from overseas.

Who, whose, and *whom* ordinarily refer to people; *which* refers to things; *that* refers to things and, in some contexts, people. The possessive *whose* (used in place of the awkward *of which*) usually refers to people but sometimes refers to things.

The poem, **whose** author is unknown, has recently been set to music.

Knowing the difference between an essential clause and a nonessential clause will help you decide whether to use *which* or *that*. A clause that a reader needs in order to identify the antecedent correctly is an **essential clause**.

The person who presented the award was last year's winner.

If the essential clause were omitted from this sentence, the reader would not know which person was last year's winner.

A **nonessential clause** is *not* needed for correct identification of the antecedent and is thus set off by commas. A nonessential clause often follows a proper noun (a specific name).

Andrea Bowen, who presented the award, was last year's winner.

If the nonessential clause were removed from this sentence, the reader would still know the identity of last year's winner.

According to a traditional grammar rule, *that* is used in essential adjectival clauses, and *which* is used in nonessential adjectival clauses.

I need a job **that** pays well.

For years, I have had the same job, **which** pays well enough.

However, some professional writers use *which* in essential clauses. Nonetheless, if you are following APA guidelines, use *which* only in nonessential clauses.

(5) Interrogative pronouns

The interrogative pronouns *what, which, who, whom,* and *whose* are question words.

Who won the award?   **Whom** did you see?

(6) Demonstrative pronouns

The demonstrative pronouns *this* and *these* indicate that someone or something is close by in time, space, or thought. *That* and *those* signal remoteness.

These are important documents; **those** can be thrown away.

(7) Indefinite pronouns

Indefinite pronouns usually do not refer to specific persons, objects, ideas, or events.

anyone	anybody	anything
everyone	everybody	everything
someone	somebody	something
no one	nobody	nothing
each	either	neither

Indefinite pronouns do not refer to an antecedent. In fact, some indefinite pronouns *serve* as antecedents.

Someone forgot **her** purse.

5b Pronoun case

To understand the uses of pronouns, you must first be able to recognize person and number. **Person** indicates whether a pronoun refers to the writer (**first person**), to the reader (**second person**), or to another person, place, thing, or idea (**third person**). **Number** reveals whether a pronoun is singular or plural.

Case refers to the form a pronoun takes to indicate its relationship to other words in a sentence. There are three cases: subjective, objective, and possessive.

> **He** [subjective] wants **his** [possessive] legislators to help **him** [objective].

CASE:	Subjective		Objective		Possessive	
NUMBER:	Singular	Plural	Singular	Plural	Singular	Plural
First person	I	we	me	us	my mine	our ours
Second person	you	you	you	you	your yours	your yours
Third person	he, she, it	they	him, her, it	them	his, her, hers, its	their theirs

(1) Pronouns in the subjective case

A pronoun that is the subject of a sentence is in the subjective case. To determine which pronoun form is correct in a compound subject (a noun and a pronoun joined by *and*), say the sentence using the pronoun alone, omitting the noun. For the following sentence, notice that "*Me* solved the problem" sounds strange, but "*I* solved the problem" sounds fine.

~~Me and~~ Marisa ^and I^ solved the problem.

Place the pronoun *I* last in the sequence. If the compound subject contains two pronouns, test each one by itself.

^He^ ~~Him~~ and I joined the club in July.

Pronouns following a *be* verb (*am, is, are, was, were, been*) should also be in the subjective case.

The first to arrive were Kevin and ^I^ ~~me~~.

> ### MULTILINGUAL WRITERS
>
> #### NOUN OR PRONOUN AS SUBJECT
>
> In some languages, a noun in the subject position may be followed by a pronoun. In Standardized English, though, such a pronoun should be omitted.
>
> My roommate ~~he~~ works in the library for three hours a week.

(2) Pronouns in the objective case

Whenever a pronoun follows an action verb or a preposition, it takes the **objective case**.

Direct object	The whole staff admired **him**.
Indirect object	The staff sent **him** a card.
Object of a preposition	The staff depended on **him**.

Pronouns in compound objects are also in the objective case.

> They will appoint you or ~~I~~ [me]. [direct objects]
>
> They lent Tom and ~~I~~ [me] money for tuition. [indirect objects]
>
> Janice sat between my brother and ~~I~~ [me]. [objects of the preposition]

To determine whether to use the subjective or objective case, remember to say the sentence with just the pronoun. Notice that "They will appoint *I*" does not sound right.

(3) Possessive forms

Possessives can be divided into two groups based on whether they are followed by nouns. *My, your, his, her, its, our,* and *their* are all followed by nouns; *mine, yours, his, hers, ours,* and *theirs* are not. (Note that *his* is in both groups.)

> **Their** budget is higher than **ours**.
> [*Their* is followed by a noun; *ours* is not.]

(4) Appositive pronouns

Appositive pronouns are in the same case as the nouns they rename.

> The red team—Rebecca, Leroy, and ~~me~~ [I]—won by only one point.
>
> A trophy was presented to the red team—Rebecca, Leroy, and ~~I~~ [me].

EXERCISE 1

Revise the following paragraph, using appropriate pronouns. Some sentences may not require editing.

¹When I was twelve, my family lived in Guatemala for a year. ²My parents taught English at a university; me and my younger brother went to a local school. ³Although the Spanish language was new to both Sam and I, we learned to speak it quickly. ⁴At first, we couldn't understand much at all, but with the help of a tutor, who we met every day after school, we started learning "survival" Spanish. ⁵After we learned to ask and answer some basic questions, we started making friends, whom eventually introduced us to they're own version of Spanish.

(5) Who/whoever and whom/whomever

To choose between *who* and *whom* or between *whoever* and *whomever,* you must first determine whether the word is functioning as a subject or an object. A pronoun functioning as the subject takes the subjective case.

Who won the award? [COMPARE: **She** won the award.]

The teachers know **who** won the award.

The student **who** won the award was quite surprised.

Whoever won the award deserves it.

When the pronoun is an object, use *whom* or *whomever*.

Whom did they hire? [COMPARE: They hired **him**.]

I do not know **whom** they hired.

The student **whom** they hired graduated in May.

Whomever they hired will have to work hard this year.

Whom may be omitted in sentences when no misunderstanding would result.

> The friend he relied on moved away.
> [*Whom* has been omitted after *friend*.]

(6) Pronouns with infinitives and gerunds

A pronoun grouped with an infinitive (*to* + the base form of a verb) takes the objective case.

> The director wanted **me** to help **him.**

A gerund (*-ing* verb form functioning as a noun) is preceded by a possessive pronoun.

> I appreciated **his** helping Denise. [COMPARE: I appreciated **Tom's** helping Denise.]

Notice that a possessive pronoun is used before a gerund but not before a present participle (*-ing* verb form functioning as an adjective).

> I saw **him** helping Luke.

(7) Pronouns in elliptical constructions

The words *as* and *than* frequently introduce **elliptical constructions**—clauses in which the writer has intentionally omitted words. To check whether you have used the correct case in an elliptical construction, read the written sentence aloud, inserting any words that have been omitted from it.

> She admires Clarice as much as **I.** [subjective case]
> Read aloud: She admires Clarice as much as *I do*.

> She admires Clarice more than **me.** [objective case]
> Read aloud: She admires Clarice more than *she admires me*.

EXERCISE 2

Correct the pronoun errors in the following sentences.

1. The board of directors has asked you and I to conduct a customer survey.
2. They also recommended us hiring someone with extensive experience in statistical analysis.
3. Whomever understands statistics should take the lead on this project.
4. Although the board asked me to be in charge, I would like you to recruit and interview candidates.

5c Pronoun-antecedent agreement

A pronoun and its antecedent (the word or word group to which it refers) agree in number (both are singular or both are plural).

The **supervisor** said **he** would help.
[Both antecedent and pronoun are singular.]

My **colleagues** said **they** would help.
[Both antecedent and pronoun are plural.]

MULTILINGUAL WRITERS

POSSESSIVE PRONOUNS

A possessive pronoun (*his, her, its, their, my, our,* or *your*), also called a **possessive determiner,** agrees with its antecedent, not with the noun it precedes.

Ken Carlson brought ~~her~~ his young daughter to the office today.
[The possessive pronoun *his* agrees with the antecedent, *Ken Carlson*, not with the following noun, *daughter*.]

(1) Indefinite pronouns

An indefinite pronoun such as *everyone, someone,* or *anybody* takes a singular verb form.

Everyone **has** [not *have*] the right to an opinion.

Difficulties arise, however, because words like *everyone* and *everybody* seem to refer to more than one person even though they take a singular verb. Thus, the definition of grammatical number and our everyday notion of number conflict. In conversation and informal writing, a plural pronoun (*they, them,* or *their*) is often used with the singular *everyone*. Nonetheless, when you write for an audience that expects you to follow traditional grammar rules, make sure to use a third-person singular pronoun.

Everyone has the combination to ~~their~~ *his or her* private locker.

You can avoid the awkwardness of using *his* or *her* by using an article instead, making both the antecedent and the possessive pronoun plural, or rewriting the sentence using the passive voice (the *be* auxiliary + the past participle).

Everyone has the combination to **a** private locker. [article]

Students have combinations to **their** private lockers. [plural antecedent and plural possessive pronoun]

The combination to a private locker **is issued** to everyone. [passive voice]

(2) Two antecedents joined by *or* or *nor*

If a singular and a plural antecedent are joined by *or* or *nor,* place the plural antecedent second and use a plural pronoun.

Either Jennifer **or** her roommates will explain how they chose their majors.

Neither the president **nor** the senators stated that they would support the proposal.

(3) Collective nouns

When an antecedent is a collective noun such as *team*, *faculty*, or *committee*, determine whether you intend the noun to be understood as singular or plural. Then, make sure that the pronoun agrees in number with the noun.

The choir decided that ~~they~~ *it* would tour during the winter.
[Because the choir decided as a group, *choir* should be considered singular.]

The committee may disagree on methods, but ~~it~~ *they* must agree on basic aims.
[Because the committee members are behaving as individuals, *committee* is regarded as plural.]

EXERCISE 3

Revise each sentence in the way indicated so that pronouns and antecedents agree.

1. Everyone should have the right to participate in a study only if they feel comfortable doing so. (Make the antecedent plural.)

2. A team of researchers should provide its volunteers with consent forms, in which they describe to the volunteers the procedures and risks involved in participation. (Make sure all pronouns are plural.)

3. Every participant should be guaranteed that the information they provide will remain confidential. (Make the antecedent plural.)

5d Clear pronoun reference

The meaning of each pronoun in a sentence should be immediately obvious. In the following sentence, the pronoun *he* clearly refers to the antecedent, *Jack*.

Jack has collected shells since **he** was eight years old.

(1) Ambiguous or unclear pronoun references

When a pronoun can refer to either of two antecedents, the ambiguity may confuse readers. To make the antecedent clear, replace the pronoun with a noun or rewrite the sentence.

Mr. Anderson told Mr. Eggers that ^Mr. Eggers ~~he~~ would be in charge of the project.

OR

Mr. Anderson put Mr. Eggers in charge of the project.

(2) Remote or awkward pronoun references

To help readers understand your meaning, place pronouns as close to their antecedents as possible. The following sentence needs to be revised so that the relative pronoun *that* is close to its antecedent, *poem*. Otherwise, the reader would wonder how a new book could be written in 1945.

The **poem**^that was originally written in 1945 has been published in a new book ~~that was originally written in 1945~~.

Notice, however, that a relative pronoun does not always have to follow its antecedent directly. In the following example, there is no risk of misunderstanding.

We slowly began to notice **changes** in our lives **that** we had never expected.

(3) Broad or implied pronoun references

Pronouns such as *it, this, that,* and *which* sometimes refer to the sense of a whole clause, sentence, or paragraph.

> Large corporations may seem stronger than individuals, but **that** is not true. [*That* refers to the sense of the whole first clause.]

In academic rhetorical situations, revise sentences that do not have specific antecedents.

> When class attendance is compulsory, some students feel that education is being forced on them. This ^perception^ is unwarranted.

[In the original sentence, *this* had no clear antecedent.]

In addition, remember to express an idea explicitly rather than merely implying it.

> My father is a music teacher. ~~It~~ ^Teaching music^ is a profession that requires much patience.

[In the original sentence, *it* had no expressed antecedent.]

Be especially careful to provide clear antecedents when you are referring to the work or possessions of others. The following sentence requires revision because *she* can refer to someone other than Jen Norton.

> In ~~Jen Norton's~~ ^her^ new book, ~~she~~ ^Jen Norton^ argues for election reform.

(4) The use of *it* without an antecedent

The expletive *it* does not have a specific antecedent. Instead, it is used to postpone, and thus give emphasis to, the subject of a sentence. If a sentence that begins with this expletive is wordy or awkward, replace *it* with the postponed subject.

<u>Trying to repair the car</u> <u>useless</u>
~~It was~~ ~~no use trying to repair the car~~.

EXERCISE 4

Edit the following sentences to make all references clear.

1. A champion cyclist, a cancer survivor, and a humanitarian, it is no wonder that Lance Armstrong is one of the most highly celebrated athletes in the world.

2. Armstrong's mother encouraged his athleticism, which led to his becoming a professional triathlete by age sixteen.

3. Though you might not believe it, Armstrong was only a senior in high school when he started training for the Olympic developmental team.

4. Not long afterward, because of intense pain, he sought medical attention, and they told him he had testicular cancer.

5. Armstrong underwent dramatic surgery and aggressive chemotherapy; this eventually helped him recover.

6. Armstrong started training five months after their diagnosis and went on to win major championships, including the Tour de France.

5e Pronoun consistency

Whenever you write, you must establish your point of view (perspective). Your point of view will be evident in the pronouns you choose. *I* or *we* indicates a first-person point of view, which is appropriate for writing that includes personal views or experiences. If you decide to address the reader as *you*, you are adopting a second-person point of view. However, because a second-person point of view is rare in academic writing, avoid using *you* unless you need to address the reader. If you select the pronouns *he, she, it, one,* and *they,* you are writing with a third-person point of view. The third-person point of view is the most common point of view in academic writing.

Although you may find it necessary to use different points of view in a paper, especially if you are comparing or contrasting other people's views with your own, be careful not to confuse readers by shifting perspective unnecessarily.

To an observer, a sleeping person appears passive, unresponsive, and essentially isolated from the rest of the world and its barrage of stimuli. While it is true that ~~you are~~ *someone asleep is* unaware of most surrounding noises ~~when you are asleep~~, *that person's* brain is far from inactive. In fact, the brain can be as active during sleep as it is ~~when you are awake~~ *in a waking state*. When ~~our brains are~~ *it is* asleep, the rate and type of electrical activity change.

EXERCISE 5

Revise the following paragraph so that there are no unnecessary shifts in point of view.

¹Many car owners used to complain about deceptive fuel-economy ratings. ²The issue was ignored until our gas prices started to rise dramatically. ³Because of increased pressure from consumer organizations, the United States Environmental Protection Agency now takes into account factors such as quick acceleration, changing road grades, and the use of air conditioning, so the new ratings should reflect your real-world driving conditions. ⁴Nonetheless, the ratings can never be exact because we all have different driving habits.

5f Use of first-person and second-person pronouns

Using *I* is appropriate when you are writing about personal experience. In academic and professional writing, the use of the first-person singular pronoun is also a clear way to distinguish your own views from those of others. However, if you frequently repeat *I feel* or *I think,* your readers may suspect that you do not understand much beyond your own experience.

We, the first-person plural pronoun, is trickier to use correctly. When you use it, make sure that your audience can tell which individuals are included in this plural reference. For example, if you are writing a paper for a college course, does *we* mean you and the instructor, you and your fellow students, or some other group (such as all Americans)? Because you may inadvertently use *we* in an early draft to refer to more than one group of people, as you edit, check to see that you have used this pronoun consistently.

If you address readers directly, you will undoubtedly use the second-person pronoun *you* (as we, the authors of this handbook, have done). There is some disagreement, though, over whether to permit the use of the indefinite *you* to mean "a person" or "people in general." If your instructor tells you to avoid using the indefinite *you*, recast your sentences. For example, use *one* instead of *you*.

Even in huge, anonymous cities, ~~you find~~ *one finds* community spirit.

If the use of *one* is too formal, try changing the word order or using different words.

Community spirit is found even in huge, anonymous cities.

EXERCISE 6

Revise the following paragraph to eliminate the use of the first- and second-person pronouns.

¹In my opinion, some animals should be as free as we are. ²For example, I think orangutans, African elephants, and Atlantic bottlenose dolphins should roam freely rather than be held in captivity. ³We should neither exhibit them in zoos nor use them for medical research. ⁴If you study animals such as these you will see that, like us, they show emotions, self-awareness, and intention. ⁵You might even find that some use language to communicate. ⁶It is clear to me that they have the right to freedom.

6 Modifiers

Modifiers are words, phrases, or clauses that modify; that is, they qualify or limit the meaning of other words. When used effectively, modifiers enliven writing with details and enhance its coherence.

6a Recognizing modifiers

You can distinguish an adjective from an adverb by determining what type of word is modified. **Adjectives** modify nouns and pronouns; **adverbs** modify verbs, adjectives, and other adverbs.

Adjectives	**Adverbs**
She looked **curious.** [modifies pronoun]	She looked at me **curiously.** [modifies verb]
productive meeting [modifies noun]	**highly** productive meeting [modifies adjective]
a **quick** lunch [modifies noun]	**very** quickly [modifies adverb]

In addition, consider the form of the modifier. Many adjectives end with one of these suffixes: *-able, -al, -ful, -ic, -ish, -less,* or *-y.*

accept**able**   rent**al**   event**ful**   angel**ic**   sheep**ish**   effort**less**   sleep**y**

Present participles (verb + *-ing*) and past participles (verb + *-ed*) can also be used as adjectives.

a **determining** factor   a **determined** effort

Be sure to include the *-ed* ending of a past participle.

Please see the ~~enclose~~ enclosed documents for more details.

Present and past participles used as adjectives cannot be used interchangeably (see **38d**).

The easiest type of adverb to identify is the adverb of manner. It is formed by adding *-ly* to an adjective.

care**ly**   unpleasant**ly**   silent**ly**

Although you may not hear the *-ly* ending when you speak, be sure to include it when you write.

They bought only ~~local~~ locally grown vegetables.

However, not all words ending in *-ly* are adverbs. Certain adjectives related to nouns also end in *-ly* (*friend, friendly; hour, hourly*). In addition, not all adverbs end in *-ly*. Adverbs that indicate time or place (*today, tomorrow, here,* and *there*) do not have the *-ly* ending. Neither does the negator *not*. A few words—for example, *fast* and *well*—can function as either adjectives or adverbs.

They like **fast** cars. [adjective]

They ran **fast** enough to catch the bus. [adverb]

(1) Modifiers of linking verbs and action verbs

An adjective used after a sensory linking verb (*look, smell, taste, sound,* or *feel*) modifies the subject of the sentence. A common error is to use an adverb after this type of verb.

I felt ~~badly~~ bad about missing the rally. [The adjective *bad* modifies *I*.]

However, when *look, smell, taste, sound,* or *feel* is used as an action verb, it can be modified by an adverb.

She looked **angrily** at the referee. [The adverb *angrily* modifies *looked*.]

BUT She looked **angry.** [The adjective *angry* modifies *she*.]

Good is an adjective and so is not used with action verbs.

The whole team played ~~good~~ well.

EXERCISE 1

In the following sentences, use appropriate adjectives and adverbs.

1. My brother said he was real nervous.
2. He did not think he could drive good enough to pass the driver's test.
3. He looked calmly, though, as he got into the tester's car.
4. As I knew he would, my brother passed his test easy.

(2) Nouns as modifiers

Adjectives and adverbs are the most common modifiers, but nouns can also be modifiers (***movie*** *critic*, ***reference*** *manual*). A string of noun modifiers can be cumbersome. The following

The ~~Friday afternoon~~ Student Affairs Committee meeting ^scheduled for Friday afternoon has been postponed.

> ### MULTILINGUAL WRITERS
> #### NOUN MODIFIERS
>
> In noun combinations, the first noun is the modifier. Different orders produce different meanings.
>
> A *company phone* is a phone that belongs to a company.
>
> A *phone company* is a company that sells phones or provides phone service.

(3) Phrases and clauses as modifiers

Participial phrases, prepositional phrases, and some infinitive phrases are modifiers.

> **Growing in popularity every year,** mountain bikes now dominate the market. [participial phrase]
>
> Mountain bikes first became popular **in the 1980s.** [prepositional phrase]
>
> Some people use mountain bikes **to commute to work.** [infinitive phrase]

Adjectival and adverbial clauses are both modifiers.

> BMX bicycles have frames **that are relatively small.** [adjectival clause]
>
> **Although mountain bikes are designed for off-road use,** many people use them on city streets. [adverbial clause]

6b Comparatives and superlatives

Many adjectives and adverbs change form to show degrees of quality, quantity, time, distance, and so on. The **positive form** of an adjective or adverb is the word you would look for in a dictionary: *hard, deserving*. The **comparative form,** which either ends in *-er* or is preceded by *more* or *less*, compares two elements: *I worked **harder** than I ever had.* The **superlative form,** which either ends in *-est* or is preceded by *most* or *least*, compares three or more elements: *Jeff is the **hardest** worker I have ever met.*

Positive	Comparative	Superlative
hard	harder	hardest
deserving	more/less deserving	most/least deserving

(1) Complete and logical comparisons

When using the comparative form of an adjective or an adverb, be sure to indicate what two elements you are comparing.

A diesel engine is **heavier** *than a gas engine*.

Occasionally, the second element in a comparison is implied. In the sentence below, the reader can infer that the grade on the second paper was better than the grade on the first paper.

She wrote **two** papers; the instructor gave her a **better** grade on the second.

A comparison should also be logical. The following example illogically compares *population* and *Wabasha*.

The **population** of Winona is larger than **Wabasha.**

You can revise this type of faulty comparison in three ways:

- Repeat the word that refers to what is being compared.

    The **population** of Winona is larger than the **population** of Wabasha.

Modifiers

- Use a pronoun that corresponds to the first element in the comparison.

    The **population** of Winona is larger than **that** of Wabasha.

- Use possessive forms.

    Winona's population is larger than **Wabasha's**.

(2) Double comparatives or superlatives

Use either an ending or a preceding qualifier, not both, to form a comparative or superlative.

The first bridge is **more narrower** than the second.

The ~~most~~ **narrowest** bridge is in the northern part of the state.

Comparative and superlative forms of modifiers that have absolute meanings, such as *a more perfect society* and *the most unique campus,* are rarely used in academic writing.

EXERCISE 2

Provide the comparative or superlative form of each modifier.

1. Amphibians can be divided into three groups. Frogs and toads are in the (common) group.
2. Because they do not have to maintain a specific body temperature, amphibians eat (frequently) than mammals do.
3. Reptiles may look like amphibians, but their skin is (dry).
4. During the Devonian period, the (close) ancestors of amphibians were fish with fins that looked like legs.

6c Double negatives

The term **double negative** refers to the use of two negative words to express a single negation. Revise any double negatives you find in your writing.

He did**n't** keep ~~no~~ _{any} records.

OR

He _{kept} ~~didn't keep~~ **no** records.

Using *not* or *nothing* with *hardly*, *barely*, or *scarcely* creates a double negative.

I could~~n't~~ **hardly** quit in the middle of the job.

OR

I could**n't** ~~hardly~~ quit in the middle of the job.

MULTILINGUAL WRITERS

NEGATION IN OTHER LANGUAGES

The use of two negative words in one sentence is common in languages such as Spanish:

*Yo **no** compré **nada**.* ["I didn't buy anything."]

If your native language allows this type of negation, be sure to revise any double negatives you find in your English essays.

6d Placement of modifiers

Effective placement of modifiers will improve the clarity and coherence of your sentences. A **misplaced modifier** obscures the meaning of a sentence.

(1) Keeping related words together

Place the modifiers *almost, even, hardly, just,* and *only* before the words or word groups they modify. Altering placement can alter meaning.

> The committee can **only** nominate two members for the position. [The committee cannot *appoint* the two members to the position.]

> The committee can nominate **only** two members for the position. [The committee cannot nominate more than two members.]

> **Only** the committee can nominate two members for the position. [No person or group other than the committee can nominate members.]

(2) Placing modifiers near the words they modify

Readers expect phrases and clauses to modify the nearest grammatical element. The revision of the following sentence clarifies that the prosecutor, not the witness, was skillful.

> With great skill, the
> ~~The~~ prosecutor cross-examined the witness ~~with great skill~~.

The following revision makes it clear that the phrase *crouched and ugly* describes the phantom, not the boy.

> The   crouched and ugly
> ~~Crouched and ugly, the~~ young boy gasped at the phantom moving across the stage.

(3) Revising squinting modifiers

A **squinting modifier** can be interpreted as modifying either what precedes it or what follows it. To avoid such lack of clarity, you can reposition the modifier, add punctuation, or revise the entire sentence.

> Even though Erikson lists some advantages **overall** his vision of a successful business is faulty.

Revisions

> Even though Erikson lists some **overall** advantages, his vision of a successful business is faulty. [modifer repositioned; punctuation added]

> Erikson lists some advantages**; however, overall,** his vision of a successful business is faulty. [sentence revised]

MULTILINGUAL WRITERS

ADVERBS OF FREQUENCY

Adverbs of frequency (such as *always, never, sometimes,* and *often*) appear before one-word verbs.

> He **rarely** goes to horror movies.

However, these adverbs appear after a form of *be* when it is the main verb.

> Novels written by Stephen King are **always** popular.

When a sentence contains more than one verb in a verb phrase, the adverb of frequency is placed after the first auxiliary verb.

> My friends have **never** read *The Shining*.

EXERCISE 3

Improve the clarity of the following sentences by moving the modifiers.

1. Alfred Hitchcock was only identified with thrillers after making his third movie, *The Lodger*.
2. Hitchcock's most famous movies revolved around psychological improbabilities that are still discussed by movie critics today.
3. Although his movies are known for suspense sometimes moviegoers also remember Hitchcock's droll sense of humor.
4. Hitchcock just did not direct movie thrillers; he also produced two television series.
5. Originally a British citizen, Queen Elizabeth knighted Alfred Hitchcock in 1980.

6e Dangling modifiers

Dangling modifiers are phrases or elliptical clauses (clauses without a subject) that lack an appropriate word to modify. To avoid including dangling modifiers in your essays, first look carefully at any sentence that begins with a phrase or an elliptical clause. If the phrase or clause suggests an action, be sure that what follows the modifier (the subject of the sentence) names the actor. If there is no actor performing the action indicated in the phrase, the modifier is dangling. To revise this type of dangling modifier, name an actor—either in the modifier or in the main clause.

Lying on the beach, time became irrelevant. [Time cannot lie on a beach.]

Revisions

While **we** were lying on the beach, time became irrelevant. [actor in the modifier]

Lying on the beach, **we** found that time became irrelevant. [actor in the main clause]

While eating lunch, the phone rang. [A phone cannot eat lunch.]

Revisions

While **we** were eating lunch, the phone rang. [actor in the modifier]

While eating lunch, **we** heard the phone ring. [actor in the main clause]

Although you will most frequently find a dangling modifier at the beginning of a sentence, you may sometimes find one at the end of a sentence.

Adequate lighting is important ~~when~~ *for anyone* studying.

[Lighting cannot study.]

EXERCISE 4

Revise any misplaced or dangling modifiers.

1. Climbing a mountain, fitness becomes all-important.
2. In determining an appropriate challenge, considering safety precautions is necessary.
3. Even when expecting sunny weather, rain gear should be packed.
4. Although adding extra weight, climbers should not leave home without a first-aid kit.
5. By taking pains at the beginning of a trip, agony can be averted at the end of a trip.

S

EFFECTIVE SENTENCES

CHAPTER 7
Sentence Unity 88

- 7a Choosing and arranging details 88
- 7b Revising mixed metaphors 89
- 7c Revising mixed constructions 89
- 7d Relating sentence parts 90
- 7e Including necessary words 93
- 7f Completing comparisons 94
- 7g Completing intensifiers 95

CHAPTER 8
Subordination and Coordination 97

- 8a Using subordination effectively 97
- 8b Using coordination effectively 98
- 8c Avoiding faulty or excessive subordination and coordination 100

CHAPTER 9
Parallelism 103

- 9a Recognizing parallel elements 103
- 9b Repeating words and grammatical forms 104
- 9c Linking two or more sentences 105
- 9d Using correlative conjunctions 106

CHAPTER 10
Emphasis 108

- 10a Placing words for emphasis 108
- 10b Using cumulative and periodic sentences 108
- 10c Ordering ideas from least to most important 109
- 10d Repeating important words 109
- 10e Inverting word order 110
- 10f Using an occasional short sentence 111

CHAPTER 11
Variety 113

- 11a Revising sentence length and form 113
- 11b Varying sentence openings 115
- 11c Using questions, exclamations, and commands 116

7 Sentence Unity

Effective academic and professional writing is composed of sentences that are consistent, clear, and complete.

7a Choosing and arranging details

Well-chosen details add interest and credibility to your writing. As you revise, you may occasionally notice a sentence that would be clearer and more believable with the addition of a phrase or two about time, location, or cause.

Missing important detail	An astrophysicist from the Harvard-Smithsonian Center has predicted a galactic storm.
With detail added	An astrophysicist from the Harvard-Smithsonian Center has predicted **that** a galactic storm **will occur within the next 10 million years.**

Without the additional information about time, most readers would wonder when the storm was supposed to occur. The added detail not only makes the sentence clearer but also helps readers accept the information.

When considering how much detail to include, be sure that every detail contributes to the central thought, as in the following excerpt.

A given mental task may involve a complicated web of circuits, which interact in varying degrees with others throughout the brain—not like the parts in a machine, but like the instruments in a symphony orchestra combining their tenor, volume, and resonance to create a particular musical effect.

—JAMES SHREEVE, *Beyond the Brain*

7b Revising mixed metaphors

When you use language that evokes images, make sure that the images are meaningfully related. Unrelated images that appear in the same sentence are called **mixed metaphors.** The following sentence includes incompatible images.

As he climbed the corporate ladder, he ~~sank into a sea of~~ <ins>incurred a large</ins> debt.

The combination of two images—climbing a ladder and sinking into a sea—could create a picture in the reader's mind of a man hanging onto a ladder as it disappears into the water. The easiest way to revise such a sentence is to replace the words evoking one of the conflicting images.

7c Revising mixed constructions

A sentence that begins with one kind of grammatical structure and shifts to another is a **mixed construction.** To untangle a mixed construction, make sure that the sentence includes a conventional subject—a noun, a noun phrase, a gerund phrase, an infinitive phrase, or a noun clause. Prepositional phrases and adverbial clauses are not typical subjects.

~~By~~ <ins>Practicing</ins> ~~practicing~~ a new language daily will help you become proficient. [A gerund phrase replaces a prepositional phrase.]

> ~~Although she won a scholarship~~ *Her scholarship award* does not give her the right to skip classes. [A noun phrase replaces an adverbial clause.]

If you find a sentence that has a mixed construction, you can either revise the subject or leave the beginning of the sentence as a modifier and add a new subject after it.

> By practicing a new language daily, **you** will become more proficient.

> Although she won a scholarship, **she** does not have the right to skip classes.

7d Relating sentence parts

When drafting, writers sometimes compose sentences in which the subject is said to be something or to do something that is not logically possible. This breakdown in meaning is called **faulty predication.** Similarly, mismatches between a verb and its complement can obscure meaning.

(1) Mismatch between subject and verb

The joining of a subject and a verb must create a meaningful idea.

Mismatch   The absence of detail screams out at the reader. [An *absence* cannot scream.]

Revision   The reader immediately notices the absence of detail.

(2) Illogical equation with *be*

When a form of the verb *be* joins two parts of a sentence (the subject and the subject complement), these two parts should be logically related.

> ~~The importance of free speech~~ *Free speech* is essential to a democracy. [*Importance* cannot be essential.]

(3) Mismatches in definitions

When you write a sentence that states a formal definition, the term being defined should be followed by a noun or a noun phrase, not an adverbial clause. Avoid using *is when* or *is where*.

> *Ecology* is ~~when you~~ the study of the relationships among living organisms and between living organisms and their environment.

> *Exploitative competition* is ~~where~~ the contest between two or more organisms ~~vie~~ vying for a limited resource such as food.

(4) Mismatch of *reason* with *is because*

You can see why *reason* and *is because* are a mismatch by looking at the meaning of *because*: "for the reason that." Saying "the reason is for the reason that" is redundant. Thus, revise any sentence containing the construction *the reason is . . . because*.

> The ~~reason the~~ old train station was closed ~~is~~ because it had fallen into disrepair.

(5) Mismatch between verb and complement

A verb and its complement should fit together meaningfully.

Mismatch	Only a few students used the incorrect use of *there*. [To "use an incorrect use" is not logical.]
Revision	Only a few students used *there* incorrectly.

To make sure that a relative pronoun in the object position is connected logically to a verb, replace the pronoun with its antecedent. In the following sentence, *the inspiration* is the antecedent for *that*.

Mismatch   The inspiration that the author created touched young writers. [To "create the inspiration" is not logical.]

Revision   The author inspired young writers.

Verbs used to report the words of others are followed by specific types of complements. A few common verbs and their typical complements are listed below.

VERBS FOR ATTRIBUTION AND THEIR COMPLEMENTS

Verb + *that* noun clause

agree	claim	report	suggest
argue	demonstrate	state	think

Example: The researcher **reported** that the weather patterns had changed.

Verb + noun phrase + *that* noun clause

convince   remind   tell

Example: He **told** the reporters that he was planning to resign.

Verb + *wh-* noun clause

demonstrate	discuss	report	suggest
describe	explain	state	wonder

Example: She **described** what had happened.

EXERCISE 1

Revise the following sentences so that each verb is followed by a conventional complement.

1. The committee chair discussed that funding requests had specific requirements.
2. He convinced that mass transit was affordable.
3. The two groups agreed how the problem could be solved.
4. Brown and Edwards described that improvements had been made to the old building.
5. They wondered that such a catastrophe could happen.

7e Including necessary words

When we speak or write quickly, we often omit small words. As you revise, be sure to include all necessary articles, prepositions, verbs, and conjunctions.

The ceremony took place in ^*an* auditorium.

We discussed a couple ^*of* issues at the meeting.

When a sentence has a **compound verb** (two verbs linked by a conjunction), you may need to supply a different preposition for each verb to make your meaning clear.

He neither **believes** ^*in* nor **approves of** exercise.

All verbs, both auxiliary and main, should be included to make sentences complete.

She <ins>has</ins> seen the movie three times.

Voter turnout has never <ins>been</ins> and will never be 100 percent.

When a sentence consists of two short clauses and the verb in both clauses is the same, the verb in the second clause can be omitted.

The wind **was** fierce and the thunder [was] deafening.

Include the word *that* before a clause when it makes the sentence easier to read. Without the added *that* in the following sentence, a reader may stumble over *discovered the fossil* before understanding that *the fossil* is linked to *provided*.

The paleontologists discovered <ins>that</ins> the fossil provided a link between the dinosaur and the modern bird.

That should always be retained when a sentence has two parallel clauses.

The graph indicated **that the population had increased** but **that the number of homeowners had not.**

7f Completing comparisons

A comparison has two parts: someone or something is compared to someone or something else. As you revise your writing, make sure that your audience knows who or what is being compared. To revise incomplete comparisons, add necessary words, phrases, or clauses.

His first novel was better <ins>than the one just published</ins>.

After you are sure that your comparisons are complete, check to see that they are also logical.

Her test scores are higher than ^those of^ the other students.

In the original sentence, *scores* were being compared to *students*. You could also rewrite that sentence as follows:

Her test scores are higher than the other students'.

Because *test scores* have already been mentioned, it is clear that *students'* (with an apostrophe) is short for *students' test scores*.

7g Completing intensifiers

In speech, the intensifiers *so, such,* and *too* are used to mean "very," "unusually," or "extremely."

That movie was **so** funny.

In academic and professional writing, however, the intensifiers *so, such,* and *too* require a completing phrase or clause.

That movie was **so** funny **that I watched it twice.**

Julian has **such** a hearty laugh **that it makes everyone else laugh with him.**

The problem is just **too** complex **to solve in one day.**

EXERCISE 2

Revise the following sentences to make them clear and complete.

1. Ralph McQuarrie sketched designs for R2D2 and Darth Vader, including his mask. Ian McCaig wanted to create something scarier for *The Phantom Menace*.
2. He drew generic male face with metal teeth and long red ribbons of hair falling in front of it.
3. He designed a face that looked as though it been flayed.
4. The evil visage of Darth Maul was so horrible. To balance the effect, McCaig added elegant black feathers.

8 Subordination and Coordination

Understanding subordination and coordination can help you indicate connections between ideas as well as add variety to your sentences.

8a Using subordination effectively

Subordinate means "being of lower rank." A subordinate grammatical structure cannot stand alone; it is dependent on the main (independent) clause. The most common subordinate structure is the dependent clause, which usually begins with a subordinating conjunction or a relative pronoun.

(1) Subordinating conjunctions

A **subordinating conjunction** specifies the relationship between a dependent clause and an independent clause. For example, it might signal a causal relationship.

The painters finished early **because** they work well together.

Here are a few of the most frequently used subordinating conjunctions:

Cause	*because*
Concession	*although, even though*
Condition	*if, unless*
Effect	*so that*
Sequence	*before, after*
Time	*when*

By using subordinating conjunctions, you can combine short sentences and indicate how they are related.

> ~~The~~ ^{After the} crew leader picked us up early on Friday_{, we}. ~~We~~ ate breakfast together at a local diner.

(2) Relative pronouns

A **relative pronoun** (*who, whom, which, that,* or *whose*) introduces a dependent clause that modifies the pronoun's antecedent.

> The temple has a portico **that faces west.**

By using an **adjectival (relative) clause**—that is, a dependent clause introduced by a relative pronoun—you can embed details into a sentence without sacrificing conciseness.

> Japanese automakers have produced a hybrid car_{, which has sold well in the United States}.

CAUTION

A relative clause beginning with *which* sometimes refers to an entire independent clause rather than modifying a specific word or phrase. Because this type of reference can be vague, you should avoid it if possible.

> ^{As} ~~He is~~ a graduate of a top university, ^{he should have} ~~which should provide him with~~ many opportunities.

8b Using coordination effectively

Coordinate means "being of equal rank." Coordinate grammatical elements have the same form. For example, they may be two words that are both adjectives, two phrases that are both prepositional, or two clauses that are both independent.

a **stunning** and **satisfying** conclusion [adjectives]

in the attic or **in the basement** [prepositional phrases]

The company was losing money, yet **the employees suspected nothing.** [independent clauses]

To indicate the relationship between coordinate words, phrases, or clauses, choose an appropriate coordinating conjunction.

Addition	*and*
Alternative	*or, not*
Cause	*for*
Contrast	*but, yet*
Result	*so*

By using coordination, you can avoid unnecessary repetition.

The hike to the top of Angels Landing has countless switchbacks. ~~It also has~~ *and* long drop-offs.

MULTILINGUAL WRITERS

CHOOSING CONJUNCTIONS

In English, use either a coordinating conjunction or a subordinating conjunction (but not both) to signal a connection between clauses.

Because he had a headache, ~~so~~ he went to the health center.

~~Because~~ *He* had a headache, **so** he went to the health center.

EXERCISE 1

Using subordination and coordination, revise the sentences in the following paragraph so that they emphasize the ideas you think are important.

¹The Lummi tribe lives in the Northwest. ²The Lummis have a belief about sorrow and loss. ³They believe that grief is a burden. ⁴According to their culture, this burden should not be carried alone. ⁵After the terrorist attack on the World Trade Center, the Lummis wanted to help shoulder the burden of grief felt by others. ⁶Some of the Lummis carve totem poles. ⁷These carvers crafted a healing totem pole. ⁸They gave this pole to the citizens of New York. ⁹Many of the citizens of New York had family members who were killed in the terrorist attacks. ¹⁰The Lummis do not believe that the pole itself heals. ¹¹Rather, they believe that healing comes from the prayers and songs said over it. ¹²For them, healing is not the responsibility of a single person. ¹³They believe that it is the responsibility of the community.

8c Avoiding faulty or excessive subordination and coordination

(1) Choosing precise conjunctions

Effective subordination requires choosing subordinating conjunctions carefully. In the following sentence, the use of *as* is distracting because it can mean either "because" or "while."

> Because
> ~~As~~ time was running out, I randomly filled in the remaining circles on the exam sheet.

Your choice of coordinating conjunction should also convey your meaning precisely. For example, to indicate a cause-and-effect relationship, *so* is more precise than *and*.

> so
> The rain continued to fall, ~~and~~ the concert was canceled.

(2) Excessive subordination and coordination

As you revise your writing, make sure that you have not overused subordination or coordination. In the following ineffective sentence, two dependent clauses compete for the reader's focus. The revision is clearer because it eliminates one of the dependent clauses.

Ineffective

Although researchers used to believe that ancient Egyptians were the first to domesticate cats, they now think that cats may have provided company for humans 5,000 years earlier **because** the intact skeleton of a cat has been discovered in a Neolithic village on Cyprus.

Revised

Although researchers used to believe that ancient Egyptians were the first to domesticate cats, they now think that cats may have provided company for humans 5,000 years earlier. They base their revised estimate on the discovery of an intact cat skeleton in a Neolithic village on Cyprus.

Overuse of coordination results in a rambling sentence in need of revision.

Ineffective

The lake was surrounded by forest, and it was large and clean, so it looked refreshing.

Revised

Surrounded by forest, the large, clean lake looked refreshing.

EXERCISE 2

Revise the following sentences to eliminate faulty or excessive coordination and subordination.

1. Duct tape was invented for the U.S. military during World War II to keep the moisture out of ammunition cases because it was strong and waterproof.

2. Duct tape was originally called "duck tape" as it was waterproof and ducks are like that too and because it was made of cotton duck, which is a durable, tightly woven material.

3. When the war was over, house builders used duck tape to connect duct work together, and the builders started to refer to duck tape as "duct tape" and eventually the color of the tape changed from the green that was used during the war to silver, which matched the ducts.

9 Parallelism

Parallelism is the use of grammatically equivalent structures to clarify meaning and to emphasize ideas.

9a Recognizing parallel elements

Two or more elements are considered parallel when they have similar grammatical forms—for example, when they are all nouns or all prepositional phrases. Parallel elements are frequently joined by a coordinating conjunction (*and, but, or, yet, so, nor,* or *for*). In the examples that follow, the elements in boldface have the same grammatical form.

Words

The dean is both **determined** and
dedicated.

Phrases

Her goals include **publicizing student and faculty research**,
increasing the funding for that research,
and **providing adequate research facilities**.

Clauses

He said **that we would conduct a similar project** but
that we would likely get different results.

Sentences

When I interviewed for the job, I tried not to sweat.
When I got the job, I managed not to shout.

9b Repeating words and grammatical forms

(1) The repetition of words

By repeating a preposition, the infinitive marker *to,* or the introductory word of a clause, you can create parallel structures that will help you convey your meaning clearly, succinctly, and emphatically.

Preposition

My embarrassment stemmed not **from** the money lost but **from** the notoriety gained.

Infinitive marker *to*

She wanted her audience **to remember** the protest song and **to understand** its origin.

Introductory word of a clause

The team vowed **that** they would support each other, **that** they would play their best, and **that** they would win the tournament.

(2) The repetition of form

Sometimes parallel structures are similar in form even though no words are repeated. The following example includes the *-ing* form (present participle) of three different verbs.

People all around me are **buying, remodeling,** or **selling** their houses.

As you edit a draft, look for sentences that include two or three structures joined by *and, but,* or *or.* Make sure the structures are parallel.

Whether **mortgage rates rise** or ~~the~~ **building codes** ~~are~~ **changed,** the real estate market should remain strong this spring.

Each part of the dependent clause in the revised sentence includes a two-word subject and a one-word predicate.

9c Linking two or more sentences

Repeating a pattern emphasizes the relationship of ideas. The following two sentences come from the conclusion of "Letter from Birmingham Jail."

> **If I have said anything** in this letter <u>that overstates the truth and indicates an unreasonable impatience,</u> **I beg you to forgive me.** **If I have said anything** <u>that understates the truth and indicates my having a patience</u> that allows me to settle for anything less than brotherhood, **I beg God to forgive me.**
>
> —MARTIN LUTHER KING, JR.

Almost every structure in the second sentence is parallel to a structure in the first. To create this parallelism, King repeats words and uses similar grammatical forms.

THINKING RHETORICALLY

PARALLELISM

Parallel elements make your writing easy to read. But consider breaking from the parallel pattern on occasion to emphasize a point. For example, to describe a friend, you could start with two adjectives and then switch to a noun phrase.

> My friend Alison is **kind, modest,** and **the smartest mathematician in the state.**

9d Using correlative conjunctions

Correlative conjunctions (or **correlatives**) are pairs of words that link other words, phrases, or clauses.

both . . . and
either . . . or
neither . . . nor
not only . . . but also
whether . . . or

Notice how the words or phrases following each conjunction in the pair are parallel.

He will major in **either** biology **or** chemistry.

Whether at home **or** at school, he is always busy.

Be especially careful when using *not only . . . but also*.

~~Not only practicing~~ <ins>His team practices not only</ins> at 6 a.m. during the week, but ~~his team~~ also ~~scrimmages~~ on Sunday afternoons.

OR

Not only <ins>does his team practice</ins> ~~practicing~~ at 6 a.m. during the week, but ~~his team~~ <ins>it</ins> also scrimmages on Sunday afternoons.

EXERCISE 1

Make the structures in each sentence parallel. In some sentences, you may have to use different wording.

1. Helen was praised by the vice president, and her assistant admired her.

2. When she hired new employees for her department, she looked for applicants who were intelligent, able to stay focused, and able to speak clearly.

3. At meetings, she was always prepared, participating actively yet politely, and generated innovative responses to department concerns.

4. In her annual report, she wrote that her most important achievements were attracting new clients and revenues were higher.

5. When asked about her leadership style, she said that she preferred collaborating with others rather than to work alone in her office.

10 Emphasis

In any piece of writing, some of your ideas will be more important than others. You can direct the reader's attention to these ideas by emphasizing them.

10a Placing words for emphasis

Words at the beginning or the end of a sentence receive emphasis. Notice how the revision of the following sentence adds emphasis to the beginning to balance the emphasis at the end.

~~In today's society, most good~~ Good jobs require a college education. today

You can also emphasize an important idea by placing it after a colon or a dash.

> At a later time [rocks and clay] may again become what they once were: dust. —LESLIE MARMON SILKO, "Interior and Exterior Landscapes"

> By 1857, miners had extracted 760 tons of gold from these hills—and left behind more than ten times as much mercury, as well as devastated forests, slopes and streams.
> —REBECCA SOLNIT, *Storming the Gates of Paradise: Landscapes for Politics*

10b Using cumulative and periodic sentences

In a **cumulative sentence,** the main idea (the independent clause) comes first; less important ideas or supplementary details follow.

> **The day was hot for June,** a pale sun burning in a cloudless sky, wilting the last of the irises, the rhododendron blossoms drooping. —ADAM HASLETT, "Devotion"

In a **periodic sentence,** however, the main idea comes last, just before the period.

> In a day when movies seem more and more predictable, when novels tend to be plotless, baggy monsters or minimalist exercises in interior emotion, **it's no surprise that sports has come to occupy an increasingly prominent place in the communal imagination.** —MICHIKO KAKUTANI, "Making Art of Sport"

Both of these types of sentences can be effective. Because cumulative sentences are more common, however, the infrequently encountered periodic sentence tends to provide emphasis.

10c Ordering ideas from least to most important

By arranging your ideas in **climactic order**—from least important to most important—you build up suspense. In the following example, the writer emphasizes a doctor's desire to help the disadvantaged and then implies that this desire has been realized through work with young Haitian doctors.

> While he was in medical school, the soon-to-be doctor discovered his calling: to diagnose infectious diseases, to find ways of curing people with these diseases, and **to bring the lifesaving knowledge of modern medicine to the disadvantaged.** Most recently, he has been working with a small group of young doctors in Haiti.

10d Repeating important words

Although effective writers avoid unnecessary repetition, they also understand that deliberate repetition emphasizes key words or ideas.

We **forget** all too soon the things we thought we could never **forget**. We **forget** the loves and betrayals alike, **forget** what we whispered and what we screamed, **forget** who we are.

—JOAN DIDION, "On Keeping a Notebook"

10e Inverting word order

Most sentences begin with a subject and end with a predicate. When you move words out of their normal order, you draw attention to them.

At the back of the crowded room sat **a newspaper reporter.** [COMPARE: **A newspaper reporter** sat **at the back of the crowded room.**]

Notice the inverted word order in the second sentence of the following passage.

¹The Library Committee met with the City Council on several occasions to persuade them to fund the building of a library annex. ²So successful were their efforts that a new wing will be added by next year. ³This wing will contain archival materials that were previously stored in the basement.

The modifier *so successful* appears at the beginning of the sentence, rather than in its normal position, after the verb: Their efforts were *so successful* that . . . . The inverted word order emphasizes the committee's accomplishment.

MULTILINGUAL WRITERS

INVERTING WORD ORDER

English sentences are inverted in various ways. Sometimes the main verb in the form of a participle is placed at the beginning of the sentence. The subject and the auxiliary verb(s) are then inverted.

> *part* *aux* *s*
> **Carved** into the bench **were someone's initials.**
> [COMPARE: Someone's initials were carved into the bench.]

An adjective may also begin a sentence. In this type of sentence, the subject and the linking verb are inverted.

> *adj* *link v* *s*
> **Crucial** to our success **was the dedication of our employees.**
> [COMPARE: The dedication of our employees was crucial to our success.]

10f Using an occasional short sentence

In a paragraph of mostly long sentences, try using a short sentence for emphasis. To optimize the effect, lead up to the short sentence with an especially long sentence.

After organizing the kitchen, buying the groceries, slicing the vegetables, mowing the lawn, weeding the garden, hanging the decorations, and setting up the grill, I was ready to have a good time when my guests arrived. **Then the phone rang.**

EXERCISE 1

Add emphasis to each of the following sentences by using the strategy indicated. You may have to add some words and/or delete others.

1. (climactic order) In the 1960 Olympics, Wilma Rudolph tied the world record in the 100-meter race, she tied the record in the 400-meter relay, she won the hearts of fans from around the world, and she broke the record in the 200-meter race.

2. (periodic sentence) Some sports reporters described Rudolph as a gazelle because of her beautiful stride.

3. (inversion) Rudolph's Olympic achievement is impressive, but her victory over a crippling disease is even more spectacular.

4. (final short sentence) Rudolph was born prematurely, weighing only four and one-half pounds. As a child, she suffered from double pneumonia, scarlet fever, and then polio.

5. (cumulative sentence) She received help from her family. Her brothers and sister massaged her legs. Her mother drove her to a hospital for therapy.

11 Variety

To make your writing lively and distinctive, include a variety of sentence types and lengths.

11a Revising sentence length and form

To avoid the choppiness of a series of short sentences, combine some of the sentences into longer sentences. You can combine sentences by using coordinating conjunctions (such as *and, but,* and *or*), subordinating conjunctions (such as *because, although,* and *when*), or relative pronouns (such as *who, that,* and *which*).

Short Minneapolis is one of the Twin Cities. St. Paul is the other. They differ in many ways.

Combined Minneapolis **and** St. Paul are called the Twin Cities, **but** they differ in many ways. [coordinating conjunctions]

Short Legislation on space tourism has not been passed. Plans for a commercial rocket service are going forward anyway.

Combined **Although** legislation on space tourism has not been passed, plans for a commercial rocket service are going forward anyway. [subordinating conjunction]

Short	Today, lawmakers discussed some new legislation. This legislation would promote the safety of rocket passengers.
Combined	Today, lawmakers discussed some new legislation **that** would promote the safety of rocket passengers. [relative pronoun]

THINKING RHETORICALLY

SHORT SENTENCES

Occasionally, a series of brief sentences produces an intended effect. The short sentences in the following passage capture the quick actions taking place as an accident is about to occur.

> "There's a truck in your lane!" my friend yelled. I swerved toward the shoulder. "Watch out!" she screamed. I hit the brakes. The wheels locked. The back of the car swerved to the right.

EXERCISE 1

Convert each set of short sentences into a single longer sentence.

1. It was the bottom of the ninth inning. The score was tied. The bases were loaded. There were two outs.
2. A young player stepped up to the plate. This was his first season. He had hit a home run yesterday. He had struck out his last time at bat.
3. He knew the next pitch could decide the game. He took a practice swing. The pitcher looked him over.
4. The pitch came in high. The batter swung low. He missed this first pitch. He also missed the second pitch.
5. He had two strikes against him. The young player hit the next ball. It soared over the right-field fence.

11b Varying sentence openings

Most writers begin more than half of their sentences with a subject. Although this pattern is common, relying on it too heavily can make writing sound dull. Experiment with the following alternatives for beginning your sentences.

(1) Beginning with an adverb

Immediately, the dentist stopped drilling and asked me how I was doing. [adverb]

(2) Beginning with a phrase

Reflecting on the election, we understood clearly how the incumbent defeated the challenger. [participial phrase]

A town of historic interest, Santa Fe also has many art galleries. [appositive phrase]

(3) Beginning with a transitional word or phrase

In each of the following examples, the transitional word or phrase shows the relationship between the ideas in the pair of sentences.

Many restaurants close within a few years of opening. **But** others, which offer good food at reasonable prices, become well established.

Independently owned restaurants struggle to get started for a number of reasons. **First of all,** they have to compete against successful restaurant chains.

(4) Beginning with a word that usually comes after the verb

I was an abysmal football player. **Soccer,** though, I could play well. [direct object]

Vital to any success I had were my mother's early lessons. [predicate adjective]

EXERCISE 2

Rewrite each sentence so that it does not begin with a subject.

1. John Spilsbury was an engraver and mapmaker from London who made the first jigsaw puzzle in about 1760.
2. He pasted a map onto a piece of wood and used a fine-bladed saw to cut around the borders of the countries.
3. The jigsaw puzzle was first an educational toy and has been a mainstay in households all over the world ever since its invention.
4. The original puzzles were quite expensive because the wooden pieces were cut by hand.
5. Most puzzles are made of cardboard today.

11c Using questions, exclamations, and commands

You can vary the sentences in a paragraph by introducing an occasional question, exclamation, or command.

(1) Raising a question or two for variety

> If people could realize that immigrant children are better off, and less scarred, by holding on to their first languages as they learn a second one, then perhaps Americans could accept a more drastic change. What if every English-speaking toddler were to start learning a foreign language at an early age, maybe in kindergarten? What if these children were to learn Spanish, for instance, the language already spoken by millions of American citizens, but also by so many neighbors to the South?
>
> —ARIEL DORFMAN, "If Only We All Spoke Two Languages"

You can either answer the question or let readers answer it for themselves, in which case it is called a **rhetorical question.**

(2) Adding an exclamatory sentence for variety

But at other moments, the classroom is so lifeless or painful or confused—and I so powerless to do anything about it—that my claim to be a teacher seems a transparent sham. Then the enemy is everywhere: in those students from some alien planet, in the subject I thought I knew, and in the personal pathology that keeps me earning my living this way. What a fool I was to imagine that I had mastered this occult art—harder to divine than tea leaves and impossible for mortals to do even passably well!
—**PARKER PALMER,** *The Courage to Teach*

(3) Including a command for variety

Now I stare and stare at people shamelessly. Stare. It's the way to educate your eye. —**WALKER EVANS,** *Unclassified*

In this case, a one-word command, "Stare," provides variety.

EFFECTIVE LANGUAGE

CHAPTER 12
Good Usage 120

- **12a** Clear style 120
- **12b** Appropriate word choice 121
- **12c** Inclusive language 122

CHAPTER 13
Precise Word Choice 127

- **13a** Accurate and precise word choice 127
- **13b** Clichés and euphemisms 129
- **13c** Idioms and collocations 130
- **13d** Clear definitions 131

CHAPTER 14
Conciseness 133

- **14a** Eliminating wordiness and other redundancies 133
- **14b** Using elliptical constructions 135

12 Good Usage

Using the right words at the right time can make the difference between having your ideas taken seriously and seeing them brushed aside. Keeping your audience and purpose in mind will help you use the right word at the right time.

12a Clear style

Although different styles are appropriate for different situations, you should strive to make your writing easy to read. To achieve a clear style, choose words that your audience understands and that are appropriate for the occasion.

Ornate The majority believes that achievement derives primarily from the diligent pursuit of allocated tasks.

Clear Most people believe that success results from hard work.

If you want readers to take your writing seriously, you must show them respect by not using obscure words when common words will do and by not using more words than necessary.

EXERCISE 1

Revise the following sentences for an audience that prefers a clear, straightforward style.

1. Expert delineation of character in a job interview is a goal that is not always possible to achieve.
2. In an employment situation, social pleasantries may contribute to the successful functioning of job tasks, but such interactions

should not distract attention from the need to complete all assignments in a timely manner.

3. Commitment to an ongoing and carefully programmed schedule of physical self-management can be a significant resource for stress reduction in the workplace.

12b Appropriate word choice

Unless you are writing for a specialized audience and have good reason to believe that this audience will welcome slang, colloquial expressions, or jargon, the following advice can help you determine which words to use and which to avoid. A good dictionary will also help you. Words labeled *dialect, slang, colloquial, nonstandard,* or *unconventional* are generally inappropriate for college and professional writing. If a word has no label, you can safely assume that it can be used in writing for school or work.

(1) Slang

The term **slang** covers a wide range of words or expressions that are considered casual or fashionable by people in a particular age group, locality, or profession. Although such words are often used in private conversation or in writing intended to mimic conversation, they are usually out of place in academic or professional writing.

(2) Conversational (or colloquial) words

Words labeled *colloquial* in a dictionary are fine for casual conversation and for written dialogues or personal essays on a light topic. Such words are sometimes used for special effect in academic writing, but you should usually replace them with more appropriate words. For example, conversational words such as *dumb* and *kid around* could be replaced by *illogical* and *tease*.

(3) Regionalisms
Regionalisms—such as *tank* for "pond" and *sweeper* for "vacuum cleaner"—can make writing lively and distinctive, but they are often considered too informal for academic and professional writing.

(4) Technical words or jargon
When writing for a diverse audience, an effective writer will not refer to the need for bifocals as *presbyopia*. However, technical language is appropriate when the audience can understand it (as when one physician writes to another) or when the audience would benefit by learning the terms in question.

12c Inclusive language

By choosing words that are inclusive rather than exclusive, you invite readers into your writing. Prejudiced or derogatory language has no place in academic or professional writing; using it undermines your authority and credibility.

(1) Nonsexist language
Effective writers show equal respect for men and women. For example, they avoid using *man* to refer to people in general because they understand that the word excludes women.

> Achievements [OR Human achievements]
> ~~Man's achievements~~ in science are impressive.

Use the following tips to ensure that your writing is respectful.

TIPS FOR AVOIDING SEXIST LANGUAGE

When reviewing drafts, revise the following types of sexist language.

- **Generic *he*:** A doctor should listen to *his* patients.

    A doctor should listen to **his or her** patients. [use of the appropriate form of *he or she*]

    Doctors should listen to **their** patients. [use of plural forms]

    By listening to patients, **doctors obtain important diagnostic information.** [elimination of *his* by revising the sentence]

- **Terms such as *man* and *mankind* or those with *-ess* or *-man* endings:** Labor laws benefit the common *man*. *Mankind* benefits from philanthropy. The *stewardess* brought me some orange juice.

    Labor laws benefit **working people.** [replacement of the stereotypical term with a gender-neutral term]

    Everyone benefits from philanthropy. [use of an indefinite pronoun]

    The **flight attendant** brought me some orange juice. [use of a gender-neutral term]

- **Stereotypical gender roles:** I was told that the university offers free tuition to faculty *wives*. The minister pronounced them *man* and *wife*.

    I was told that the university offers free tuition to faculty **spouses.** [replacement of the stereotypical term with a gender-neutral term]

    The minister pronounced them **husband** and wife. [use of a term equivalent to *wife*]

- **Inconsistent use of titles:** *Mr. Holmes* and his *wife,* Mary, took a long trip to China.

    Mr. and Mrs. [or Ms.] Holmes took a long trip to China. [consistent use of titles]

    OR **Peter and Mary Holmes** took a long trip to China. [removal of titles]

    OR **Peter Holmes** and **Mary Wolfe** took a long trip to China. [use of full names]

(Continued on page 124)

(Continued from page 123)

- **Unstated gender assumption:** Have your *mother make your costume* for the school pageant.

  Have your **parents provide you with a costume** for the school pageant. [replacement of the stereotypical words with gender-neutral ones]

EXERCISE 2

Revise the following sentences to eliminate sexist language.

1. The ladies met to discuss the company's operating budget.
2. Mothers should read to their small children.
3. Some fans admired the actress because of her movies; others praised her for her environmental activism.
4. For six years, he worked as a mailman in a small town.

(2) Nonracist language

Rarely is it necessary to identify anyone's race or ethnicity in academic or professional writing. However, you may need to use appropriate racial or ethnic terms if you are writing a demographic report, an argument against existing racial inequities, or a historical account of a particular event involving ethnic groups. Determining which terms a particular group prefers can be difficult because preferences sometimes vary within a group and change over time. One conventional way to refer to Americans of a specific descent is to include an adjective before the word *American*: *African American, Asian American, European American, Latin American, Mexican American, Native American*. These words are widely used; however, members of a particular group may identify themselves in more than one way. In addition to *African American* and *European American*, *Black* (or *black*) and *White* (or *white*) have long been used. People of Spanish-speaking descent may prefer *Chicano/Chicana*,

Hispanic, Latino/Latina, Puerto Rican, or other terms. Members of cultures that are indigenous to North America may prefer a specific name such as *Cherokee* or *Haida,* though some also accept *American Indian* or *Native People.*

(3) Writing about any difference respectfully

If a writing assignment requires you to distinguish people based on age, ability, geographical area, religion, or sexual orientation, show respect to the groups or individuals you discuss by using the terms they prefer.

(a) Referring to age

Although some people object to the term *senior citizen,* a better alternative has not emerged. When used respectfully, the term refers to a person who has reached the age of retirement (but may not have decided to retire) and is eligible for certain privileges granted by society. However, if you know your audience would object to this term, find out which alternative is preferred.

(b) Referring to disability or illness

A current recommendation for referring to disabilities and illnesses is "to put the person first." In this way, the focus is placed on the individual rather than on the limitation. Thus, *persons with disabilities* is preferred over *disabled persons.* You can find out whether such person-first expressions are preferred by noting whether they are used in the articles and books (or by the people) you consult.

(c) Referring to geographical areas

Certain geographical terms need to be used with special care. Though most frequently used to refer to people from the United States, the term *American* may also refer to people from Canada, Mexico, and Central or South America. If your audience may be confused by this term, use *people from the United States* or *U.S. citizens* instead.

The term *Arab* refers to people who speak Arabic. If you cannot use specific terms such as *Iraqi* or *Saudi Arabian,* be sure you know that a country's people speak Arabic and not another language. Iranians, for example, are not Arabs because they speak Farsi.

British, rather than *English,* is the preferred term for referring to people from the island of Great Britain or from the United Kingdom.

(d) Referring to religion
Reference to a person's religion should be made only if it is relevant. If you must mention religious affiliation, use only those terms considered respectful. Because religions have both conservative and liberal followers, be careful not to make generalizations about political stances.

(e) Referring to sexual orientation
If your purpose for writing makes it necessary to identify sexual orientations, choose terms used by the people you are discussing.

13 Precise Word Choice

By choosing the right word and putting it in the right place, you can communicate exactly what you mean and make your writing memorable to your intended audience.

13a Accurate and precise word choice

(1) Denotations and connotations

Denotations are definitions of words, such as those that appear in dictionaries. For example, the noun *beach* denotes a sandy or pebbly shore. Select words whose denotations convey your point exactly.

Yosemite National Park ~~is really great.~~ *astounds even an indifferent tourist like me.*

[Because *great* can mean "extremely large" as well as "outstanding" or "powerful," its use in this sentence is imprecise.]

Connotations are the associations evoked by a word. The context in which a word appears affects the associations it evokes. In a treatise on shoreline management, *beach* has scientific and geographic connotations; in a fashion magazine, this word is associated with bathing suits, sunglasses, and sunscreen. The challenge for writers is to choose the words that are most likely to spark the appropriate connotations in their readers' minds.

Mr. Kreuger's ~~relentlessness~~ *persistence* has earned praise from his supervisors.

[*Relentlessness* has negative connotations, which make it an unlikely quality for which to be praised.]

(2) Providing readers with helpful details

A **general word** is all-inclusive, indefinite, and sweeping in scope. A **specific word** is precise, definite, and limited in scope.

General	Specific	More Specific/Concrete
food	fast food	cheeseburger
place	city	Atlanta

An **abstract word** refers to a concept or idea, a quality or trait, or anything else that cannot be touched, heard, or seen. A **concrete word** signifies a particular object, a specific action, or anything that can be touched, heard, or seen.

Abstract	democracy, evil, strength, charity
Concrete	mosquito, hammer, plastic, fog

As you select words to fit your context, be as specific and concrete as you can. Ask yourself one or more of these questions about what you want to say: Exactly who? Exactly what? Exactly when? Exactly where? Exactly how? In the following example, notice what a difference concrete words can make in expressing an idea and how adding details can expand or develop it.

Vague	She has kept no reminders of performing in her youth.
Specific	She has kept no sequined costume, no photographs, no fliers or posters from that part of her youth. —LOUISE ERDRICH, "The Leap"

(3) Figurative language

Figurative language is the use of words in an imaginative rather than a literal sense. Similes and metaphors are the chief **figures of speech**. A **simile** is a comparison of dissimilar things that includes *like* or *as*. A **metaphor** is an implied comparison of dissimilar things, without *like* or *as*.

Simile

He was **like a piece of rare and delicate china which was always being saved from breaking and finally fell.**

—ALICE WALKER, "To Hell with Dying"

Metaphor

His **money was a sharp pair of scissors** that snipped rapidly through tangles of red tape. —HISAYE YAMAMOTO, *The Brown House*

Single words can be used metaphorically.

> These roses must be **planted** in good soil. [literal]
>
> Keep your life **planted** wherever you can put down the most roots. [metaphorical]

13b Clichés and euphemisms

When forced or overused, certain expressions lose their impact. For example, the expressions *bite the dust, breath of fresh air,* and *smooth as silk* were once striking and thus effective. Excessive use, though, has drained them of their original force and made them **clichés.** Newer expressions such as *put a spin on something* and *think outside the box* have also lost their vitality because of overuse. Nonetheless, clichés are so much a part of the language that nearly every writer uses them from time to time. But effective writers often give a fresh twist to an old saying.

> I seek a narrative, a fiction, to order days like the one I spent several years ago, on a gray June day in Chicago, when I took a roller-coaster ride on the bell curve of my experience.
> —GAYLE PEMBERTON, "The Zen of Bigger Thomas"

[Notice how much more effective this expression is than a reference to "being on an emotional roller coaster."]

Sometimes writers coin new expressions to substitute for words that have coarse or unpleasant connotations. These expressions, called **euphemisms,** occasionally become standardized. To avoid the word *dying,* for example, a writer might say that someone was *terminally ill.* However, although euphemisms sound more pleasant than the words they replace, they sometimes obscure facts. Euphemisms such as *revenue enhancement* for *tax hike* and *pre-owned* for *used* are considered insincere or deceitful.

EXERCISE 1

Replace the following overused expressions with carefully chosen words. Then use the replacements in sentences.

1. an axe to grind
2. hit the nail on the head
3. eat like a pig
4. business as usual

13c Idioms and collocations

Idioms are fixed expressions whose meanings cannot be entirely determined by knowing the meanings of their parts—*bear in mind, fall in love, in a nutshell, stand a chance*. **Collocations** are combinations of words that frequently occur together. Unlike idioms, they have meanings that *can* be determined by knowing the meanings of their parts—*depend on, fond of, little while, right now*. Regardless of whether you are using an idiom or a collocation, if you make even a small inadvertent change to the expected wording, you may distract or confuse your readers.

She tried to keep a ~~small~~ low profile.

They had ~~an invested~~ a vested interest in the project.

As you edit your writing, keep an eye out for idioms or collocations that might not be worded correctly. Then check a general dictionary or the **Glossary of Usage** at the end of this book to ensure that your usage is appropriate. Writers sometimes have trouble with the following collocations, all of which contain prepositions.

CHOOSING THE RIGHT PREPOSITION

Instead of	Use
according **with**	according **to** the source
accused **for**	accused **of** the crime
based **off of**	based **on** the novel
in accordance **to**	in accordance **with** policy
independent **to**	independent **of** his family
happened **on**	happened **by** accident
superior **than**	superior **to** others

13d Clear definitions

When words have more than one meaning, establish which meaning you have in mind in a particular piece of writing. A definition can set the terms of the discussion.

In this paper, I use the word *communism* **in the Marxist sense of social organization based on the holding of all property in common.**

A **formal definition** first states the term to be defined, then puts it into a class, and finally differentiates it from other members of that class.

> A *phosphene* [term] is **a luminous visual image** [class] that **results from applying pressure to the eyeball** [differentiation].

A short dictionary definition may adequately convey the meaning of a word unfamiliar to readers.

> Here, *galvanic* means **"produced as if by electric shock."**

A synonym can easily clarify the meaning of a term.

> *Machismo,* **confidence with an attitude,** can be a pose rather than a reality.

Examples also help readers understand the meaning of a word.

> Many homophones **(such as *be* and *bee*, *in* and *inn*, or *see* and *sea*)** are not spelling problems.

14 Conciseness

To facilitate readers' understanding, effective writers convey their thoughts clearly and efficiently, choosing each word wisely.

14a Eliminating wordiness and other redundancies

After writing a first draft, review your sentences to make sure that they contain only the words necessary to make your point.

(1) Redundancy
Restating a key point in different words can help readers understand it. But if you rephrase readily understood terms, your work will suffer from **redundancy**—repetition for no good reason.

Ballerinas auditioned ~~in the tryouts~~ for *The Nutcracker*.

MULTILINGUAL WRITERS

USING RELATIVE PRONOUNS

Review your sentences to make sure that no clause includes both a personal pronoun (*I, me, he, him, she, her, it,* etc.) and a relative pronoun (*who, that, which*) referring to the same antecedent.

The drug **that** we were testing ~~it~~ has not been approved by the Food and Drug Administration.

(2) Unnecessary words and wordy phrases

As you edit a draft, delete words that add no meaning to adjacent words and shorten wordy expressions.

> ~~In the event that~~ _{If} taxes are raised, ~~expect complaints on the part of the voters.~~ _{voters will complain.}

In addition, watch for vague words such as *area, aspect, factor, feature, kind, situation, thing,* and *type.* They may signal wordiness.

> ~~In an employment situation, effective~~ _{Effective} communication is essential at work.

REPLACEMENTS FOR WORDY EXPRESSIONS

Instead of	Use
at this moment (point) in time	now, today
due to the fact that	because
for the purpose of	for
it is clear (obvious) that	clearly (obviously)
without a doubt	undoubtedly
in the final analysis	finally

USELESS WORDS IN COMMON PHRASES

yellow [in color]	connect [up together]
at 9:45 a.m. [in the morning]	[really and truly] fearless
[basic] essentials	circular [in shape]

(3) *There are* and *it is*

There or *it* may function as an **expletive**—a word that signals that the subject of the sentence will follow the verb, usually a form of *be*. Writers use expletives to emphasize words that would not be emphasized in the typical subject-verb order.

> Three children were playing in the yard. [typical order]
>
> There were three children playing in the yard. [use of expletive]

However, if you find that you have drafted several sentences that begin with expletives, revise a few of them.

> Hundreds were
> ~~There were hundreds~~ of fans ˄crowding onto the field.
>
> Joining the crowd
> ˄It was frightening ~~to join the crowd~~.

(4) Relative pronouns

If a relative pronoun (*who, which, that*) is followed by a form of the verb *be* (*am, is, are, was,* or *were*), you can often omit the relative pronoun and sometimes the verb as well.

> The change ~~that~~ the young senator proposed yesterday angered most legislators.
>
> Bromo, ~~which is~~ Java's highest mountain, towers above its neighbors.

14b Using elliptical constructions

An **elliptical construction** is one that deliberately omits words that can be understood from the context.

> Speed is the goal for some swimmers, endurance ~~is the goal~~ for others, and relaxation ~~is the goal~~ for still others.

Sometimes, as an aid to clarity, commas mark omissions in elliptical constructions.

> My family functioned like a baseball team: my mom was the coach; my brother, the pitcher; and my sister, the shortstop. [Use semicolons to separate items with internal commas.]

EXERCISE 1

Rewrite the sentences below to make them less wordy.

1. He put in an application for every job offered.
2. Prior to the time of the ceremony, he had not received an award.
3. The library is located in the vicinity of the post office.
4. The fans who were watching television made a lot of noise.
5. There was nobody home.
6. It is important to register early.

P

PUNCTUATION

CHAPTER 15
The Comma 138

- **15a** Before a coordinating conjunction linking independent clauses 138
- **15b** After an introductory word or word group 139
- **15c** Separating elements in a series 141
- **15d** With nonessential elements 142
- **15e** With geographical names and items in dates and addresses 145
- **15f** With direct quotations 146
- **15g** Unnecessary or misplaced commas 147

CHAPTER 16
The Semicolon and the Colon 149

- **16a** The semicolon 149
- **16b** The colon 151

CHAPTER 17
The Apostrophe 154

- **17a** Indicating ownership and other relationships 154
- **17b** Marking omissions of letters or numbers 158
- **17c** Forming certain plurals 158

CHAPTER 18
Quotation Marks 160

- **18a** Direct quotations 160
- **18b** Titles of short works 162
- **18c** With other punctuation marks 163

CHAPTER 19
The Period and Other Punctuation Marks 166

- **19a** The period 166
- **19b** The question mark 167
- **19c** The exclamation point 167
- **19d** The dash 168
- **19e** Parentheses 169
- **19f** Square brackets 170
- **19g** Ellipsis points 171
- **19h** The slash 173

The Comma

Pauses are often signaled by commas; however, they are not the most reliable guide for comma placement, because commas are often called for where speakers do not pause and pauses can occur where no comma is necessary. A better guide is an understanding of some basic principles of comma usage.

15a Before a coordinating conjunction linking independent clauses

Use a comma before a coordinating conjunction (*and, but, for, nor, or, so,* or *yet*) that links two independent clauses. An **independent clause** is a group of words that can stand as a sentence. It consists of a subject and predicate.

INDEPENDENT CLAUSE**,** **CONJUNCTION**
INDEPENDENT CLAUSE.

	and	
	but	
	for	
Subject + predicate,	**nor**	subject + predicate.
	or	
	so	
	yet	

The Iditarod Trail Sled Dog Race begins in March**,** **but** training starts much sooner.

When the independent clauses are short, the comma is often omitted before *and, but,* or *or.*

My friend races **but** I don't.

If a coordinating conjunction joins two parts of a compound predicate (which means there is only one subject), a comma is not normally used before the conjunction.

The race starts in Anchorage~~,~~ and ends in Nome.

> **EXERCISE 1**
>
> Insert commas where needed.
>
> 1. Dinosaurs lived for 165 million years and then became extinct.
> 2. No one knows why dinosaurs became extinct but several theories have been proposed.
> 3. According to some theorists a huge meteor hit the earth so the climate may have changed dramatically.
> 4. Another theory suggests that dinosaurs did not actually become extinct but simply evolved into lizards and birds.
> 5. Another theory suggests that dinosaurs just grew too big but not all of the dinosaurs were huge.

15b After an introductory word or word group

If the subject of the main part of your sentence (the independent clause) is preceded by a word or a group of words, place a comma after the word or word group.

Apparently, she believed the rest of the world was like her own small town. [word]

Despite a downturn in the national economy, the number of students enrolled in this university has increased. [phrase]

15b The Comma

Although the safest automobile on the road is expensive, the protection it offers justifies the cost. [clause]

If you begin a sentence with a short introductory word group, you may omit the comma as long as the resulting sentence is not difficult to read.

In 2009 the enrollment at the university increased.

BUT

In 2009, 625 new students enrolled in courses. [A comma separates two numbers.]

Use a comma to set off interjections, **vocatives** (words used to address someone directly), or transitional words.

Oh, I forgot about the board meeting. [interjection]

Bob, I want you to know that your design impressed everyone on the board. [vocative]

Moreover, the design will increase efficiency in the office. [transitional word]

EXERCISE 2

Insert commas wherever necessary in the following paragraph. Explain why each comma is needed. Some sentences may not require editing.

[1]If you had to describe sound would you call it a wave? [2]Although sound cannot be seen people have described it this way for a long time. [3]Envisioning waves in the air the Greek philosopher Aristotle hypothesized that sound would not be able to pass through a vacuum because there would be no air to transmit it. [4]Aristotle's hypothesis was not tested until nearly two thousand years later. [5]In 1654 Otto von Guericke found that he could not hear a bell ringing inside the vacuum he had created.

15c Separating elements in a series

A comma appears after each item in a series except the last one.

Ethics are based on **moral, social,** or **cultural values.**

The company's code of ethics encourages **seeking criticism of work, correcting mistakes,** and **acknowledging the contributions of everyone.**

Several circumstances can lead to unethical behavior: **people are tempted by a desire to succeed, they are pressured by others into acting inappropriately,** or **they are simply trying to survive.**

THINKING RHETORICALLY

COMMAS AND CONJUNCTIONS IN A SERIES

How do the following sentences differ?

We discussed them all: life, liberty, **and** the pursuit of happiness.
We discussed them all: life **and** liberty **and** the pursuit of happiness.
We discussed them all: life, liberty, the pursuit of happiness.

The first sentence follows conventional guidelines; that is, a comma and a conjunction precede the last element in the series. Having two conjunctions and no commas, the second sentence slows down the pace of the reading, causing stress to be placed on each of the three elements in the series. In contrast, the third sentence, with commas but no conjunctions, speeds up the reading, as if to suggest that the rights listed do not need to be stressed because they are so familiar.

Two or more adjectives that precede the same noun are called **coordinate adjectives.** To test whether adjectives are coordinate, either interchange them or put *and* between them. If the altered version of the phrase is acceptable, the adjectives are coordinate and should be separated by a comma.

> Crossing the **rushing, shallow** creek, I slipped off a rock and fell into the water.
> [COMPARE: a rushing and shallow creek OR a shallow, rushing creek]

If the adjectives cannot be interchanged or joined by *and*, they should not be separated by a comma.

> Sitting in the water, I saw an **old wooden** bridge.
> [NOT a wooden old bridge OR an old and wooden bridge]

15d With nonessential elements

Nonessential (nonrestrictive) elements provide supplemental information, that is, information a reader does not need in order to identify who or what is being discussed. Use commas to set off nonessential words or word groups.

> The Hilltop Folk Festival, **planned for late July,** should attract many tourists.

In the preceding sentence, the phrase placed between commas, *planned for late July*, conveys nonessential information: the reader knows which festival will attract tourists without being told when it will be held. When a phrase follows a specific name, such as *The Hilltop Folk Festival,* it is usually nonessential. In the following sentence, the phrase *planned for late July* is necessary for the reader to be able to identify the festival as the one scheduled for late July, not for a different time.

> The festival **planned for late July** should attract many tourists.

(1) Nonessential elements used as modifiers

Nonessential modifiers are often **adjectival** (**relative**) **clauses**—those clauses usually introduced by the relative pronoun *who, which,* or *that.* In the following sentence, a comma sets off the adjectival clause because the reader does not need the content of that clause in order to identify the mountain.

> We climbed Mt. McKinley**,** **which is over 15,000 feet high.**

Nonessential modifiers also include **participial phrases** (phrases introduced by a present or past participle).

> Mt. McKinley**,** **towering above us,** brought to mind our abandoned plan for climbing it. [participial phrase beginning with a present participle]
>
> My sister**,** **slowed by a knee injury,** rarely hikes anymore. [participial phrase beginning with a past participle]

An **adverbial clause** begins with a subordinating conjunction signaling cause (*because*), purpose (*so that*), or time (*when, after, before*). This type of clause is usually considered essential and thus is not set off by commas when it appears at the end of a sentence.

> Dinosaurs may have become extinct **because their habitat was destroyed.**

In contrast, an adverbial clause that provides nonessential information, such as an extra comment, should be set off from the main clause.

> Dinosaurs are extinct**,** **though they are alive in many people's imaginations.**

(2) Nonessential appositives

Appositives refer to the same person, place, object, idea, or event as a nearby noun or noun phrase but with different words. Nonessential appositives provide extra details about nouns or noun phrases and are set off by commas. In the following sentence, the title of the article is mentioned, so the reader does not need the information provided by the appositive in order to identify the article. The appositive is thus set off by commas.

> "Living on the Line," **Joanne Hart's most recent article,** describes the lives of factory workers in China.

In the next sentence, *Joanne Hart's article* is nonspecific, so an essential appositive containing the specific title of the article is integrated into the sentence. It is not set off by commas. Without the appositive, the reader would not know which of Hart's articles describes the lives of factory workers in China.

> Joanne Hart's article "Living on the Line" describes the lives of factory workers in China.

(3) Absolute phrases
An **absolute phrase** (the combination of a noun and a modifying word or phrase) provides nonessential details and so should always be set off by a comma or commas.

> The actor, **his hair wet and slicked back,** began his audition.

(4) Transitional expressions and other parenthetical elements
Commas customarily set off transitional words and phrases such as *for example, that is,* and *namely*.

> An airline ticket, **for example,** can be delivered electronically.

Because they generally indicate little or no pause in reading, transitional words and phrases such as *also, too, at least,* and *thus* need not be set off by commas.

> Traveling has **thus** become easier in recent years.

Use commas to set off other parenthetical elements, such as words or phrases that provide commentary you wish to stress.

> Over the past year, my flights have, **miraculously,** been on time.

(5) Contrasted elements

Commas set off sentence elements in which words such as *never* and *unlike* express contrast.

> A planet**,** **unlike** a star**,** reflects rather than generates light.

In sentences in which contrasted elements are introduced by *not only . . . but also,* place a comma before *but* if you want to emphasize what follows it. Otherwise, leave the comma out.

> Planets **not only** vary in size**,** **but also** travel at different speeds. [Comma added for emphasis.]

EXERCISE 3

Set off nonessential clauses, phrases, and appositives with commas.

1. Maine Coons long-haired cats with bushy tails have adapted to a harsh climate.
2. These animals which are extremely gentle despite their large size often weigh twenty pounds.
3. Maine Coons unlike most cats will play fetch with their owners.

15e   With geographical names and items in dates and addresses

Use commas to make geographical names, dates, and addresses easy to read.

(1) City and state

> **Nashville, Tennessee,** is the largest country-and-western music center in the United States.

(2) Day and date

> Martha left for Peru on **Wednesday, February 12, 2009,** and returned on March 12.

(3) Addresses
In a sentence containing an address, the name of the person or organization, the street address, and the name of the town or city are all followed by commas, but the abbreviation for the state is not.

> I had to write to **Ms. Melanie Hobson, Senior Analyst, Hobson Computing, 2873 Central Avenue, Orange Park, FL 32065.**

15f With direct quotations

Many sentences containing direct quotations also contain attributive tags such as *The author claims* or *According to the author*.

(1) Attributive tag at the beginning of a sentence
Place the comma directly after the attributive tag, before the quotation marks.

> According to Jacques Barzun, "It is a false analogy with science that makes one think latest is best."

(2) Attributive tag in the middle of a sentence
Place the first comma inside the quotation marks that precede the attibutive tag; place the second comma directly after the tag, before the next set of quotation marks.

> "It is a false analogy with science," claims Jacques Barzun, "that makes one think latest is best."

(3) Attributive tag at the end of a sentence
Place the comma inside the quotation marks before the attributive tag.

> "It is a false analogy with science that makes one think latest is best," claims Jacques Barzun.

15g Unnecessary or misplaced commas

(1) No comma between a subject and its verb or a verb and its object

Although speakers often pause before or after a verb, such a pause should not be indicated by a comma.

> In this climate, rain at frequent intervals ~~,~~ produces mosquitoes.
>
> The forecaster said ~~,~~ that rain was likely.

(2) No comma following a coordinating conjunction

Avoid using a comma after a coordinating conjunction (*and, but, for, nor, or, so,* or *yet*).

> We worked very hard on her campaign for state representative **,** but ~~,~~ the incumbent was too strong to defeat in the northern districts.

(3) No comma separating elements in a compound predicate

In general, avoid using a comma between two elements of a compound predicate (a predicate in which both verbs agree with the same subject).

> I **read** the comments carefully ~~,~~ and then **started** my revision.

(4) No comma setting off essential words, phrases, or clauses

In the following sentences, the elements in boldface are essential and so should not be set off by commas.

> Zoe was born ~~,~~ **in Chicago during the Great Depression.**
>
> Everyone ~~,~~ **who has a mortgage** ~~,~~ is required to have fire insurance.
>
> Someone ~~,~~ **wearing an orange wig** ~~,~~ greeted us at the door.

(5) No comma preceding the first item of a series or following the last

Make sure that you place commas only between elements in a series, not before or after them.

She was known for her photographs, sketches, and engravings.

The exhibit included her most exuberant, exciting, and expensive photographs.

16 The Semicolon and the Colon

Although semicolons and colons both link independent clauses, they signal different grammatical relationships.

16a The semicolon

The semicolon most frequently connects two independent clauses when the second clause supports or contrasts with the first, but it can be used for other purposes as well.

(1) Connecting independent clauses

A semicolon placed between two independent clauses indicates that they are closely related. The second of the two clauses generally supports or contrasts with the first.

> For many cooks, basil is a key ingredient; it appears in recipes worldwide. [support]
>
> Sweet basil is used in many Mediterranean dishes; Thai basil is used in Asian and East Indian recipes. [contrast]

Sometimes, a transitional expression such as *for example* or *however* accompanies a semicolon and further establishes the relationship between the ideas.

> Basil is omnipresent in the cuisine of some countries; **for example,** Italians use basil in salads, soups, and many vegetable dishes.
>
> The culinary uses of basil are well known; **however,** this herb also has medicinal uses.

A comma is usually inserted after a transitional word, though it can be omitted if doing so will not lead to a misreading.

(2) Separating elements that contain commas

In a series of phrases or clauses that contain commas, semicolons indicate where each phrase or clause ends and the next begins.

> To survive, mountain lions need a large area in which to range**;** a steady supply of deer, skunks, raccoons, foxes, and opossums**;** and the opportunity to find a mate, establish a den, and raise a litter.

Semicolons do not set off phrases or dependent clauses unless they contain commas. Use commas for these purposes.

> We consulted Alinka Kibukian~~;~~**,** the local horticulturalist.

> Our trees survived~~;~~**,** even though we live in a harsh climate.

EXERCISE 1

Revise the following sentences, using semicolons to separate independent clauses or elements that contain internal commas.

1. Soccer is a game played by two opposing teams on a rectangular field, each team tries to knock a ball, roughly twenty-eight inches in circumference, through the opponent's goal.

2. The game is called *soccer* only in Canada and the United States, elsewhere it is known as *football*.

3. Generally, a team consists of eleven players: defenders (or fullbacks), who defend the goal by trying to win control of the ball, midfielders (or halfbacks), who play both defense and offense, attackers (or forwards), whose primary responsibility is scoring goals; and a goalkeeper (or goalie), who guards the goal.

4. In amateur matches, players can be substituted frequently, however, in professional matches, the number of substitutions is limited.

16b The colon

A colon calls attention to what follows. It also separates numbers in parts of scriptural references and titles from subtitles.

(1) Directing attention to an explanation, a summary, or a quotation

When a colon appears between two independent clauses, it signals that the second clause will explain or expand on the first.

> No one expected the game to end as it did: after seven extra innings, the favored team collapsed.

A colon is also used after an independent clause to introduce a direct quotation.

> Marcel Proust explained the importance of mindfulness: "The true journey of discovery consists not in seeking new landscapes but in having fresh eyes."

CAUTION

The rules for using an uppercase or a lowercase letter to begin the first word of an independent clause that follows a colon vary across style manuals.

MLA The first letter should be lowercase unless (1) it begins a word that is normally capitalized, (2) the independent clause is a quotation, or (3) the clause expresses a rule or principle.

APA The first letter should be uppercase.

CMS The first letter should be lowercase unless (1) it begins a word that is normally capitalized, (2) the independent clause is a quotation, or (3) two or more related sentences follow the colon.

(2) Signaling that a list follows

Writers frequently use colons to introduce lists. Note that an independent clause precedes the list.

> Three students received internships: Asa, Vanna, and Jack.

Avoid placing a colon between a verb and its complement or after the words *including* and *such as*.

> The winners were: Asa, Vanna, and Jack.
> Many vegetarians do not eat dairy products such as: butter and cheese.

(3) Separating a title and a subtitle

Use a colon between a work's title and its subtitle.

> *Collapse: How Societies Choose to Fail or Succeed*

(4) Citing scriptural references

Colons are often used between numbers in scriptural references.

> Psalms 3:5   Gen. 1:1

However, MLA requires the use of periods instead of colons.

> Psalms 3.5   Gen. 1.1

(5) Specialized uses in business correspondence

A colon follows the salutation of a business letter and any notations.

> Dear Dr. Horner: Dear Maxine: Enc:

A colon introduces the headings in a memo.

> To: From: Subject: Date:

EXERCISE 2

Insert colons where they are needed in the following sentences.

1. Before we discuss marketing, let's outline the behavior of consumers consumer behavior is the process individuals go through as they select, buy, or use products or services to satisfy their needs and desires.

2. The process consists of six stages recognizing a need or desire, finding information, evaluating options, deciding to purchase, purchasing, and assessing purchases.

3. When evaluating alternatives, a house hunter might use some of the following price, location, size, age, style, and landscaping design.

17 The Apostrophe

Apostrophes serve a number of purposes. For example, you can use them to show that someone owns something *(my neighbor's television),* that someone has a specific relationship with someone else *(my neighbor's children),* or that someone has produced or created something *(my neighbor's recipe).* Apostrophes are also used in contractions *(can't, don't)* and in certain plural forms *(x's and y's).*

17a Indicating ownership and other relationships

An apostrophe, often followed by an *s,* signals the possessive case of nouns. Possessive nouns are used to express a variety of meanings.

Ownership	**Fumi's** computer, the **photographer's** camera
Origin	**Einstein's** ideas, the **student's** decision
Human relationships	**Linda's** sister, the **employee's** supervisor
Possession of physical or psychological traits	**Mona Lisa's** smile, the **team's** spirit
Association between abstractions and attributes	**democracy's** success, **tyranny's** influence

Identification of documents	**driver's** license, **bachelor's** degree
Identification of things or days named after people	**St. John's** Cathedral, **Valentine's** Day
Specification of amounts	a **day's** wages, an **hour's** delay

(1) Singular nouns, indefinite pronouns, abbreviations, and acronyms

Add an apostrophe and an *s* to indicate the possessive case of singular nouns, indefinite pronouns, abbreviations, and acronyms.

the dean**'s** office [noun]

Yeats**'s** poems [noun]

anyone**'s** computer [indefinite pronoun]

the NFL**'s** reputation [abbreviation]

OPEC**'s** price increase [acronym]

Walter Bryan Jr.**'s** letter

When a singular proper noun ends in *s*, you will have to consult the style guide for the discipline in which you are writing. The *MLA Handbook for Writers of Research Papers* recommends always using *'s*, as in *Illinois's legislature* and *Dickens's novels*. CMS allows exceptions to this rule. An apostrophe without an *s* may be acceptable in the following circumstances: (1) when a name ends in a syllable pronounced "eez" *(Sophocles' poetry)*, (2) when a singular common noun ends in *s (physics' contribution)*, and (3) when the name of a place or an organization ends in *s* but refers to a single entity *(United States' foreign aid)*.

Possessive pronouns *(my, mine, our, ours, your, yours, his, her, hers, its, their, theirs,* and *whose)* are not written with apostrophes.

The committee concluded **its** discussion.

> **CAUTION**
>
> Be careful not to confuse possessive pronouns with contractions. Whenever you write a contraction, you should be able to substitute the complete words for it without changing the meaning.
>
> | Possessive pronoun | Contraction |
> |---|---|
> | **Its** motor is small. | **It's** [It is] a small motor. |
> | **Whose** turn is it? | **Who's** [Who is] representing us? |

(2) Plural nouns ending in s

Add only an apostrophe to indicate the possessive case of plural nouns that end in *s*.

the boys' game   the babies' toys   the Joneses' house

Plural nouns that do not end in *s* need both an apostrophe and an *s*.

men's lives   women's health   children's projects

> **CAUTION**
>
> An apostrophe is not needed to make a noun plural. To make most nouns plural, add *s* or *es*. Add an apostrophe only to signal ownership, origin, and other similar relationships.
>
> The ~~protesters'~~ protesters met in front of the conference center.
>
> The protesters' meeting was on Wednesday.
>
> To form the plural of a family name, use *s* or *es,* not an apostrophe.
>
> The ~~Johnson's~~ Johnsons participated in the study.
> [COMPARE: The Johnsons' participation in the study was crucial.]

(3) To show collaboration or joint ownership

An apostrophe and an *s* follow the second of two singular nouns. Just an apostrophe follows the second of two plural nouns that already ends in *s*.

the carpenter and the **plumber's** decision [They made the decision collaboratively.]

the Becks and the **Lopezes'** cabin [They own one cabin jointly.]

(4) To show separate ownership or individual contributions

Each plural noun is followed by an apostrophe; each singular noun is followed by *'s*.

the **Becks'** and the **Lopezes'** cars [Each family owns a car.]

the **carpenter's** and the **plumber's** proposals [They each made a proposal.]

(5) Compound nouns

An apostrophe and an *s* follow the last word of a compound noun.

my brother-in-**law's** friends, the attorney **general's** statements [singular]

my brothers-in-**law's** friends, the attorneys **general's** statements [plural]

To avoid awkward constructions such as the last two, consider using a prepositional phrase beginning with *of* instead: *the statements of the attorneys general.*

(6) Nouns preceding gerunds

Depending on its number, a noun that precedes a gerund takes either an apostrophe and an *s* or just an apostrophe.

Lucy**'s having** to be there seemed unnecessary. [singular noun preceding gerund]

The family appreciated the lawyers**' handling** of the matter. [plural noun preceding gerund]

Sometimes you may find it difficult to distinguish between a gerund and a participle. A good way to tell the difference is to note whether the emphasis is on an action or on a person. In a sentence containing a gerund, the emphasis is on the action; in a sentence containing a participle, the emphasis is on the person.

> Our successful completion of the project depends on **Terry's providing** the illustrations. [gerund]
>
> I remember my **brother telling** me the same joke last year. [participle]

(7) Names of products and geographical locations

Follow an organization's preference for its name or the name of a product; follow local conventions for a geographical location.

> Consumers Union   Actors' Equity   Taster's Choice
> Devil's Island   Devils Tower   Devil Mountain

17b Marking omissions of letters or numbers

Apostrophes mark omissions in contractions, numbers, and words mimicking speech.

> they're [they are]   class of '09 [class of 2009]
> y'all [you all]   singin' [singing]

17c Forming certain plurals

These plurals are generally formed by adding *s* only:

> 1990s   fours and fives   YWCAs   two *and*s   the three Rs

Lowercase letters and abbreviations that include a combination of uppercase and lowercase letters are made plural by adding both an apostrophe and an *s*.

x's and *y*'s   PhD's

The MLA differs from this style in recommending the use of apostrophes for the plurals of uppercase letters (*A*'s and *B*'s) as well as lowercase letters.

EXERCISE 1

Insert apostrophes where needed in the following sentences.

1. Whose responsibility is it to see whether its working?
2. Hansons book was published in the early 1920s.
3. NPRs fund drive begins this weekend.
4. Few students enrolled during the academic year 06–07.
5. There cant be more *x*s than there are *y*s in the equation.

18 Quotation Marks

Quotation marks indicate that the words between them were first written or spoken by someone else or that they are being used in an unconventional way.

18a Direct quotations

Double quotation marks set off direct quotations, including those in dialogue. Single quotation marks enclose a quotation within a quotation.

(1) Direct quotations

Double quotation marks enclose only quotations, not any expression such as *she said* or *he replied*. When a sentence ends with quoted material, place the period inside the quotation marks.

"I believe that we learn by practice," writes Martha Graham. "Whether it means to learn to dance by practicing dancing or to learn to live by practicing living, the principles are the same."

When using direct quotations, reproduce all quoted material exactly as it appears in the original. Quotation marks are not used with indirect quotations or paraphrases (restatements of what someone else has said or written).

Martha Graham believes that practice is necessary for learning, regardless of what we are trying to learn.

(2) Quotations within quotations

If the quotation you are using includes another direct quotation, use single quotation marks for the embedded quotation.

> According to Anita Erickson, "when the narrator says, 'I have the right to my own opinion,' he means that he has the right to his own delusion" (22).

However, if the embedded quotation appears in a block quotation, use double quotation marks. (Note that double quotation marks are not used to mark the beginning and end of a block quotation.)

> Anita Erickson claims that the narrator uses the word *opinion* deceptively.
>
> > Later in the chapter, when the narrator says, "I have the right to my own opinion," he means that he has the right to his own delusion. Although it is tempting to believe that the narrator is making decisions based on a rational belief system, his behavior suggests that he is more interested in deception. (22)

(3) Dialogue

When creating a dialogue, enclose in quotation marks what each person says. Use a separate paragraph for each speaker, beginning a new paragraph whenever the speaker changes.

> Farmer looked up, smiling, and in a chirpy-sounding voice he said, "But that feeling has the disadvantage of being . . ." He paused a beat. "Wrong."
> "Well," I retorted, "it depends on how you look at it."
> —TRACY KIDDER, *Mountains Beyond Mountains*

When quoting more than one paragraph by a single speaker, put quotation marks at the beginning of each paragraph. However, place closing quotation marks only at the end of the last paragraph.

(4) Thoughts resembling speech
Quotation marks set off thoughts that resemble speech.

> "His silence on this topic has surprised everyone," I noted to myself as I surveyed the faces of the other committee members.

Thoughts are usually marked by such phrases as *I thought, he felt*, and *she believed*.

(5) Short excerpts of poetry included within a sentence
When quoting fewer than four lines of poetry, enclose them in quotation marks; use a slash to indicate a line division.

> After watching a whale swim playfully, the speaker in "Visitation" asks, "What did you think, that joy / was some slight thing?"

18b Titles of short works

Quotation marks enclose the title of a short work, such as a story, an essay, a poem, or a song. The title of a larger work, such as a book, magazine, newspaper, or play, should be italicized.

Short stories	"The Lottery"	"The Fall of the House of Usher"
Essays	"Walden"	"Play-by-Play"
Articles	"Small World"	"Arabia's Empty Quarter"
Book chapters	"Rain"	"Cutting a Dash"
Short poems	"Orion"	"Mending Wall"
Songs	"Lazy River"	"The Star-Spangled Banner"
TV episodes	"Show Down!"	"The Last Time"

Use single quotation marks for a title within a longer title that is enclosed in double quotation marks.

"Irony in 'The Sick Rose'" [article about a poem]

> **CAUTION**
>
> Avoid using quotation marks around words that may not be appropriate for your audience or purpose. Instead, take the time to choose suitable words. The revised sentence in the following pair is more effective than the first.
>
> **Ineffective**   He is too much of a "wimp" to be a good leader.
> **Revised**   He is too indecisive to be a good leader.

18c With other punctuation marks

To decide whether to place some other punctuation mark inside or outside quotation marks, note whether the punctuation mark is part of the quotation or part of the surrounding context.

(1) With commas and periods

Quoted material is usually accompanied by an attributive tag such as *she said* or *he replied*. When your sentence starts with such an expression, place a comma after it to separate the tag from the quotation. Place a period inside closing quotation marks.

She replied, "There's more than one way to slice a pie."

If your sentence starts with the quotation instead, place the comma inside the closing quotation marks.

"There's more than one way to slice a pie," she replied.

When quoting material from a source, provide the relevant page number(s). If you are following MLA guidelines, note the page number(s) in parentheses after the final quotation marks. Place the period that ends the sentence after the final parenthesis, unless the quotation is a block quotation.

> According to Diane Ackerman, "Love is a demanding sport involving all the muscle groups, including the brain" (86).

CAUTION

Do not put a comma after *that* when it precedes a quotation.

> Diane Ackerman claims that ⨂ "[l]ove is a demanding sport involving all the muscle groups, including the brain" (86).

(2) With semicolons and colons

Place semicolons and colons outside quotation marks.

> His favorite song was "Cyprus Avenue"; mine was "Astral Weeks."

> Because it is repeated, one line stands out in "The Conductor": "We are never as beautiful as now."

(3) With question marks, exclamation points, and dashes

If the direct quotation includes a question mark, an exclamation point, or a dash, place that punctuation *inside* the closing quotation marks.

> Jeremy asked, "What is truth?"
>
> Gordon shouted, "Congratulations!"
>
> Laura said, "Let me tell—" just as Dan walked into the room.

Use just one question mark inside the quotation marks when a question you write ends with a quoted question.

> Why does the protagonist ask, "Where are we headed?"

If the punctuation is not part of the quoted material, place it *outside* the closing quotation marks.

Who wrote "The Figure a Sentence Makes"?

You have to read "Awareness and Freedom"!

EXERCISE 1

Revise sentences in which quotation marks are used incorrectly and insert quotation marks where they are needed. Do not alter sentences that are written correctly. (The numbers in parentheses are page numbers, placed according to MLA guidelines.)

1. Have you read Nicholas Negroponte's essay Creating a Culture of Ideas?

2. Negroponte states, Innovation is inefficient (2).

3. However, he also believes that "without innovation we are doomed—by boredom and monotony—to decline" (2).

4. Negroponte suggests that new ideas are fostered by 'providing a good educational system, encouraging different viewpoints, and fostering collaboration' (3).

5. According to the author, "More than ever before, in the new "new economy," research and innovation will need to be housed in those places where there are parallel agendas and multiple means of support" (3).

19 The Period and Other Punctuation Marks

To indicate the end of a sentence, you can use one of three punctuation marks: the period, the question mark, or the exclamation point. Within sentences, you can use dashes, parentheses, square brackets, ellipsis points, and slashes.

Both CMS and MLA guidelines recommend using only one space after a period, a question mark, or an exclamation point, although the MLA style manual allows two spaces as long as they are used consistently. APA guidelines recommend two spaces after end punctuation marks.

19a The period

(1) A period at the end of a sentence
Use a period at the end of a sentence.

Many adults in the United States are overfed yet undernourished.

In addition, place a period at the end of an instruction or recommendation.

Eat plenty of fruits and vegetables.

(2) Periods after some abbreviations

Dr. Jr. a.m. p.m. vs. etc. et al.

Only one period follows an abbreviation that ends a sentence.

The tour begins at 1:00 p.m.

19b The question mark

Place a question mark after a direct question.

> How does the new atomic clock work? Who invented this clock?

Use a period, instead of a question mark, after an indirect question—that is, a question embedded in a statement.

> I asked whether the atomic clock could be used in cell phones.
> [COMPARE: Can the atomic clock be used in cell phones?]

MULTILINGUAL WRITERS

INDIRECT QUESTIONS

In English, the subject and verb in indirect questions are not inverted as they would be in the related direct question.

> We do not know when ~~will~~ the meeting ^will^ end.
> [COMPARE: When will the meeting end?]

Place a question mark after each question in a series of related questions, even when they are not full sentences.

> Will the new atomic clock be used in cell phones? Word processors? Car navigation systems?

19c The exclamation point

An exclamation point often marks the end of a sentence, but its primary purpose is rhetorical—to create emphasis.

> Whoa! What a game!

Use the exclamation point sparingly so that you do not diminish its value. If you do not intend to signal strong emotion, place a comma after an interjection and a period at the end of the sentence.

Well, no one seriously expected this victory.

19d The dash

A dash (or em dash) marks a break in thought, sets off a nonessential element for emphasis or clarity, or follows an introductory list or series. To use your keyboard to create a dash, type two hyphens with no spaces between, before, or after them. Most word-processing programs can be set to convert these hyphens automatically to an em dash.

(1) Marking a break in the normal flow of a sentence
Use a dash to indicate a shift in thought or tone.

I was awed by the almost superhuman effort Stonehenge represents—but who wouldn't be?

(2) Setting off a nonessential element
Use a dash or a pair of dashes to set off extra comments or details.

Dr. Kruger's specialty is mycology—the study of fungi.

The trail we took into the Grand Canyon—steep, narrow, winding, and lacking guardrails—made me wonder whether we could call a helicopter to fly us out.

(3) Following an introductory list or series
If you decide to place a list or series at the beginning of a sentence in order to emphasize it, the main part of the sentence (after the dash) should sum up the meaning of the list or series.

Eager, determined to succeed, and scared to death—all of these describe how I felt on the first day at work.

> **THINKING RHETORICALLY**
>
> **COMMAS, DASHES, AND COLONS**
>
> Although a comma, a dash, or a colon may be followed by an explanation, an example, or an illustration, is the rhetorical impact the same?
>
> > He never failed to mention what was most important to him**,** the bottom line.
> >
> > He never failed to mention what was most important to him—the bottom line.
> >
> > He never failed to mention what was most important to him**:** the bottom line.
>
> The comma, one of the most common punctuation marks, barely draws attention to what follows it. The dash, in contrast, signals a longer pause and so places more emphasis on the information that follows. The colon is more direct and formal than either of the other two punctuation marks.

19e Parentheses

Use parentheses to set off information that is not closely related to the main point of a sentence or paragraph but that provides an interesting detail, an explanation, or an illustration.

> We might ask why affairs of state are classified as important and their discussants intelligent, while discussion of family and human interaction (what we disparagingly call "gossip") is dismissed as idle chatter. —**ROBIN LAKOFF**, *Language and Woman's Place*

In addition, place parentheses around an acronym or an abbreviation when introducing it after its full form.

The Search for Extraterrestrial Intelligence (SETI) uses the Very Large Array (VLA) outside Sicorro, New Mexico, to scan the sky.

If you use numbers or letters in a list within a sentence, set them off by placing them within parentheses.

Your application should include (1) a current résumé, (2) a statement of purpose, and (3) two letters of recommendation.

> **THINKING RHETORICALLY**
>
> **DASHES AND PARENTHESES**
>
> Dashes and parentheses are both used to set off part of a sentence, but they differ in the amount of emphasis they signal. Whereas dashes call attention to the material that is set off, parentheses usually deemphasize such material.
>
> Her grandfather—born during the Great Depression—was appointed to the Securities and Exchange Commission.
>
> Her grandfather (born in 1930) was appointed to the Securities and Exchange Commission.

19f Square brackets

Square brackets set off additions or alterations used to clarify direct quotations. In the following example, the bracketed noun specifies what is meant by the pronoun *They*.

"They [hyperlinks] are what turn the Web from a library of pages into a web" (Weinberger 170).

Square brackets also indicate that a letter in a quotation has been changed from uppercase to lowercase, or vice versa.

> David Weinberger claims that "[e]ven our notion of self as a continuous body moving through a continuous map of space and time is beginning to seem wrong on the Web" (10).

To avoid the awkwardness of using brackets in this way, you may be able to quote only part of a sentence so that no change in capitalization is needed.

> David Weinberger claims that "our notion of self as a continuous body moving through a continuous map of space and time is beginning to seem wrong on the Web" (10).

Within parentheses, square brackets are used to avoid the confusion of having two sets of parentheses.

> People frequently provide personal information online. (See, for example, David Weinberger's *Small Pieces Loosely Joined* [Cambridge: Perseus, 2002].)

Angle brackets (< >) are used to enclose any Web address included in an MLA works-cited list so that the period at the end of an entry is not confused with the dot(s) in the URL: <http://www.mla.org>.

19g Ellipsis points

Ellipsis points indicate an omission from a quoted passage or a reflective pause or hesitation.

(1) Marking an omission from a quoted passage

The following examples illustrate how to use ellipsis points in quotations from a passage by Patricia Gadsby.

Original

> Cacao doesn't flower, as most plants do, at the tips of its outer and uppermost branches. Instead, its sweet white buds hang from the trunk and along a few fat branches, popping out of patches of

> bark called cushions, which form where leaves drop off. They're tiny, these flowers. Yet once pollinated by midges, no-see-ums that flit in the leafy detritus below, they'll make pulp-filled pods almost the size of rugby balls.
>
> —PATRICIA GADSBY, "Endangered Chocolate"

Whenever you omit anything from material you are quoting, replace the omitted material with ellipsis points—three equally spaced periods.

> Patricia Gadsby notes that cacao flowers "once pollinated by midges . . . make pulp-filled pods almost the size of rugby balls."

Do not use ellipsis points to indicate that you have deleted words from the beginning of a quotation.

> According to Patricia Gadsby, cacao flowers will become "pulp-filled pods almost the size of rugby balls."

To indicate omitted words from the end of a sentence, put a space between the last word and the set of three spaced ellipsis points. Then add the end punctuation mark (a period, a question mark, or an exclamation point). If the quoted material is followed by a parenthetical source or page reference, the end punctuation comes after the second parenthesis.

> Claiming that cacao flowers differ from those of most plants, Patricia Gadsby describes how "the sweet white buds hang from the trunk and along a few fat branches . . . ."
>
> OR ". . . branches . . . " (2).

To signal the omission of a sentence or more (even a paragraph or more), place an end punctuation mark (usually a period) before the ellipsis points.

> Patricia Gadsby describes the flowering of the cacao plant: "its sweet white buds hang from the trunk and along a few fat branches, popping out of patches of bark called cushions, which form where leaves drop off. . . . Yet once pollinated

by midges, no-see-ums that flit in the leafy detritus below, they'll make pulp-filled pods almost the size of rugby balls."

To signal the omission of a full line or more in quoted poetry, use spaced periods covering the length of either the line above it or the omitted line.

The yellow fog that rubs its back upon the window-panes,

. . . .

Curled once about the house, and fell asleep.
—T. S. ELIOT, "The Love Song of J. Alfred Prufrock"

(2) Indicating an unfinished sentence or marking a pause

Use ellipsis points to indicate that you are intentionally leaving a sentence incomplete or to signal a reflective pause.

Read aloud the passage that begins "The yellow fog . . ."

Keith saw four menacing youths coming toward him . . . and ran.

19h The slash

A slash between words, as in *and/or* and *he/she,* indicates that either word is applicable in the given context. There are no spaces before and after a slash used in this way. Because extensive use of the slash can make writing choppy, use it judiciously and sparingly. (If you are following APA or MLA guidelines, avoid using *he/she, him/her,* and so on.)

A slash is also used to mark line divisions in quoted poetry. A slash used in this way is preceded and followed by a space.

Wallace Stevens refers to the listener who, "nothing himself, beholds / Nothing that is not there and the nothing that is."

EXERCISE 1

Add appropriate dashes, parentheses, square brackets, and slashes to the following sentences.

1. Researchers in an exciting field Artificial Intelligence AI are working on devices to assist the elderly.
2. One such device is Pearl a robotic nurse that helps around the house.
3. Another application is cooking software that checks for missing and or incorrect ingredients.
4. The actual cost of such devices expensive now but more affordable later is yet to be determined.

M
MECHANICS

CHAPTER 20
Spelling, the Spell Checker, and Hyphenation 176

- **20a** Spelling and pronunciation 176
- **20b** Words that sound alike 177
- **20c** Prefixes and suffixes 178
- **20d** Confusion of *ei* and *ie* 180
- **20e** Hyphens 181

CHAPTER 21
Capitals 183

- **21a** Proper names 183
- **21b** Titles and subtitles 184
- **21c** Beginning a sentence 185
- **21d** Computer keys, menu items, and icon names 187

CHAPTER 22
Italics 188

- **22a** Titles of works published or produced separately 188
- **22b** Other uses of italics 189
- **22c** Words not italicized 190

CHAPTER 23
Abbreviations, Acronyms, and Numbers 191

- **23a** Abbreviations with names 191
- **23b** Addresses in correspondence 192
- **23c** Acceptable abbreviations in academic and professional writing 192
- **23d** Acronyms 193
- **23e** General uses of numbers 194
- **23f** Special uses of numbers 195

Spelling, the Spell Checker, and Hyphenation

Proofreading for spelling mistakes is essential as you near the end of the writing process. Your teachers, employers, or supervisors will expect you to submit polished work.

> **TIPS FOR USING A SPELL CHECKER**
>
> The spell checker is a wonderful invention, though you must use it with care.
>
> - If a spell checker regularly flags a word that is not in its dictionary but is spelled correctly, add that word to its dictionary by clicking on the Add button. From that point on, the spell checker will accept the word you added.
> - Reject any offers the spell checker makes to correct all instances of a particular error.
> - Use a dictionary to evaluate the alternative spellings the spell checker provides, because some of them may be erroneous.

20a Spelling and pronunciation

Many words in English are not spelled the way they are pronounced, so pronunciation is not a reliable guide to correct spelling. Here are a few words typically misspelled because they include unpronounced letters:

condem*n*   foreign   lab*o*ratory   mus*c*le   solem*n*

Here are a few more that include letters that are often not heard in rapid speech.

can*d*idate   diff*e*rent   gove*r*nment   sep*a*rate

You can teach yourself the correct spellings of words by pronouncing them to yourself the way they are spelled, that is, by pronouncing each letter mentally so that you "hear" even silent letters.

> **CAUTION**
>
> The words *and, have,* and *than* are often not stressed in speech and are thus misspelled.
>
> They would rather ~~of~~ (have) written two papers ~~then~~ (than) taken midterm ~~an~~ (and) final exams.

20b Words that sound alike

Words that sound alike but are spelled differently are frequently confused. Many of these words are listed with explanations in this handbook's **Glossary of Usage**. Also troublesome are two-word sequences that can be written as compound words or as separate words.

Everyday life was grueling.	She attended class **every day.**
They do not fight **anymore.**	They could not find **any more** evidence.

Other examples are *awhile/a while, everyone/every one, maybe/may be,* and *sometime/some time.*

Singular nouns ending in *-nce* and plural nouns ending in *-nts* are easily confused.

Assistance is available.	I have two **assistants.**
His **patience** wore thin.	Some **patients** waited for hours.

Be sure to write contractions but not possessive pronouns with an apostrophe.

Contractions	it's, you're, there's, who's
Possessives	its, your, theirs, whose

20c Prefixes and suffixes

When a prefix is added to a base word (often called the **root**), the spelling of the base word is unaffected.

necessary, **un**necessary   moral, **im**moral

However, adding a suffix to the end of a base word often changes the spelling.

(1) Dropping or retaining a final e

- If a suffix begins with a vowel, the final *e* of the base word is dropped: bride, brid**al;** come, com**ing**. However, to keep the /s/ sound of *ce* or the /j/ sound of *ge*, retain the final *e* before *-able* or *-ous*: notic**eable,** courag**eous.**
- If a suffix begins with a consonant, the final *e* of the base word is retained: entire, entire**ly;** rude, rude**ness.** Some exceptions are *argument, ninth, truly,* and *wholly.*

(2) Doubling a final consonant

- If a consonant ends a one-syllable word with a single vowel or ends a stressed syllable with a single vowel, double the final consonant: stop, sto**pped;** omit, omi**tted.**
- If there are two vowels before the consonant, the consonant is not doubled: remain, remain**ed,** remain**ing.**
- If the final syllable is not stressed, the consonant is not doubled: edit, edit**ed,** edit**ing;** picket, picket**ed,** picket**ing.**

(3) Changing or retaining a final y

- Change a final *y* following a consonant to *i* when adding a suffix (except *-ing*): lazy, laz**ily;** defy, def**ied,** BUT defy**ing.**

- Retain the final *y* when it follows a vowel: gray, gray**ish**; stay, stay**s**, stay**ed**; obey, obey**s**, obey**ed**.
- Some verb forms are irregular and thus can cause difficulties. For a list of irregular verbs, see pages 35–36.

(4) Retaining a final *l*

The letter *l* at the end of a word is retained when *ly* is added.

cool, coo**lly**   formal, form**ally**   real, real**ly**   usual, usua**lly**

EXERCISE 1

Add the specified suffix to the words that follow it.

Example

-ly: late, casual, psychological
   lately casually psychologically

1. *-ment*: manage, commit, require, argue
2. *-ous*: continue, joy, acrimony, libel
3. *-ed*: race, tip, permit, carry, pray

---

(5) Forming plurals

- Add *es* to most nouns ending in *s, z, ch, sh,* or *x:* box, box**es**.
- If a noun ends in a consonant and *y*, change the *y* to *i* and add *es:* company, compan**ies**; ninety, nine**ties**.
- If a noun ends in a consonant and *o*, add *es:* hero, hero**es**. Note that sometimes just *s* is added (photo, photo**s**) and other times either *s* or *es* can be added (motto**s**, motto**es**).
- Certain nouns have irregular plural forms: woman, wom**en**; child, child**ren**; foot, f**ee**t.
- Add *s* to most proper nouns: the Kennedy**s**. Add *es* to most proper nouns ending in *s, z, ch, sh,* or *x:* the Jones**es**.

Words borrowed from Latin or Greek generally form their plurals as they did in the original language.

Singular

criterion   alumnus, alumna   analysis   datum   species

Plural

criter**ia**   alumn**i**, alumn**ae**   analys**es**   dat**a**   species

Sometimes two different forms are acceptable: the plural form of *syllabus* is either *syllabuses* or *syllabi*.

> **EXERCISE 2**
> Provide the plural forms for the following words.
> 1. virus   2. phenomenon   3. copy   4. delay   5. portfolio

20d Confusion of *ei* and *ie*

An old rhyme will help you remember the order of letters in most words containing *e* and *i*:

> Put *i* before *e*
> Except after *c*
> Or when sounded like *a*
> As in *neighbor* and *weigh*.

Words with *i* before *e*: bel**ie**ve, ch**ie**f, pr**ie**st, y**ie**ld

Words with *e* before *i*, after *c*: conc**ei**t, perc**ei**ve, rec**ei**ve

Words with *ei* sounding like *a* in *cake*: **ei**ght, r**ei**n, th**ei**r, h**ei**r

Words that are exceptions to the rules in the rhyme include *either, neither, species, foreign*, and *weird*.

20e Hyphens

Hyphens link two or more words functioning as a single word and separate word parts to clarify meaning. They also have many conventional uses in numbers, fractions, and measurements.

(1) Linking two or more words

If two or more words serve as a single adjective before a noun, they should be hyphenated. If the words follow the noun, they are not hyphenated.

> You submitted an **up-to-date** report.
>
> The report was **up to date**.

When the second word in a hyphenated expression is omitted, the first word is still followed by a hyphen.

> They discussed both **private-** and **public-sector** partnerships.

A hyphen is not used after adverbs ending in *ly* (*poorly planned event*).

(2) Other uses of the hyphens

A hyphen is also used after certain prefixes and in certain numbers.

Between repeated letters	anti-intellectual
To clarify meaning	re-sign (NOT resign) the petition
After *self-* or *ex-*	self-esteem, ex-wife
In numbers twenty-one through ninety-nine	one hundred thirty-two
In fractions	three-fourths, one-half

When you form a compound modifier that includes a number and a unit of measurement, place a hyphen between them: *two-year-old boy*.

EXERCISE 3

Convert the following word groups into hyphenated compounds.

Example

a movie lasting two hours   *a two-hour movie*

1. a man who is fifty years old
2. a street that runs only one way
3. history from the twenty-first century
4. a paper that is well written

21 Capitals

Capital letters draw attention to significant details—for example, the beginnings of sentences or the names of particular people, places, and products.

21a Proper names

Proper nouns are specific names. They are capitalized, even when they are used as modifiers (*Mexico, Mexican government*). Words such as *college, company, park,* and *street* are capitalized only if they are part of a name (*a university* but *Oregon State University*).

The following names and titles should be capitalized: personal names, including titles; names of deities, religions, religious followers, and sacred works; names of awards, products, and companies; names of countries, ethnic or cultural groups, and languages; names of bridges, buildings, monuments, and geographical features or regions; names of universities and specific courses; names of days of the week, months, and holidays (but not seasons); names of historical documents, periods, and events; names of political parties and government agencies; and military terms.

Capitalized	Not capitalized
Noam Chomsky, Chomskyan	a linguist, a theoretical perspective
Uncle Rory	my uncle
President Lincoln	the president

Capitalized	Not capitalized
God (a name)	a god
Bible, Koran, Talmud	sacred works
Academy Award	an award
Nike, Nike Free	a company, a running shoe
Japan, Japanese	a country, a language
Empire State Building	a building
Grand Canyon	a canyon
the West	a western state
Howard University	a university
Biology 101	a biology course
Fourth of July	a holiday
May	a month in spring
Bill of Rights	a historical document
Renaissance	the sixteenth century
Great Depression	a recession
Democratic Party	democratic process
Internal Revenue Service	a government agency
Gulf War	a war
U.S. Army	an army

21b Titles and subtitles

The first and last words in titles and subtitles are capitalized, as are major words—that is, all words other than articles (*a, an,* and *the*), coordinating conjunctions (*and, but, for, nor, or, so,* and *yet*), prepositions (such as *in, on,* and *of*), and the infinitive marker *to*.

Dictation: A Quartet

"To Be a Student or Not to Be a Student"

"Stop-and-Go Signals"

The American Psychological Association (APA) differs from the Modern Language Association (MLA) in recommending capitalizing any word in a title, including a preposition, that has four or more letters.

Southwestern Pottery from Anasazi to Zuni [MLA]

Southwestern Pottery From Anasazi to Zuni [APA]

21c Beginning a sentence

Of course a sentence begins with a capital letter, but there are certain types of sentences that deserve special note.

(1) A quoted sentence

Capitalize only the first word in a quoted sentence, even if you interrupt the sentence with commentary.

> When asked to name the books she found most influential, Nadine Gordimer responded, "**I**n general, the works that mean most to one—change one's thinking and therefore maybe one's life—are those read in youth."

> "**O**ddly," states Ved Mehta, "**l**ike my earliest memories, the books that made the greatest impression on me were the ones I encountered as a small child."

MLA recommends that you use a bracketed lowercase letter when integrating someone else's sentence into a sentence of your own.

> Nadine Gordimer believes that "[i]n general, the works that mean most to one—change one's thinking and therefore maybe one's life—are those read in youth" (102).

(2) A freestanding parenthetical sentence

Capitalize the first word of a freestanding sentence inside parentheses.

> Lance Armstrong won the Tour de France a record-breaking seven times. (**P**revious record holders include Jacques Anquetil, Bernard Hinault, Eddy Merckx, and Miguel Indurain.)

If the sentence inside the parentheses occurs within a sentence of your own, the first word should not be capitalized.

> Lance Armstrong won the Tour de France a record-breaking seven times (**p**reviously, he shared the record with four other cyclists).

(3) An independent clause following a colon

According to the *Chicago Manual of Style* (CMS), if only one independent clause (a clause with a subject and a predicate) follows a colon, the first word should be lowercased. However, if two or more independent clauses follow the colon, the first word of each clause is capitalized.

> The ear thermometer is used quite frequently now: **t**his type of thermometer records a temperature more accurately than a glass thermometer.

> Two new thermometers are replacing the old thermometers filled with mercury: **T**he digital thermometer uses a heat sensor to determine body temperature. **T**he ear thermometer is actually an infrared thermometer that detects the temperature of the eardrum.

The APA manual recommends capitalizing the first word of *any* independent clause following a colon. The MLA manual advises capitalizing the first word only when what follows is a rule or principle.

> Think of fever as a symptom, not as an illness: **I**t is the body's response to infection. [APA]

He has two basic rules for healthy living: **E**at sensibly and exercise strenuously at least three times a week. [APA and MLA]

(4) An abbreviated question
The first words of all abbreviated questions are capitalized when the intent is to draw attention to the questions.

How do we distinguish the legal codes for families? For individuals? For genetic research?

21d Computer keys, menu items, and icon names

When referring to specific computer keys, menu items, and icon names, capitalize the first letter of each.

To find the thesaurus, press Shift and the function key F7.

Instead of choosing Copy from the Edit menu, you can press Ctrl+C.

EXERCISE 1

Edit the capitalization errors in the following paragraph. Be prepared to explain any changes that you make.

¹Diana taurasi (Her teammates call her dee) plays basketball for the Phoenix mercury. ²She has all the skills she needs to be a Star Player: She can pass and shoot, as well as rebound, block, and steal. ³In april of 2004, taurasi played on the u.s. national team against japan, and, in the Summer of 2004, she made her olympic debut in Athens.

22 Italics

Italics indicate that a word or a group of words is being used in a special way, for example, to indicate titles or foreign words.

22a Titles of works published or produced separately

Italics indicate the title of a work published or produced as a whole rather than as part of a larger work. A newspaper, for example, is a separate work, but an editorial in a newspaper is not; thus, the title of the newspaper is italicized, and the title of the editorial is enclosed in quotation marks.

The titles of the following kinds of separate works are italicized:

Books	*The Hours*	*Unaccustomed Earth*
Magazines	*Wired*	*National Geographic*
Newspapers	*USA Today*	*Wall Street Journal*
Plays, films, videotapes	*Death of a Salesman*	*Akeelah and the Bee*
Television and radio shows	*American Idol*	*A Prairie Home Companion*
Recordings	*Kind of Blue*	*Great Verdi Overtures*
Works of art	*American Gothic*	*David*
Long poems	*Paradise Lost*	*The Divine Comedy*
Pamphlets	*Saving Energy*	*Tips for Gardeners*
Comic strips	*Peanuts*	*Doonesbury*

According to the MLA, titles of Web sites are also italicized. When an italicized title includes the title of a separate work within it, the embedded title is not italicized.

Modern Interpretations of Paradise Lost

Neither italics nor quotation marks are necessary for titles of major historical documents or religious texts.

The Bill of Rights contains the first ten amendments to the U.S. Constitution.

The Bible, a sacred text just as the Koran or the Torah is, begins with the Book of Genesis.

According to MLA and CMS guidelines, an initial *the* in a newspaper or periodical title is not italicized.

The story was published in the *New York Times*.

22b Other uses of italics

Use italics for foreign words; genus and species names; legal cases; names of ships, submarines, aircraft, and spacecraft; words, letters, or figures referred to as such; and emphasized words.

Foreign word	*fútbol*
Genus and species	*Homo sapiens*
Legal case	*Miranda v. Arizona*
Name of ship or submarine	USS *Enterprise* USS *Hawkbill*
Name of aircraft or spacecraft	*Enola Gay* *Atlantis*
Reference to word	The word *love* is hard to define.
Reference to letter or figure	The number *2* and the letter *Z* often look similar.
Emphasized word	These *are* the right files.

22c Words not italicized

Italics are not used for a reference to a legal case by an unofficial name.

All the major networks covered the O. J. Simpson trial.

But do italicize the shortened name of a well-known legal case.

The Supreme Court decision in *Brown* forced racial integration of schools.

Italics are also not used for the names of trains, the models of vehicles, and the trade names of aircraft.

Orient Express   Ford Mustang   Boeing 747

EXERCISE 1

Identify words that require italics in the following sentences.

1. Information about museum collections and exhibits can be found in art books, museum Web sites, and special sections of magazines and newspapers such as Smithsonian Magazine and the New York Times.
2. The title page of William Blake's Songs of Innocence is included in Masterpieces of the Metropolitan Museum of Art.
3. This book includes a photograph of a beautiful script used in the Koran; the script is known as the maghribi, or Western, style.
4. In 1998, the Songwriters Hall of Fame honored John Williams, who has written music for such movies as Jaws, Star Wars, and E.T.
5. The Smithsonian Institution's National Air and Space Museum houses an impressive collection of aircraft and spacecraft, including Spirit of St. Louis and Gemini 4.

Abbreviations, Acronyms, and Numbers

An **abbreviation** is a shortened version of a word or phrase: *assn.* (association), *dept.* (department), *et al.* (*et alii,* or "and others"). An **acronym** is formed by combining the initial letters and/or syllables of a series of words: *AIDS* (**a**cquired **i**mmune **d**eficiency **s**yndrome), *sonar* (**so**und **na**vigation **r**anging).

23a Abbreviations with names

Certain abbreviations are used before and/or after a person's name.

Ms. Gretel Lopez	**Mrs.** Marcus
Kim Beck, **MD**	Lee Evans, **PhD**
Dr. Redshaw	Samuel Levy **Jr.**
Mark Ngo **Sr.**	

A comma may be used to set off *Jr.* or *Sr.* However, these abbreviations are increasingly considered part of the names they follow.

Civil or military titles should not be abbreviated.

Senator Larry Johnson	Captain James
Professor Sue Li	Ambassador Aluarez

23b Addresses in correspondence

The names of states and words such as *Street, Road,* and *Company* are written out when they appear in a letter, including in the address at the top of the page. However, they are abbreviated when used in the address on an envelope.

Derson Manufacturing Co.
200 Madison St.
Watertown, MN 55388

When addressing correspondence within the United States, use the two-letter state abbreviations established by the U.S. Postal Service.

23c Acceptable abbreviations in academic and professional writing

Some abbreviations have become so familiar that they are considered acceptable substitutes for full words.

(1) Abbreviations for special purposes

Words such as *volume, chapter,* and *page* are abbreviated (*vol., ch.,* and *p.*) in bibliographies and in citations of research sources, but they are written out within sentences.

(2) Abbreviations for time periods and zones

82 BC [OR BCE] for before Christ [OR before the common era]

AD 95 [OR 95 CE] for *anno Domini,* "in the year of our Lord" [OR the common era]

7:40 a.m. for *ante meridiem*, before noon
4:52 EST for Eastern Standard Time

(3) The abbreviation for the United States (U.S. or US) as an adjective

the U.S. Navy, the US economy
[COMPARE: They moved to the United States in 1990.]

The abbreviation *U.S.* or *US* should be used only as an adjective. When using *United States* as a noun, spell it out. MLA lists *US* as the preferred abbreviated form, but APA uses *U.S.*

(4) Some abbreviations for Latin expressions

Certain abbreviations for Latin expressions are common in academic writing.

cf. [compare]	et al. [and others]	i.e. [that is]
e.g. [for example]	etc. [and so forth]	vs. OR v. [versus]

23d Acronyms

Introduce an acronym by placing it in parentheses after the group of words it stands for.

The Federal Emergency Management Administration (FEMA) was criticized by many after Hurricane Katrina.

> **MULTILINGUAL WRITERS**
>
> **USING ARTICLES WITH ABBREVIATIONS, ACRONYMS, OR NUMBERS**
>
> When you use an abbreviation, an acronym, or a number, you sometimes need an indefinite article. Choose *a* or *an* based on the pronunciation of the initial sound of the abbreviation, acronym, or number: use *a* before a consonant sound and *an* before a vowel sound.
>
> **an IBM** computer [*IBM* begins with a vowel sound.]
>
> **a NASA** engineer [*NASA* begins with a consonant sound.]
>
> **a 1964** Mustang [*1964* begins with a consonant sound.]

23e General uses of numbers

Depending on their uses, numbers are treated in different ways. MLA recommends spelling out numbers that are expressed in one or two words (*nine, ninety-one, nine hundred, nine million*). A numeral is used for any other number (*9½, 9.9, 999*), unless it begins a sentence.

The register recorded 164 names.

APA advises spelling out only numbers below ten. Both MLA and APA recommend using words rather than numerals at the beginning of a sentence.

One hundred sixty-four names were recorded in the register.

When numbers or amounts refer to the same entities throughout a passage, use numerals when any of the numbers would be more than two words long if spelled out.

Only 5 of the 134 delegates attended the final meeting. The remaining 129 delegates will be informed by e-mail.

23f Special uses of numbers

Numerals can be used for the following:

Times of day	9:30 p.m.
Dates	September 11, 2001 OR 11 September 2001 OR 9/11
Decades	1999 to 2003 OR 1999–2003
Addresses	25 Arrow Drive, Apartment 1
Identification of proper nouns	Edward III Highway 61
Parts of books and plays	chapter 1, page 15 act 2, scene 1 OR Act II, Scene I
Decimals	a 2.5 average
Percents	12 percent

When monetary amounts are mentioned frequently, they can be expressed with numerals and symbols: $20.00, 99¢ or $0.99.

MULTILINGUAL WRITERS

COMMAS AND PERIODS WITH NUMERALS

In American usage, a decimal point (period) indicates a number or part of a number that is smaller than one, and a comma divides large numbers into units of three digits.

7.65 (seven and sixty-five one-hundredths)   10,000 (ten thousand)

In some other cultures, these usages of the decimal point and the comma are reversed.

7,65 (seven and sixty-five one-hundredths)   10.000 (ten thousand)

EXERCISE 1

Edit the following sentences to correct the usage of abbreviations and numbers.

1. A Natl. Historic Landmark, Hoover Dam is located about 30 miles s.e. of Las. Vegas, Nev.

2. The dam is named after Herbert Hoover, the 31st pres. of the U.S.

3. It is administered by the U.S. Dept. of the Interior.

4. Built by the fed. gov. between nineteen thirty-three and 1935, this dam is still considered one of the greatest achievements in the history of civ. engineering.

5. Spanning the Colorado River, Hoover Dam created Lake Mead—a reservoir covering 247 sq. miles.

WRITING

CHAPTER 24
Writing and Reading Rhetorically 198

- **24a** Understanding the rhetorical situation 198
- **24b** Addressing exigence with a specific purpose 200
- **24c** Considering audience 201
- **24d** Writing and reading a message within a context 203

CHAPTER 25
Planning and Drafting Essays 204

- **25a** Stages of the writing process 204
- **25b** Focusing a topic into a clearly stated thesis 205
- **25c** Creating an outline 206
- **25d** Drafting well-developed paragraphs 207

CHAPTER 26
Revising and Editing Essays 209

- **26a** Revising for unity and coherence 209
- **26b** Editing and proofreading 212
- **26c** Sample final draft 213

CHAPTER 27
Using Visuals 217

- **27a** Using graphics 217
- **27b** Using pictures 218

CHAPTER 28
Writing Arguments 221

- **28a** Determining the purpose of your argument 221
- **28b** Considering differing viewpoints 222
- **28c** Distinguishing between fact and opinion 223
- **28d** Taking a position or making a claim 223
- **28e** Providing evidence for an effective argument 224
- **28f** Using the rhetorical appeals to ground your argument 226
- **28g** Arranging an effective argument 227
- **28h** Sample argument 228

CHAPTER 29
Writing in Business 236

- **29a** Business letters 237
- **29b** Business memos 240
- **29c** Résumés 242
- **29d** Letters of application 245

24 Writing and Reading Rhetorically

Rhetoric, the purposeful use of language, pervades your daily life. Whether you are reading textbooks or e-mails, writing assignments for class or text messaging your friends, composing with words or visuals, you are actively engaging the main elements of the **rhetorical situation** (see fig. 24.1).

Figure 24.1. The rhetorical situation.

24a Understanding the rhetorical situation

The rhetorical situation—the set of cirumstances under which one writes or reads a text—is composed of six elements: exigence, writer, audience, message, purpose, and context. In a rhetorical situation, a **writer** (or reader) identifies an **exigence**, a reason to write (or read) something. Whether you want to solve a problem (the landlord has not provided enough parking spaces) or learn something new (how to upload photos to Snapfish), you use words to do so. You might compose a **message** (a visual and/or verbal text) in order to fulfill your purpose: persuading the landlord to open up two blocked parking spaces. Or you might read instructions from Snapfish that explain exactly how to upload pictures. First, though you might **preview** the Snapfish Web site, skimming over all the information to locate the specific content you need ("Need help uploading your photos?"). Then you will read it carefully, and even reread it until you understand how to perform the task.

In cases like these, you are writing or reading for a specific **purpose,** that of addressing and maybe even resolving the exigence. To fulfill the purpose, the message must reach an **audience** (such as the landlord or yourself) that can help address or resolve the problem. Every audience—no matter how willing or reluctant to help—reads, hears, or sees a message within a specific **context.** The landlord may be blocking those parking spaces for some reason or may have forgotten they exist. You might be trying to upload your photographs to a computer with out-of-date software, too narrow a bandwidth, or insufficient memory, or you might be unaware of the helpful instructions Snapfish provides.

In other words, every context for communication (writing or reading) includes resources (positive influences) and constraints (obstacles) that influence the rhetorical situation. Such resources and constraints include the history of what has been said about the problem, how well the writer communicates with the intended audience, how receptive the audience is, and the writer's reputation in relation to the audience.

In your role as an academic reader, you will follow the same steps as when finding and reading instructions from Snapfish. You will start by previewing or skimming the entire text. You'll examine the title of the text or the individual chapter titles to see whether the text is likely to contain the information you are searching for. Then, if possible, you will read the inside back cover or the author bio to learn about the author's reputation and credentials. What does the preface tell you about the author or text? An index or a bibliography can help you determine the breadth and depth of research that went into the text itself.

As you preview a text, you work to get a sense of what the author is trying to say. What is the author's purpose? Who is the audience? In order to determine these components of any rhetorical situation you enter, you need to stay alert for the author's major points. Often, transitional words—that is, words indicating purpose, result, summary, causation, repetition, exemplification, or intensification—alert you to important points.

24b Addressing exigence with a specific purpose

The purposeful use of words can help resolve a particular problem or exigence. Once you have determined the exigence for writing or reading, you are in a position to gauge all the elements of the text—from choice of words to organizational pattern—in terms of overall purpose and intended audience. Knowing the reason for an author's written work will help orient you to what you might expect from reading (and rereading) the entire text. The simple question on the Snapfish site—"Need help uploading your photos?"—serves to orient your reading; the words and images themselves fulfill the purpose of instructing you, someone who needs help. In your academic reading, you may determine that an author is writing to explain a point or a process (for instance, how bridge safety is ensured or how Gettysburg National Battlefield Park became a national memorial).

Successful writers always work to clarify their purpose in terms of who makes up their intended audience and how they want to influence the thinking, understanding, or behavior of that audience. Thus, depending on the writer's overall purpose, the message may be classified as **expressive**, emphasizing the writer's feelings about and reaction to a person or an event. The Declaration of Independence is a powerful example of expressive writing. A message may also be **expository,** focusing more on objects, events, or ideas than on the writer's feelings about them. An example is a description or an analysis of typical American Fourth of July celebrations. Messages may also be classified as **argumentative**, or intended to influence the audience's attitudes or actions. Frederick Douglass's 1852 speech, "What to the Slave Is the Fourth of July?" exemplifies an argumentative text.

Whatever their purpose, writers can develop a message using one or more of the following methods, which are familiar to you from your own reading and writing: narration, description, cause-and-effect analysis, comparison and contrast, and so on. Whether writing or reading rhetorically, you need to assess the overall rhetorical purpose of the message in order to evaluate whether that message is aligned with that purpose. For instance, if you are writing in response to a specific assignment, talk with your instructor or examine the assignment sheet to review which elements of the rhetorical situation (purpose, context, and audience) have already been established for you. If you are reading rhetorically, take time to underline, highlight, or add comments or questions to the passages that suggest the writer's purpose, context, intended audience, and response to a problem. After all, reading rhetorically means reading actively. Writing rhetorically means writing with purposeful awareness.

24c Considering audience

A clear understanding of the audience—its values, concerns, and knowledge—helps a writer tailor a message in terms of length, quality and quantity of details, word choice, and inclusion of effective examples. Of course, the audience is anyone who reads a text, but the rhetorical, or intended, audience consists of those people whom the writer considers capable of being influenced by the words or who are capable of bringing about change. If you're reading rhetorically, you may become a member of the writer's rhetorical audience.

Writers usually consider three kinds of audiences. A **specialized audience** has a demonstrated interest or expertise in the subject and can help resolve the exigence. Only someone who has an interest in downloading photos will read the information on the Snapfish Web site. A **diverse audience** consists of readers with differing levels of expertise and varying interest in the subject. When you're in a doctor's waiting room, reading whatever is available (*People, Newsweek, GQ*), you are part of a diverse audience. **Multiple audiences** are composed of a primary target audience of readers and a secondary audience who has access to and may read the text. E-mails are usually sent to a primary audience and often circulated to a secondary audience, whom the writer of the message may not have taken into consideration.

As a writer, you need to think clearly about who exactly will be reading (or who might end up reading) what you write and ask yourself whether your language choices and examples are appropriate for that audience, especially if it is an unintended audience. As a reader, you want to weigh the opinions the author holds and determine the message the author is trying to impart. In other words, how well supported are those opinions? How reliable or believable does the author seem? You also want to determine how the author is addressing you as a member of the audience. How does the author's choice of words, tone, examples, and organization connect—or not—with your values and your opinions?

24d Writing and reading a message within a context

Context includes the time and place in which a message is read or written, the writer and the audience of that message, and the medium of delivery—it is the entire set of the circumstances under which writer and reader communicate. Social, political, religious, and other cultural factors all influence the context by helping or hindering successful communication. After all, your background and beliefs often shape the attitude you take whether you are writing or reading, just as the medium (print, online, or visual) in which you are writing or reading influences how you produce or interpret the message. Writing material for a Web page, for instance, requires you to think differently about organization, design, and style than does writing a traditional academic essay or a letter to your landlord. Reading a novel in book format or an article online requires you to adjust your expectations: reading a stable print text is a markedly different experience from reading an online text, which may be enhanced by visual, video, and audio elements.

Writers who consider the context—as well as their own attitude toward the subject—are more likely to communicate the ideas to the audience effectively. Readers who consider the context in which the writer has produced a message are more likely to read actively by responding to, questioning, and agreeing or disagreeing with the text. Writing and reading rhetorically are imperative to clear communication and understanding—and to your success in college.

25 Planning and Drafting Essays

Writing is a process. Effective writers know they cannot do everything at once, so they generate, organize, develop, and clarify their ideas as well as polish their prose during a series of sometimes separate—but often overlapping—steps.

25a Stages of the writing process

Prewriting is the initial stage of the writing process. Consider what is expected of you in terms of your intended audience, context, and overall purpose. Then jump-start your thinking by talking with others working on the same assignment, keeping a journal, freewriting, or questioning.

Drafting involves writing down as much as you can without worrying about being perfect or staying on topic. The more ideas you get down on paper, the more options you will have as you begin to clarify your thesis and purpose for writing. Progress is your goal at this stage, not perfection.

Revising offers you the opportunity to focus your purpose for writing, establish a clear thesis statement, and organize your ideas toward those ends. During revision, you can start stabilizing the overall structure of your essay, the structure of the individual paragraphs, and your introduction and conclusion. Revising means producing another draft for further revision and editing.

Editing focuses on surface features: punctuation, spelling, word choice, grammar, sentence structure, and all the rest of the details of Standardized English.

25b Focusing a topic into a clearly stated thesis

To bring your topic into focus, consider your interests, purpose, the needs of your audience, and the time and space available. Once you have focused your subject into a topic, you have come a long way toward developing the main idea you want to convey as well as your purpose for writing (to explain, teach, analyze, argue, or compare). Your subject, purpose, supporting information, and focus all come together in a controlling idea, or **thesis statement,** an explicit declaration (usually in one sentence) of the main idea.

An explicitly formulated thesis statement helps keep your writing on target, unifies your writing, and guides your readers through the content that follows.

CHECKLIST for Assessing a Topic

- Are you interested in the topic?
- Is the topic appropriate for your audience?
- Can you interest the audience in your topic?
- What is your purpose in writing about this topic?
- Can you do justice to the topic in the time and space available to you? Or should you narrow it down or expand it?
- Do you know enough about the topic to write a paper of the required length? If not, how will you get additional information?
- Are you willing to learn more about the topic?

TIPS FOR DEVELOPING A THESIS STATEMENT

- Decide which feature of the topic interests you most.
- Write down your point of view or assertion about that feature.
- Mark the passages in your rough draft that support your position.
- Draft a thesis statement, and consider whether it is too broad or too narrow to be developed sufficiently.
- After your initial drafts, ask yourself whether the scope of your thesis should be adjusted to reflect the direction your essay has taken.
- If you are still unhappy with your thesis, start again with the first tip and be even more specific.

25c Creating an outline

Many writers need a working plan to direct their ideas and keep their writing on course. Others rely on outlines.

When Richard Petraglia was assigned to assess the reasons for studying a foreign language, he drafted the following tentative outline:

TENTATIVE THESIS STATEMENT: Studying a foreign language is the best way to learn about English.

I. Many Americans don't think they need to learn another language.
   A. English is the language of global communication.
   B. English speakers always have an advantage in intercultural communication.
II. English-only speakers miss out on benefits of learning another language.
   A. Learning another language is not just about being able to talk to people in different countries.

> B. Studying another language increases a student's knowledge of another culture and so promotes tolerance and understanding.
>
> C. Knowing the language enriches a student's stay in a foreign country.
>
> III. Students who take a foreign language do better on standardized tests.
>
> A. Students can compare grammars to better remember the rules of their own language.
>
> B. Studying a foreign language opens up a student's mind to different ways of speaking and expressing ideas.
>
> C. Studying a foreign language helps students acquire better reading skills.

25d Drafting well-developed paragraphs

You compose a draft by developing the information that will constitute the paragraphs of your essay.

(1) Using details

The following well-developed paragraph uses details to bring an idea to life:

> I stood in front of the mirror and looked at myself and laughed. My hair was one of those odd, amazing, unbelievable, stop-you-in-your-tracks creations—not unlike a zebra's stripes, an armadillo's ears, or the feet of the electric-bluefooted boobie—that the Universe makes for no reason other than to express its own limitless imagination. I realized I had never been given the opportunity to appreciate hair for its true self. That it did, in fact, have one. I remembered years of enduring hairdressers—from my mother onward—doing missionary work on my hair. They dominated,

suppressed, controlled. Now, more or less free, it stood this way and that. I would call up my friends around the country to report on its antics. It never thought of lying down. Flatness, the missionary position, did not interest it. It grew. Being short, cropped off near the root, another missionary "solution," did not interest it either. It sought more and more space, more light, more of itself. It loved to be washed; but that was it.

—ALICE WALKER, "Oppressed Hair Puts a Ceiling on the Brain"

(2) Providing examples

Like details, examples contribute to paragraph development by making specific what otherwise might seem general and hard to grasp. The author of the following paragraph uses both methods:

It began with coveting our neighbor's chickens. Lily would volunteer to collect the eggs, and then she offered to move in with them. Not the neighbors, the chickens. She said if she could have some of her own, she would be the happiest girl on earth. What parent could resist this bait? Our lifestyle could accommodate a laying flock; my husband and I had kept poultry before, so we knew it was a project we could manage, and a responsibility Lily could handle largely by herself. I understood how much that meant to her when I heard her tell her grandmother, "They're going to be just *my* chickens, grandma. Not even one of them will be my sister's." To be five years old and have some other life form entirely under your control—not counting goldfish or parents—is a majestic state of affairs.

—BARBARA KINGSOLVER, "Lily's Chickens"

26 Revising and Editing Essays

Revising entails rethinking what you have already written in terms of your overall purpose: how successfully you have addressed your audience, how clearly you have stated your thesis, how effectively you have arranged your information, and how thoroughly you have developed your assertions. When you are **editing,** you are polishing your writing: you choose words more precisely, shape prose more distinctly, and structure sentences more effectively. When you are **proofreading,** you focus even more sharply to eliminate surface errors in grammar, punctuation, and mechanics.

26a Revising for unity and coherence

When revising the body of an essay, writers are likely to discover ways to make each paragraph more **unified** by relating every sentence within the paragraph to the single main idea of the topic sentence. After weeding out unrelated sentences, writers concentrate on **coherence,** ordering the sentences so that ideas progress logically and smoothly from one sentence to the next. A successful paragraph is well developed, unified, and coherent.

(1) Stating the main idea
Much like the thesis statement of an essay, a **topic sentence,** such as the one in italics in the following paragraph, states the main idea of a paragraph and comments on that main idea.

> *I think we are innately suspicious of... rapid cognition.* We live in a world that assumes that the quality of a decision is directly related to the time and effort that went into making it. When doctors are faced with a difficult diagnosis, they order more tests, and when we are uncertain about what we hear, we ask for a second opinion. And what do we tell our children? Haste makes waste. Look before you leap. Stop and *think.* Don't judge a book by its cover. We believe that we are always better off gathering as much information as possible and spending as much time as possible in deliberation. We really only trust conscious decision making. But there are moments, particularly in times of stress, when haste does not make waste, when our snap judgments and first impressions can offer a much better means of making sense of the world. —MALCOLM GLADWELL, *Blink*

You can also end a paragraph with a topic sentence:

> The first time I visited Texas, I wore a beige polyester-blend lab coat with reinforced slits for pocket access and mechanical-pencil storage. I was attending a local booksellers' convention, having just co-written a pseudo-scientific book . . . , and my publicist suggested that the doctor getup would attract attention. It did. Everyone thought I was the janitor. *Lesson No. 1: When in Texas, do not dress down.* —PATRICIA MARX, "Dressin' Texan"

(2) Unifying each paragraph

Paragraphs are **unified** when every sentence relates to the main idea. The following tips may help you improve paragraph unity.

TIPS FOR IMPROVING PARAGRAPH UNITY

Identify	Identify the topic sentence for each paragraph.
Relate	Read each sentence in a paragraph and decide if and how it relates to the topic sentence.
Eliminate	Any sentence that violates the unity of a paragraph should be cut (or saved for use elsewhere).

Clarify	Any sentence that "almost" relates to the topic sentence should be revised until it does relate. You may need to clarify details or add information or a transitional word or phrase to make the relationship clear.
Rewrite	If more than one idea is conveyed in a single paragraph, either split the paragraph in two or rewrite the topic sentence so that it establishes a relationship between both ideas.

(3) Establishing coherence

Some paragraphs are unified but not coherent. In a unified paragraph, every sentence relates to the main idea of the paragraph. In a **coherent** paragraph, the relationship among the ideas is clear, and the progression from one sentence to the next is easy for readers to follow, as in the following paragraph.

> When we moved into our new apartment, we found that the kitchen was in horrible shape. The previous tenant had left behind lots of junk that we had to get rid of, from dented canisters and broken can openers to dirty dish towels and towel rack parts. The inside of the refrigerator was covered with black mold, and it smelled as if something had been rotting in there for years. The stove was as dirty as the refrigerator. So we set to work. All the drawers and cabinets had to be washed. I put new paper down on all the shelves, and my roommate took care of lining the drawers. We had to scrub the walls with a brush and plenty of Lysol to get rid of the grease.

To achieve coherence and unity in your paragraphs, make conscious decisions about how to order the information. Use **chronological order** (particularly useful in narration) to arrange ideas according to the order in which things happened. With **spatial order** (effective in description), you orient the reader's focus from right to left, near to far, top to bottom, and so on. With **emphatic order** (useful in expository and persuasive writing), information is arranged in order of importance, usually from least to most important, which helps readers understand logical relationships. And, sometimes, information is presented in **logical order,** from specific to general or from general to specific, as in the following paragraph.

> It was not the only disappointment my mother felt in me. In the years that followed, I failed her so many times, each time asserting my own will, my right to fall short of expectations. I didn't get straight As. I didn't become class president. I didn't get into Stanford. I dropped out of college. —AMY TAN, "Two Kinds"

26b Editing and proofreading

If you are satisfied with the revised structure of your essay and the content of your paragraphs, you can edit individual sentences for clarity, effectiveness, and variety and then proofread the entire draft for correctness.

CHECKLIST for Editing

Sentences
- What is the unifying idea of each sentence?
- Are the sentences varied in length?
- How many of your sentences use subordination? Coordination? If you overuse any one sentence structure, revise for variation.
- Which sentences should have parallel structure?
- Do any sentences contain misplaced modifiers?
- Does each verb agree with its subject? Does every pronoun agree with its antecedent?

Diction
- Have you unintentionally repeated any words?
- Are any of your word choices vague or too general?
- Is the vocabulary you have chosen appropriate for your audience, purpose, and context?
- Have you defined any technical or unfamiliar words for your audience?

CHECKLIST for Proofreading

Spelling

- Have you double-checked the words you frequently misspell and any the spell checker may have missed (for example, misspellings that still form words, such as *form* for *from*)?
- If you used a spell checker, did it overlook homophones (such as *there/their, who's/whose,* and *it's/its*)?
- Have you double-checked the spelling of all foreign words and all proper names?

Punctuation and Capitalization

- Does each sentence have appropriate closing punctuation, and have you used only one space after each end punctuation mark?
- Is all punctuation within sentences—commas, semicolons, apostrophes, hyphens, and dashes—used appropriately and placed correctly?
- Are direct quotations carefully and correctly punctuated? Where have you placed end punctuation with a quotation? Are quotations capitalized properly?
- Are all proper names, people's titles, and titles of published works correctly capitalized?
- Are titles of works identified with quotation marks, underlining, or italics?

26c Sample final draft

The essay that Richard Petraglia ultimately submitted to his teacher follows.

Petraglia 1

Richard Petraglia
Professor Glenn
English 15
20 October 2008

Why Take a Foreign Language?

Native English speakers have an advantage when it comes to intercultural communication: English is the language of business, diplomacy, and global communication in general. It is therefore tempting to think that English speakers don't need to learn a foreign language. But they do—and for reasons other than being able to communicate with people in foreign countries. Students who study a foreign language in school often have better writing skills, reading comprehension, and scores on standardized tests.

One good reason for American students to study a foreign language is that learning a second or even third language helps them learn more about English. For me, learning about English has been the most rewarding part of studying foreign languages continuously since middle school. Students need to look beyond the idea that all they will learn in a foreign language class is how to speak someone else's language and realize that learning another language has the fortunate effect of teaching them more about their own.

For example, there is an ongoing debate about just how useful teaching grammar is in improving student writing. Because students intuitively know how to conjugate English verbs and generally make themselves understood, it can seem pointless and frustrating for them to be taught the minutiae of the language they already speak. But, as students learn how to express themselves in a foreign language, they also indirectly learn about their own language's structure. Therefore, learning German grammar improves writing in English because it improves the student's knowledge of grammatical structures.

By gaining a better understanding of their own language through studying the language of another country, students begin to understand the subtle changes of meaning that happen with changes of grammar. As they absorb the subtleties of grammar, students write and speak with more variety and precision and use their own language more effectively.

Statistics indicate that students who pursue several years of foreign languages in high school tend to score higher on standardized tests. One might conclude that more highly motivated students will be the ones who pursue an elective like Spanish or French all four years and that language study is just a characteristic of the more motivated students who will score higher on standardized tests anyway. But their success is at least partially due to the way studying a foreign language builds awareness of their own language. Studying a foreign language improves reading comprehension because students begin to think about how ideas are expressed through language. Once a student has this awareness, he or she can more easily grasp the ideas a writer is trying to convey.

Studying a foreign language also makes students better learners because it teaches them to learn in a combination of ways. First, students practice learning intuitively, using the knowledge of their native language to make educated guesses about the way the foreign language will work. In conjunction with this intuitive method, foreign language learning develops the students' ability to follow complex rules. Another language often expresses ideas in a different way than English does, using unfamiliar grammatical rules and structures. The students are therefore forced to rely on their knowledge of complex grammatical rules to express ideas in a foreign language. Because learning a foreign language teaches students to learn by a combination of both intuitive and rule-based methods, it makes them better learners in general. A student can carry this knowledge of being able to apply complex rules as well as the ability to learn intuitively to any other discipline.

27 Using Visuals

In today's visual culture, it is hard to find a report, an essay, or an article that does not include graphics or images. Tables, charts, graphs, and pictures are the most common visual elements used in text documents.

27a Using graphics

Many academic and professional documents that are primarily composed of text also include substantial visual displays, or **graphics,** to clarify written material. Different types of graphics—tables, charts, and graphs—serve different purposes, and some may serve multiple purposes in a given document.

(1) Tables

Tables use a row-and-column arrangement to organize data (numbers or words) spatially; they are especially useful for presenting great amounts of numerical information in a small space, enabling the reader to draw direct comparisons among pieces of data or even to locate specific items. When you design a table, be sure to label all of the columns and rows accurately and to provide both a title and a number for the table. The table number and title traditionally appear above the table body, as table 27.1 demonstrates, and any notes or source information should be placed below it.

(2) Charts and graphs

Charts and graphs display relationships among statistical data in visual form by using lines, bars, or other visual elements rather than just letters and numbers. **Pie charts** are especially useful

Using Visuals

Table 27.1 MODIFIED MONTHLY TORNADO STATISTICS

Month	2007 Final	2006 Final	2005 Final	2004 Final	4-Year Average
Jan	21	47	33	3	26
Feb	52	12	10	9	21
Mar	171	150	62	50	108
Apr	165	245	132	125	167
May	250	139	123	509	255
Jun	128	120	316	268	208
Jul	69	71	138	124	101
Aug	73	80	123	179	114
Sep	51	84	133	295	141
Oct	87	76	18	79	65
Nov	7	42	150	150	87
Dec	19	40	26	26	28
Total	1093	1106	1264	1817	1321

Source: National Weather Service.

for showing the relationship of parts to a whole (see fig. 27.1), but they can only be used to display sets of data that add up to 100 percent (a whole).

Bar charts show correlations between two variables that do not change smoothly over time. For instance, a bar chart might illustrate the relative speeds of various computer processors or statistics about the composition of the U.S. military (see fig. 27.2).

27b Using pictures

Pictures include photos, sketches, technical illustrations, paintings, icons, and other visual representations. Photographs are often used to reinforce textual descriptions or to show a reader

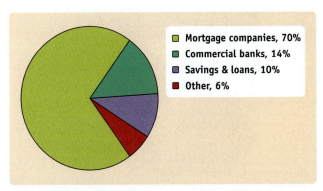

Figure 27.1. Pie chart showing issuers of mortgage-based securities.

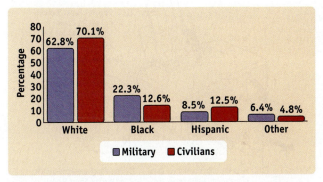

Figure 27.2. Bar chart illustrating the composition of the U.S. military.

exactly what something looks like. But photographs are not always the most informative type of picture. Compare the two images in fig. 27.3. Although the photograph is a more realistic image of the actual printer, the illustration more clearly shows the printer's important features: buttons, panels, and so forth. Line drawings enable the designer of a document, such as a user manual, to highlight specific elements of an object while deemphasizing or eliminating unnecessary information.

Figure 27.3 A photo and a drawing of the same printer.

28   Writing Arguments

When you express a point of view and use logical reasoning to invite a specific audience to accept that point of view or adopt a course of action, you are writing an **argument.** Arguments serve three basic purposes: to analyze a complicated issue or question an established belief, to express or defend a point of view, and to invite or convince an audience to change a position or adopt a course of action.

28a   Determining the purpose of your argument

What is your topic? What is at stake? What is likely to happen as a result of making this argument? Who is in a position to act or react in response to your argument?

When writing an argument, you need to establish the relationships among your topic, purpose, and audience.

- If there is little likelihood that you can convince members of your audience to change a strongly held opinion, you might achieve a great deal by inviting them to understand your position.
- If the members of your audience are not firmly committed to a position, you might be able to convince them to agree with the opinion you are expressing or defending.
- If the members of your audience agree with you in principle, you might invite them to undertake a specific action—such as voting for the candidate you are supporting.

No matter how you imagine those in your audience responding to your argument, you must establish **common**

ground with them, stating a goal toward which you both want to work or identifying a belief, assumption, or value that you both share.

28b Considering differing viewpoints

If everyone agreed on everything, there would be no need for argument, for taking a position. Therefore, a good deal of the writing you will do in school or at work will require you to take an arguable position on a topic.

Behind any effective argument is a question that can generate more than one reasonable answer. Answers differ because people approach questions with various backgrounds, experiences, and assumptions. As a consequence, they are often tempted to use reasoning that supports what they already believe. As a writer, employing such reasoning is a good place to start. But as you expand your argument, you will want to demonstrate not only that you are knowledgeable about your topic but also that you have given fair consideration to other views about it.

When you choose a topic for argumentation, you will want to take a stance that provides you an exigence (or reason) for writing. First, you focus on a topic, on the part of some general subject that you will address in your essay, and then you pose a question about it. As you craft your question, consider the following: (1) your own values and beliefs with respect to the question, (2) how your assumptions might differ from those of your intended audience, and (3) how you might establish common ground with members of your audience, while at the same time respecting any differences between your opinion and theirs. The question you raise will evolve into your **thesis,** an arguable statement. To determine whether a topic might be suitable, make a statement about the topic ("I believe strongly that . . . " or "My view is that . . . ") and then check to see if that statement can be argued.

28c Distinguishing between fact and opinion

When you develop your thesis statement into an argument, you use both facts and opinions. **Facts** are reliable pieces of information that can be verified through independent sources or procedures. **Opinions,** on the other hand, are assertions or inferences that may or may not be based on facts. Opinions that are widely accepted may seem to be factual when they are not. Facts are significant only when they are used responsibly to support a claim; otherwise, a thoughtful and well-informed opinion might have more impact.

28d Taking a position or making a claim

When making an argument, a writer takes a position (called the **claim**) on a particular topic, which clearly states what the writer wants the audience to do with the information being provided. The claim is the thesis of the argument.

Claims can be absolute or moderate, large or limited. Absolute claims assert that something is always true or false, completely good or bad; moderate claims make less sweeping assertions.

Absolute claim	College athletes are never good students.
Moderate claim	Most colleges have low graduation rates for their athletes.

The stronger the claim, the stronger the evidence needed to support it. Be sure to consider the quality and the significance of the evidence you use—not just its quantity.

Claims also vary in terms of how much they encompass. **Substantiation claims,** for instance, assert that something exists or is evident. Without making a value judgment, such a claim makes a point that can be supported by evidence.

The job market for those who just received a PhD in English is limited.

The post office is raising rates again.

Evaluation claims assert that something has a specific quality, is good or bad, effective or ineffective, attractive or unattractive, successful or unsuccessful.

The graduation rate for athletes at Penn State is very high compared with that at the other Big Ten universities.

The public transportation system in Washington DC is reliable and safe.

Finally, **policy claims** call for a specific action.

We must find the funds to hire better qualified high school teachers.

We need to build a light-rail system linking downtown with the airport and the western suburbs.

28e Providing evidence for an effective argument

Effective arguments are well developed and supported by intelligent and ethical evidence. They also take into consideration the reasons others might disagree.

(1) Establishing reasons for the claim

If you want readers to take your ideas seriously, you must communicate the reasons that have led to your position as well as the values and assumptions that underlie your thinking. When you are exploring your topic, make a list of the reasons that have led to your belief. For example, when Anna Seitz was working on her argumentative essay (presented at the end of this chapter), she listed the following reasons for her belief that universities should not allow individuals or corporations to buy naming rights to campus buildings:

1. By purchasing naming rights, donors gain influence over educational policy decisions, even though they are not qualified to make such decisions.
2. Significant donations can adversely affect overall university finances by replacing existing funding sources.
3. Donors who purchase naming rights are associated with the university, in spite of the fact that they or their corporations may subscribe to a different set of values.

Although it is possible to base an argument on one good reason (such as "The selling of naming rights distracts from the educational purposes of universities"), doing so can be risky. When you show that you have more than one reason for believing as you do, you increase the likelihood that your audience will find merit in your argument. Sometimes, however, one reason is more appropriate than several others you could advance. To develop an argument for which you have only one good reason, explore the bases underlying your reason: the values and assumptions that led you to take your stand.

Whether you have one reason or several, be sure to provide sufficient evidence from credible sources to support your claim: facts, statistics, examples, and testimony from personal experience or professional expertise.

This evidence must be accurate, representative, and sufficient. Accurate information should be verifiable by others. Recognize, however, that even if the information a writer provides is accurate, it may not be representative or sufficient if it was drawn from an exceptional case, a biased sample, or a one-time occurrence. Whatever form of evidence you use—facts, statistics, examples, or testimony—you need to make clear to your audience exactly *why* and *how* the evidence supports your claim.

(2) Responding to diverse views

Effective arguments consider and respond to other points of view, fairly and respectfully. The most common strategy for addressing opposing points of view is **refutation:** you introduce diverse views and then respectfully demonstrate why you disagree with or accept each of them. When you find yourself agreeing with a point that supports another side of the issue, you can benefit from offering a **concession,** which can demonstrate your fair-mindedness. If you admit that others are partially right, they are more likely to admit that you could be partially right as well.

28f | Using the rhetorical appeals to ground your argument

Effective arguments always incorporate a combination of three persuasive strategies: the **rhetorical appeals** of ethos, logos, and pathos. **Ethos** (an ethical appeal) establishes the speaker's or writer's credibility and trustworthiness. An ethical appeal demonstrates goodwill toward the audience, good sense or knowledge of the subject at hand, and good character. Establishing common ground with the audience is another feature of ethos. **Logos,** a logical appeal, demonstrates an effective use of reason and judicious use of evidence, whether that evidence consists of facts, statistics, comparisons, anecdotes, expert opinions, personal experiences, or observations. You employ logos in the process of supporting claims, drawing reasonable conclusions, and avoiding rhetorical fallacies. **Pathos** (an emotional appeal) involves using language that will engage (not manipulate) the feelings of the audience by establishing empathy and authentic understanding. The most effective arguments combine these three persuasive appeals responsibly and knowledgeably.

28g Arranging an effective argument

No single arrangement is right for every written argument. The decisions you make about arrangement should be based on several factors: your topic, your audience, and your purpose. You can develop a good plan by listing the major points you want to make, deciding what order to put them in, and determining where to include refutation or concession. You must also decide where to place your thesis statement or claim.

Your conclusion should move beyond what has already been stated to reinforce your rhetorical purpose: the course of action you want your audience to take, an invitation to further understanding, or the implications of your claim.

(1) The classical arrangement
One way to organize your argument is to use classical arrangement, which assumes that an audience is prepared to follow a well-reasoned argument.

(2) Placement of the refutation and concession
Classical arrangement places the refutation after the proof or confirmation of the argument, an arrangement that usually works well. Sometimes, however, that refutation can come too late to be effective. Therefore, when you are taking a controversial stand on an emotionally loaded subject, strive to establish common ground, state your position (offering one strong reason for it), and then acknowledge and respond to opposing viewpoints. Keep at least one other reason in reserve (often one that relies on pathos) so that you can present it after responding to opposing views, thereby ending with an emphasis on confirmation.

FEATURES OF THE CLASSICAL ARRANGEMENT

Introduction	Introduce your issue and capture the attention of your audience. Begin establishing your credibility (using ethos) and common ground.
Background information	Provide your audience with a history of the situation and state how things currently stand. Define any key terms. Draw the attention of your audience to those points that are especially important and explain why they are meaningful.
Proposition	Introduce the position you are taking: present the argument itself and provide the basic reasons for your belief. Frame your position as a thesis statement or a claim.
Proof or confirmation	Discuss the reasons that have led you to take your position. Each reason must be clear, relevant, and representative. Provide facts, expert testimony, and any other evidence that supports your claim.
Refutation	Recognize and disprove the arguments of people who hold a different position and with whom you continue to disagree.
Concession	Concede any point with which you agree or that has merit; show why this concession does not damage your own case.
Conclusion	Summarize your most important points and appeal to your audience's feelings, making a personal connection. Describe the consequences of your argument in a final attempt to encourage your audience to consider (if not commit to) a particular course of action.

28h Sample argument

As you read the following essay by Anna Seitz, note her use of classical rhetorical appeals (ethos, logos, and pathos), her reasoning, and her arrangement. Also, identify the kinds of evidence she uses (facts, examples, testimony, or authority).

Seitz 1

Anna Seitz

Professor Byerly

Library Science 313

30 November 2007

Naming Opportunities: Opportunities for Whom?

All over the nation, football stadiums, business schools, law schools, dining halls, and even coaching positions have become naming opportunities (also known as "naming rights" and "legacy opportunities"). Since the first college deal in 1979—when Syracuse University signed a deal with the Carrier Corporation for lifetime naming rights to its sports stadium, the Carrier Dome—naming has become a common practice with an alleged two-fold payoff: universities raise money, and donors get their names writ large. Universities use the money, from naming opportunities to hire more faculty, raise salaries, support faculty research, provide travel opportunities for students, and build stadium suites and boxes for game watching. Reser Stadium (Oregon State), The Donald Bren School of Law (University of California–Irvine), or the Malloy Paterno Head Football Coach Endowment (Penn State University)—all these naming opportunities seem like a good solution for raising money, especially at a time when state legislatures have cut back on

Introduction

university funding and when wealthy alumni are being besieged for donations from every college they have ever attended. Naming opportunities seem like a good solution for donors, too, because their donations will be broadly recognized. While naming opportunities may seem like a perfect solution for improving colleges and universities and simplifying funding, in reality they are not. In this paper, I argue against naming opportunities on college and university campuses because they create more problems than they solve.

Background information

The naming of sports stadiums is a familiar occurrence; after all, universities commonly highlight the sponsors of their athletic programs. But naming opportunities in other spheres of academic life are unfamiliar to most people, even though such naming is an established practice. A quick search of the Web pages of university libraries reveals that many of them, especially those in the midst of major development campaigns, have created a price list just for naming opportunities. Entire buildings are available, of course. For example, a $5 million donation earns the right to name the music library at Northwestern University (Northwestern). But parts of buildings are also available these days. North Carolina State University will name an atlas stand according to the donor's wishes for only $7,500 or put a specific name on a lectern for $3,500 (North Carolina).

Seitz 3

Naming opportunities can clearly bring in a good deal of money. It has become commonplace for schools to offer naming opportunities on planned construction in exchange for 51 percent of the cost of the building! That's a big head start to a building project, and naming opportunities may be what allow some schools to provide their students with better facilities than their unnamed counterparts. In fact, donors are often recruited for the opportunity to pay for named faculty chairs, reading rooms, or major library or art collections—all of which enhance student life.

Background information

Clearly the more opportunities and resources any university can offer current and potential students and even alumni, the more that university enhances its own growth and that of its faculty. Library donors and recipients say that if it is possible for a library to pay for a new computer lab just by adding a sign with someone's name over the door, the advantages often seem to outweigh the disadvantages. Proponents of naming opportunities point out that small donors are often hailed as library supporters, even when big donors are maligned as corporate flag-wavers.

Few would argue that these donations necessarily detract from the educational mission of the institution. However, selling off parts of a university library, for example, does not always please people, especially those whose responsibility includes managing that donation. The curator of rare books and manuscripts at a prominent state university told me that one of the most frustrating parts of her job is dealing with "strings-attached" gifts, which is what too many library donations turn out to be (and why she wishes to remain anonymous). Some major donors like to make surprise visits, during which they monitor the prominence of their "legacy opportunity." Others like to create rules which limit the use of their funds to the purchase of certain collections or subjects; still others just need constant personal maintenance, including lunches, coffees, and regular invitations to events. But meddling in their donation after the fact is just a minor inconvenience compared to some donors' actions.

Donors who fund an ongoing educational program and give money on a regular basis often expect to have regular input. Because major donors want major prestige, they try to align themselves with successful programs. Doing that can result in damage to university budgets. First, high-profile programs can become increasingly well funded, while less prominent, less glamorous ones are ignored. Second, regularly available corporate or private funds can erode existing funding sources. Simply put, if a budgeted program becomes funded by donation, the next time the program needs funding, the department or unit will likely be told that finding a donor is their only option. Essentially, once donor-funded, always donor-funded.

Additionally, many academics feel that selling off naming rights can create an image problem for a university. While buildings, schools, endowed chairs, even football stadiums were once named for past professors, university presidents, or others with strong ties to the university, those same facilities are now named for virtually anyone who can afford to donate, especially corporations. Regular input from a corporation creates the appearance of a conflict of interest in a university, which is exactly the reason such arrangements are so often vehemently opposed by the university community. Boise State University in Idaho received such negative press for negotiating a deal with labor-unfriendly Taco Bell that it was finally pressured to terminate the $4 million contract (Langrill 1).

Given these drawbacks, many universities are establishing guidelines for the selection of appropriate donors for named gifts. To that end, fundraising professional and managing director of Changing Our World, Inc. Robert Hoak suggests that naming opportunities should be mutually beneficial for the donor (whether a corporation or an individual) and the organization (university, for instance) and that these opportunities should be viewed as the start of a long-term relationship between the

Seitz 6

two, not the final gift. Additionally, he cautions that even if the donor seems the right fit for the organization, it is in the best interest of both parties to add an escape clause to the contract in order to protect either side from potential embarrassment or scandal. He provides the example of Seton Hall University, which regrettably had both an academic building and the library rotunda named for Tyco CEO Dennis Kozlowski. When Kozlowski was convicted of grand larceny, the university pulled the names (Hoak).

Although many people prefer that naming be a recognition of an accomplished faculty member or administrator, most realize that recruiting named gift donors is good business. Whether it is "good education" is another question. Naming university property for major donors should not be merely a sales transaction. New College in Cambridge, Massachusetts, was just that—until local clergyman John Harvard died and left half his estate and his entire library to what would soon become Harvard College. Modern naming opportunities, however, do not necessarily recognize and remember individuals who had significant influence on university life; rather, they create obligations for the university to operate in such a way as to please living donors or their descendants. Pleasing wealthy donors should not replace educating students as a university's primary goal.

Seitz 7

Works Cited

Hoak, Robert. "Making the Most of Naming Opportunities." *onPhilanthropy*. Changing Our World, 28 Mar. 2003. Web. 5 Nov. 2007.

Langrill, Chereen. "BSU Faculty Says 'No Quiero' to Taco Bell." *Idaho Statesman* [Boise] 27 Oct. 2004: 1+. Print.

North Carolina State University Libraries. "NCSU Libraries East Wing Renovation: Naming Opportunities." *NCSU Libraries*. North Carolina State U, n.d. Web. 5 Nov. 2007. <http://www.lib.ncsu.edu/renovation/namingOp/>.

Northwestern University Library. "Making a Gift: Naming Opportunities." *Naming Opportunities: Library Development Office*. Northwestern U, 2007. Web. 20 Nov. 2007.

29 Writing in Business

Writing in business requires the same attention to audience, purpose, and context as writing in any other situation or discipline. However, the nature of authorship differs: although you are the writer, you must project both your own image and that of your employer as credible and reliable. The strategies presented in the following box will help you produce comprehensive, concise, and well-organized documents by introducing you to some of the stylistic characteristics of effective business communication.

> **STRATEGIES FOR EFFECTIVE BUSINESS COMMUNICATION**
>
> **Be direct.**
>
> - Know who your audience members are and consider their needs.
> - State the purpose of your document in your opening sentence or paragraph.
> - Write straightforward sentences, beginning with a subject and an active verb.
> - Use technical language sparingly, unless the document is intended for a specialized audience.
>
> **Be concise.**
>
> - Compose direct sentences that are neither too long nor too complicated.
> - Include only necessary details.
> - Use numbers, bullets, or descriptive headings that help readers locate information easily.
> - Use graphs, tables, and other visual elements that convey information succinctly.

Use conventional formatting.

- Follow the standard formats developed for your type of business or company or use those outlined in this chapter.
- Avoid using informal language, unless you know that a casual tone is acceptable.
- Edit carefully for errors; typos, grammatical mistakes, sentence fragments, and missing words detract significantly from your ethos as a businessperson and as a representative of your employer.

29a Business letters

Regardless of its purpose, a business letter usually fits on a single sheet of paper, is single-spaced, and follows a standard block format.

ELEMENTS OF A STANDARD BUSINESS LETTER

- **Return address.** Your employer may require you to use letterhead stationery. If not, type your mailing address one inch from the top of the paper, flush left on a one-inch margin, and single-spaced.
- **Date.** Type the date beneath your return address. If you are using letterhead stationery, type the date one or two lines below the letterhead's last line.
- **Recipient's name and address.** Provide the full name and address of the recipient. Single-space these lines, and allow an extra line of space above them. If you do not know the person's name, try to find it by checking the company's Web site or calling the company. If you cannot find the recipient's name, use an appropriate title such as *Personnel Director* or *Customer Service Manager* (not italicized).

(Continued on page 238)

(Continued from page 237)

- **Greeting.** Type your greeting two lines below the last line of the recipient's address. The conventional greeting is *Dear* _____ (not italicized) followed by a colon. If you and the recipient use first names to address each other, use the person's first name. Otherwise, use *Mr., Ms., Mrs., or Miss* and the last name. (Choose *Ms.* when you do not know a woman's preference.)

- **Body of the letter.** Begin the first paragraph two lines below the greeting. Single-space lines within a paragraph; double-space between paragraphs. If your letter must continue on a second page, include the recipient's last name, the date, and the page number in three single-spaced lines at the top left on the second page.

- **Closing.** Close your letter two lines after the end of the body with an expression such as *Sincerely* or *Cordially* (not italicized) followed by a comma.

- **Signature.** Type your full name four lines below the closing. Then, in the space above your typed name, sign your full name, using blue or black ink. If you have addressed the recipient by his or her first name, sign just your first name.

- **Additional information.** If you are enclosing extra material such as a résumé, type the word *Enclosure* or the abbreviation *Encl.* (not italicized) two lines below your name. You may also note the number of enclosures or the identity of the document(s): for example, *Enclosures (3)* or *Encl.: 2002 Annual Year-End Report*. If you would like the recipient to know the names of people receiving copies of the letter, use the abbreviation *cc* (for "carbon copy") and a colon followed by the other recipients' names. Place this element on the line directly below the enclosure line or, if there is no enclosure, two lines below your name.

The following sample **letter of inquiry** (a letter intended to elicit information) illustrates the parts of a typical business letter.

Letter of inquiry

550 First Avenue
Ellensburg, WA 98926
February 4, 2008

Mr. Mark Russell
Bilingual Publications
5400 Sage Avenue
Yakima, WA 98907

Dear Mr. Russell:

I am a junior in the Bilingual Education Program at Central Washington University. For my coursework, I am investigating positions in publishing that include the use of two languages. Your name and address were given to me by my instructor, Marta Cole, who worked for you from 2002 through 2006.

I have learned something about your publications on your Web site. I am most interested in dual documents—one in English and one in Spanish. Could you please send me samples of such documents so that I can have a better idea of the types of publications you produce?

I am also interested in finding out what qualifications I would need to work for a business like yours. I am fluent in both Spanish and English and have taken a course in translation. If possible, I would like to ask you a few questions about your training and experience. Would you have time for an interview some day next week?

Sincerely,

Chris Humphrey

Chris Humphrey

— Return address and date
— Name and address of recipient
— Greeting
— Body of letter
— Closing
— Signature

29b Business memos

A **memo** (short for *memorandum*) is a brief document sent electronically or on paper within a business to announce a meeting, set a schedule, or request information or action. The basic guidelines for writing memos also apply to e-mail messages.

ELEMENTS OF A STANDARD BUSINESS MEMO

- **Heading.** On four consecutive lines, type *To* (not italicized) followed by a colon and the name(s) of the recipient(s), *From* followed by a colon and your name and title (if appropriate), *Date* followed by a colon and the date, and *Subject* followed by a colon and a few words identifying the memo's subject. (The abbreviation *Re*, for "regarding," is sometimes used instead of *Subject*.) This information should be single-spaced. If you are sending copies to individuals whose names are not included in the *To* line, place those names on a new line beginning with *cc* (for "carbon copy") and a colon.
- **Body.** Use the block format, single-spacing lines within each paragraph and double-spacing between paragraphs. Double-space between the heading and the body of the memo.

Business memo

> To: Intellectual Properties Committee
> From: Leo Renfrow, Chair of Intellectual Properties Committee
> Date: March 15, 2008
> Subject: Review of Policy Statement
>
> *Heading*
>
> At the end of our last meeting, we decided to have our policy statement reviewed by someone outside our university. Clark Beech, chair of the Intellectual Properties Committee at Lincoln College, agreed to help us. Overall, as his review shows, the format of our policy statement is sound. Dr. Beech believes that some of the content should be further developed, however. It appears that we have used some ambiguous terms and included some conditions that would not hold up in court.
>
> Early next week, my assistant will deliver a copy of Dr. Beech's review to each of you. Please look it over by our next meeting, on March 29. If you have any questions or comments before then, please call me at ext. 1540.
>
> *Body of memo*

Because most regular users of e-mail receive a large volume of messages, you should announce your topic in the subject line and then arrange and present it in concise, readable chunks that help recipients locate important information.

> **TIPS FOR SENDING ATTACHMENTS WITH E-MAIL MESSAGES**
>
> - Before you send any attachment, consider the size of the file—many inboxes have limited space and cannot accept or store large files that contain streaming video, photographs, or sound clips. If you want to send a large file or multiple files, call or e-mail your recipient first to ask permission.
> - If you do not know the type of operating system or software installed on your recipient's computer, send text-only documents in rich text format (**.rtf**), which preserves most formatting and is recognized by many word-processing programs.
> - Because attachments are notorious for transmitting computer viruses, never open an attachment sent by someone you do not know. Before opening an attachment, make sure that you are working on a computer with antivirus software that scans all incoming files for viruses.

29c Résumés

A **résumé** is designed to emphasize a person's job qualifications by highlighting his or her experience and abilities. Be sure to include dates, job titles, and responsibilities, emphasizing specific information according to what the job advertisement says about desired experience and traits. You can organize your résumé chronologically, functionally, or in combination. Keep your overall design simple.

Sample résumé

Joseph F. Delaney III
138 Main Street, Apt 10D
Cityville, PA 16800
(555) 544-9988
JoeDel4@psu.edu

Objective

To obtain a position specializing in project and risk management

Education

Pennsylvania State University, University Park, PA, 2003–2007
Majors: IST BS (Information Context Option),
Psychology BS (Quantitative Option)
Dean's List: Summer 2006, Fall 2006, and Spring 2007
Cumulative GPA: 3.60
Relevant Classes:
- Project Management in Technology—dealt with the application of basic concepts, methodologies, and tools of project management in the field of information sciences and technology
- Database Management—managed a project team that applied MySql, PHP, and HTML in completing Rabble Mosaic Creator, which is described at www.schoolproject.psu.edu/~100

Computer and Technical Skills

- MySql, PHP, GD Library, C++ (2 years experience), Java (1 year experience)
- TCP/IP, network security, LANs and WANs
- HTML, XML, and project and risk management

Clubs/Activities

IST Student Government:
- Active and voting member of my college's student government
- Regular participant in the student government's Academic Committee
- Student resource for the IST Student Executive Board

IST Academic Committee:
- Participated in regularly scheduled meetings with Dean Henry C. Foley and Professor-in-Charge John Yen
- Worked with the administration to address students' problems

Work Experience
Penn State Pollock Library, University Park, PA, May–July 2006
- Assisted patrons of the library in using computers, printers, and the Internet via a wireless network using VPN
- Coordinated computers in my designated area and assisted with defragmenting, rebooting, reformatting, charging, and normal maintenance of laptops

Honors
- 2005 scholarship student in the College of IST; recipient of the Cingular Wireless Trustee Scholarship
- Pollock Library 2006 student employee of the year

TIPS FOR RÉSUMÉ WRITING

- Include your name, address, telephone number, and an e-mail address or fax number, if available.

- Identify your career or job objective simply. If you do not have such an objective, do not mention one in the résumé. You can provide details about your future plans when asked about them during an interview.

- Whenever possible, establish a clear relationship between jobs you have had and the job you are seeking. Offer details of the responsibilities in each of your jobs that most closely correspond with the position you seek.

- List your college or university degree and any pertinent areas in which you have had special training. Decide what details about your education best show your qualifications for the job at hand. Consider including your GPA (your overall GPA or your GPA in your major, whichever is more impressive), particular coursework (list

specific classes or note areas of specialization, such as twenty hours of coursework in accounting), and relevant class projects.
- Do not include personal data such as age, marital status, race, religion, or ethnicity.
- Even if an advertisement or posting asks you to state a salary requirement, any mention of salary is usually deferred until an interview.
- The names and addresses of **references** (people who have agreed to speak or write on your behalf) are not usually listed on a résumé, though you may want to mention that references are available on request. Instead, job candidates are advised to take a list of references to interviews. Make sure that the individuals on your list understand the nature of the position you are seeking. The list should include their names and addresses as well as their telephone numbers and/or e-mail addresses.
- To show that you are well organized, use a clean, clear format.
- Meticulously proofread your résumé before sending it and have others read it carefully as well. Errors in business writing always detract from your credibility, but errors in a résumé or letter of application can ruin your chances of getting an interview.

29d Letters of application

Writing a letter of application gives you the opportunity to present yourself as articulate, interesting, and professional.

Address your letter to a specific person. You can assume that the recipient will be reviewing many letters, so try to keep yours to one page. In your opening paragraph, identify the position you are applying for, explain how you learned about it, and—in a single sentence—state why you believe you are qualified to fill it. In the paragraphs that follow, describe the experience and abilities that qualify you for the job. In your closing paragraph, make a direct request for an interview; be specific about how you can be reached.

Model letter of application

Return address and date

Joseph F. Delaney III
138 Main Street, Apt. 10D
Cityville, PA 16800
June 4, 2007

Name and address of recipient

Mr. Jim Konigs, Human Resource Director
E. G. Hickey Technical Enterprise
333 Cumberville State Road, Suite 110
West Cumberville, PA 19428-2949

Greeting

Dear Mr. Konigs:

Body of letter

I am applying for the position of project manager advertised on Monster.com. I graduated on May 15 with a BS degree in information sciences and technology from Pennsylvania State University. I believe that my in-depth research and education in information technology make me an ideal candidate for this position.

I have completed the required coursework and an internship in information technology, consulting, and security, working under such distinguished professors as James Wendle and David Markison. I am currently a teaching instructor with Dr. Markison, responsible for student evaluation and advising. I have served as a project team leader in database management; my team created Rabble Mosaic Creator, a Web site that allows users to create mosaics out of images.

In addition to my studies, I have applicable experience as a member of the student government's Academic Committee, which manages students' problems through policy and hands-on work before presenting the issues to the dean and professor in charge.

I would appreciate the opportunity to talk with you about the position. I can be reached at the phone number or e-mail address at the top of my résumé.

Closing

Sincerely,

Signature

Joseph F. Delaney

Joseph F. Delaney III

Enclosure line

Encl.: résumé

R

RESEARCH

CHAPTER 30
Finding Sources in Print, Online, and in the Field 248

- 30a Research and the rhetorical situation 248
- 30b Finding books 250
- 30c Finding articles 252
- 30d Finding online sources 253
- 30e Field research 255

CHAPTER 31
Evaluating Print and Online Sources 259

- 31a Credibility of authors 259
- 31b Credibility of publishers 261
- 31c Online sources 262
- 31d Relevance and timeliness 262

CHAPTER 32
Using Sources Effectively and Responsibly 264

- 32a The rhetorical situation and the research paper 264
- 32b Organizing notes 265
- 32c Working bibliography and annotated bibliography 267
- 32d Integrating sources 268
- 32e Avoiding plagiarism 274
- 32f Responding to sources 276

Finding Sources in Print, Online, and in the Field

To conduct useful and authoritative research efficiently, you must develop skills in accessing information.

30a Research and the rhetorical situation

To make the most of the time you spend doing research, determine your rhetorical situation early in the research process.

(1) Identifying an exigence to form a research question

The starting point for any research project is your exigence—the issue or problem that has prompted you to write; to locate, analyze, and substantiate information before you write; and to craft a challenging question that guides your research and focuses your working thesis.

> **TIPS FOR FINDING A CHALLENGING RESEARCH QUESTION**
>
> - What problem or issue from one of your classes would you like to address?
> - What have you read or observed recently that piqued your curiosity?
> - What local or campus problem would you like to explore?
> - Is there anything (lifestyles, political views, global events) that you find unusual or intriguing and would like to investigate?

(2) Establishing a purpose

You also need to establish the rhetorical purpose of your research, which could be any of the following:

- *To inform an audience.* The researcher reports current thinking on a specific topic, including opposing views, without analyzing them or siding with a particular position.
- *To analyze and synthesize information and then offer possible solutions.* The researcher analyzes a topic and synthesizes the available information about it, looking for points of agreement and disagreement and for gaps in coverage. Sometimes the researcher offers possible ways to address any problems found.
- *To convince or issue an invitation to an audience.* The researcher states a position and backs it up with data, statistics, testimony, corroborating texts or events, or supporting arguments. The researcher's purpose is to persuade readers to take the same position.

(3) Using primary and secondary sources

Experienced researchers consult both primary and secondary sources. **Primary sources** for researching topics in the humanities are generally documents such as archived letters, records, and papers, as well as literary, autobiographical, and philosophical texts. In the social sciences, primary sources can be field observations, case histories, and survey data. In the

Primary sources, such as a report from an archeological dig, are useful for many research projects.

natural sciences, primary sources are generally empirical and include field observations, measurements, or discoveries and experimental results. **Secondary sources** are commentaries on primary sources.

30b Finding books

Three types of books are commonly used in the research process. **Scholarly books** are written by experts to advance knowledge of a certain subject. Most include original research and are reviewed by scholars in the same field as the author(s). **Trade books** may also be written by experts, scholars, journalists, or freelance writers. Authors of trade books write to inform a general audience of research that has been done by others. **Reference books** such as encyclopedias and dictionaries provide factual information in short articles or entries written and reviewed by experts in the field.

(1) Locating sources through an online catalog

The easiest way to find books related to your research question is to consult your library's online catalog, doing either keyword searches or subject searches. To perform a **keyword search,** choose a word or phrase that you think might be found in the title of a book or in notes in the catalog's records. By using a word or part of a word followed by asterisks, you can find all sources that include that root, even when suffixes have been added. For example, if you entered *environment***, you would find not only sources with *environment* in the title, subject headings, and content notes, but also sources with *environments, environmental,* or *environmentalist* in those locations.

You can also use a **Boolean search.** Combining words or phrases using *and, or, not,* or *near* will limit or widen a search. For example, you could try *Marion and Ohio, Buckeye or Ohio, Marion not Ohio,* or *Marysville near Marion.*

Once you find the online catalog record for a book you would like to use, write down its **call number,** which indicates where the book is shelved.

(2) Specialized reference books

A specialized encyclopedia or dictionary can provide background information related to the topic you are researching. To find such sources using an online search page, enter the type of reference book and one or two keywords identifying your topic.

USEFUL REFERENCE BOOKS

For a detailed list of reference books and a short description of each, consult *Guide to Reference Books* by Robert Balay and *American Reference Books Annual* (*ARBA*). A few widely used reference books are listed here.

Specialized Dictionaries and Encyclopedias
- *Dictionary of American History*
- *Dictionary of Art*
- *Encyclopedia of Bioethics*
- *Encyclopedia of Higher Education*
- *Encyclopedia of Psychology*

Collections of Biographies
- *American National Biography*
- *Dictionary of Scientific Biography*
- *Notable American Women*
- *Who's Who in America*

30c Finding articles

Articles can be found in various **periodicals** (publications that appear at regular intervals), which offer information that is often more recent than that found in books. **Scholarly journals** contain reports of original research written by experts for an academic audience. **Professional,** or **trade, magazines** feature articles written by staff writers or industry specialists. **Popular magazines** and **newspapers,** generally written by staff writers, carry a combination of news stories and essays.

The best strategy for finding print articles is to use your library's **electronic database,** which is a collection of articles indexed according to author, title, date, keywords, and other features. Similar to an online catalog, an electronic database allows you to search for sources by author, title, keyword, and so on.

College libraries subscribe to a wide variety of database services, but the following are the most common:

ERIC: Articles related to education

JSTOR: Articles from journals in the arts, humanities, ecology, and social sciences

PsycINFO: Articles related to psychology

InfoTrac: Articles on a wide variety of subjects from journals and magazines

Vendors such as EBSCO and Lexis Nexis offer a variety of databases.

> **TIPS FOR CONDUCTING A SEARCH FOR PERIODICAL LITERATURE**
> - Identify keywords that clearly represent the topic.
> - Determine the databases you want to search.
> - Refine your search strategy if the first search returns too many, too few, or (worse) irrelevant citations.
> - Download and print the relevant articles.

30d Finding online sources

Most researchers start their online research by using **search engines,** electronic indexes of words and terms from Web pages. The following are the addresses for some commonly used search engines:

Ask	www.ask.com
Google	www.google.com
Bing	www.bing.com
Lycos	www.lycos.com
Yahoo	www.yahoo.com

Unlike search engines, **subject directories** are collections of Web sources arranged topically. The following are some useful subject directories for academic and professional research:

Academic Info	www.academicinfo.net
The Internet Public Library	www.ipl.org/ref
Librarians' Index to the Internet	lii.org
The WWW Virtual Library	vlib.org

(1) Keeping track of your sources on the Web

As you click from link to link, you can keep track of your location by looking at the Web address, or **URL (uniform resource locator),** at the top of the screen. Web addresses generally include the following information: server name, domain name, directory (and perhaps subdirectory) name, file name, and file type.

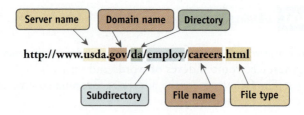

Because sites change and even disappear, some scholarly organizations require that bibliographic entries for Web sites include both the **access date** (the date on which the site was visited) and the **publication date** (the date when the site was published or last modified). When you print out material from the Web, the access date usually appears at the top or bottom of the printout. The publication date often appears on the site itself. Keeping a separate record of this information can help you when you need to verify information on a site or list it in a bibliography.

(2) Using U.S. Government Web sites

If you need information on particular federal laws, court cases, or population statistics, U.S. Government documents may be your best sources. You can find these documents by using online databases such as these:

FirstGov	**www.firstgov.gov**
U.S. Government Printing Office	**www.gpoaccess.gov**
U.S. Courts	**www.uscourts.gov**
FedWorld	**www.fedworld.gov**

(3) Using images

If your rhetorical situation calls for the use of images, the Internet offers you billions from which to choose. If an image you choose is copyrighted, you need to contact the author, artist, or designer for permission to use it. You do not need to obtain permission to use public domain images or those that are cleared for reuse. Collections of specific types of images are available at the following Web sites:

Advertisements

Ad*Access	**library.duke.edu/ digitalcollections/ adaccess**
Adflip	**www.adflip.com**
Advertising World	**advertising.utexas.edu/ world**

Art

The Artchive	**www.artchive.com**
The Web Gallery of Art	**www.wga.hu**

Clip art

The Icon Browser	**www.ibiblio.org/gio/ iconbrowser**
Webclipz	**www.webclipz.com**

Photography

The New York Public Library Picture Collection Online	**digital.nypl.org/mmpco**
Smithsonian Images	**smithsonianimages.com**

30e Field research

Interviews, discussions, questionnaires, and observations are the most common methods of **field research** to gather information in a natural setting.

(1) Interviewing an expert

After you have consulted some sources on your topic, you may still have questions that might best be answered by someone who has firsthand experience in the area you are researching: a teacher, government official, business owner, or another person with the relevant background.

To arrange an interview, introduce yourself, briefly describe your project, and then explain your reasons for requesting the interview. Try to accommodate the person you hope to interview by asking him or her to suggest an interview date. If you intend to tape your interview, ask for permission ahead of time.

Start preparing your list of questions before the day of the interview, using a blend of open (or broad) questions and focused (or narrow) questions that begin with *why, when, what, who, where,* or *how.* By doing so, you give your interviewee a chance to elaborate. Take notes or record the interview. After the interview, review and expand your notes or transcribe the relevant parts of the recording. Write extensively about the interview, asking yourself what you found most important, most surprising, and most puzzling.

(2) Participating in an online discussion group

Online discussion groups, or forums, allow you to read messages posted to all the members of a group interested in a specific topic and to post messages or questions yourself. You can find addresses of online discussion groups at **www.forumone.com** or **groups.google.com**.

(3) Using a questionnaire

Whereas an interview elicits information from one person whose name you know, a questionnaire provides information from a number of anonymous people. To be effective, a questionnaire should be short and focused. If the list of questions is too long, people may not be willing to take the time to answer them all. If the questions are not focused on your research topic, you will find it difficult to integrate the results into your paper.

EXAMPLES OF TYPES OF SURVEY QUESTIONS

Questions that require a simple yes-or-no answer:

Do you commute to work in a car? (Circle one.)

Yes   No

Multiple-choice questions:

How many people do you commute with? (Circle one.)

0   1   2   3   4

Questions with answers on a checklist:

How long does it take you to commute to work? (Check one.)

___ 0–30 minutes   ___ 60–90 minutes
___ 30–60 minutes   ___ 90–120 minutes

Questions with a ranking scale:

Other than a car, which of the following types of transportation do you rely on? (Rank the choices from 1 for most frequently used to 4 for least frequently used.)

___ bus   ___ shuttle van   ___ subway   ___ taxi

Open questions:

What feature of commuting do you find most irritating?

Begin your questionnaire with an introduction stating the purpose of the questionnaire, how the results will be used, and how many questions it contains or approximately how long it should take to complete. In the introduction, assure participants that their answers will remain confidential. Before you distribute your questionnaire, check with the institutional review board (IRB) on your campus to make certain that you have followed its guidelines.

It is a good idea to send out twice as many copies of the questionnaire as you would like returned because the proportion of responses is generally low. If you mail out a questionnaire, provide a self-addressed envelope and directions for returning it. Questionnaires can sometimes be distributed in college dormitories, in classes, or through listservs (if approved by school officials).

Once the questionnaires have been completed and returned, tally the results for all but the open questions. To find patterns in the responses to the open questions, first read through them all, and try to create categories for the responses, which will help you tally the answers.

CHECKLIST for Creating a Questionnaire

- Does each question relate directly to the purpose of the survey?
- Are the questions easy to understand?
- Are they designed to elicit short, specific responses?
- Are they designed to collect concrete data that can be analyzed easily?
- Have respondents been given enough space to write their answers to open questions?
- Do you have access to the group you want to survey?
- Have you asked a few classmates to "test-drive" your questionnaire?

31 Evaluating Print and Online Sources

As you find sources that seem to address your research question and support your working thesis, you have to evaluate them to determine whether the information they contain is credible, relevant, and timely.

31a Credibility of authors

Credible (or trustworthy) authors present facts accurately, support their opinions with compelling evidence, connect their ideas reasonably, and demonstrate respect for any opposing views. To evaluate the credibility of the authors of your sources, find out what their credentials are, consider what world view informs their ideas, and note how other readers respond to their work. Credentials include academic or professional training, publications, and experience. The author's credentials may be found on the jacket or in the preface of a book, in a note in an article, or on a page devoted to providing background on contributors.

CHECKLIST for Assessing an Author's Credentials

- Does the author's education or profession relate to the subject of the work?
- With what institutions, organizations, or companies has the author been affiliated?
- What awards has the author won?
- What other works has the author produced?
- Do other experts speak of the author as an authority?

An author's values and beliefs about the world constitute his or her **world view,** which underpins his or her research and publications. To determine what these values and beliefs are, consider the author's purpose and intended audience. So as you read and use sources, keep in mind that they reflect the world views of the authors and often of the audience for whom they were written. By identifying these values and beliefs, you can responsibly represent and report the information in your sources.

> **CHECKLIST for Determining an Author's World View**
>
> - What is the author's educational and professional background?
> - With what types of organizations do the author and publisher affiliate themselves?
> - What is the editorial slant of the organization publishing the author's work? Where does it lie on the political spectrum from conservative to liberal?
> - What, if any, signs of bias on the part of the author or the publisher can you detect?
> - Is the information purported to be factual? Objective? Personal?
> - Who advertises in the source?
> - To what types of Web sites do any links lead?
> - How can you use the source? As fact? Opinion? Example? Authoritative testimony? Material to be refuted?

You can learn even more about an author's background or other works by searching the Internet for information, using a general search engine such as Google or a specialized search engine such as the People search option offered by Lycos (**www.whowhere.com**).

Book reviews, both in print and online, often include information for determining whether an author is credible. Even a work by a credible author may get some negative responses, but dismiss from further consideration any writer whom more than one reviewer characterizes as ill-informed, careless with facts, biased, or dishonest in any way.

31b Credibility of publishers

When you are doing research, consider not only the credibility of authors but also the credibility of the media through which their work is made available to you. Some publishers hold authors accountable to higher standards than others do.

When evaluating books, you can usually assume that publishers associated with universities demand a high standard of scholarship. Books published by commercial (or trade) presses, in contrast, typically do not undergo the same type of review. Thus, to determine how a trade book has been received by others writing in the same area, you have to rely on book reviews.

An article published in a scholarly journal is generally considered more credible than one published in a popular magazine because it has been both written and reviewed by an expert. Authors of scholarly journal articles are expected to include both in-text citations and bibliographies so that other researchers can consult the sources used.

Articles that appear in popular magazines and newspapers may also be reliable but are usually written quickly and chosen for publication by someone on the periodical's staff—not by an expert in the field. Because magazines and newspapers often report research results that were initially published elsewhere, you should try to find the original source to ensure the accuracy of their reports.

When evaluating an article in a magazine or newspaper, also take into account the reputation of the publication itself, examining several issues in terms of the space devoted to various stories, the tone of the commentary on the editorial pages, and the extent to which staff members (as opposed to wire services) are responsible for stories.

31c Online sources

If you are evaluating a periodical source that you obtained online, you can follow the guidelines for print-based sources. But if you are evaluating a Web site, you also need to consider the nature of the site and its sponsor. Although many sites are created by individuals working on their own, many others are sponsored by colleges or universities, professional or nonprofit organizations, and commercial enterprises. The type of sponsor is typically indicated in the site's address (URL) by a suffix that represents the domain. Colleges and universities are indicated by the suffix **.edu**, government departments and agencies by **.gov**, professional and nonprofit organizations by **.org**, network sites by **.net**, and businesses by **.com**. As you access the various types of sites to evaluate their content, remember that every site is shaped to achieve a specific purpose and to address a specific audience.

31d Relevance and timeliness

A source is useful only when it is relevant to your research question and working thesis. As you conduct research, draft, and revise, you may reject some sources altogether and use only parts of others. Seldom will an entire book, article, or Web site be useful for a specific research project.

Useful sources are also timely. You should always seek up-to-date information. However, if you are writing about a specific era in the past, you should also consult sources written during that period.

CHECKLIST for Establishing Relevancy and Timeliness

- Does the table of contents, index, or directory of the work include key words related to your research question?
- Does the abstract of a journal article contain information on your topic?
- If an abstract is not available, are any of the article's topic sentences relevant to your research question?
- Do the section heads of the source include words connected to your topic?
- On a Web site, are there hyperlinks that lead you to relevant information?
- Is the work recent enough to provide up-to-date information?
- If you need a source from another time period, is the work from the right period?

32 Using Sources Effectively and Responsibly

To use sources effectively, you need to remember that you are a *writer,* not just a compiler of data. To use sources responsibly, you acknowledge others' ideas and words as you incorporate them into your paper. But even when you use sources responsibly, your voice remains the most important voice in the paper.

32a The rhetorical situation and the research paper

Like any other paper, a research paper should respond to an exigence with a purpose appropriate for a particular audience and context. In a research paper, you discuss what others have discovered, creating a conversation in which you play an essential role: you orchestrate how your sources interact with one another and at the same time talk back to them. You also establish yourself as a credible author. By conducting research and citing sources, you demonstrate that you have

- educated yourself about your topic,
- drawn accurately on the work of others (including diverse points of view),
- understood what you have discovered,
- integrated research data into a paper that is clearly your own, and
- provided all the information readers will need to consult the sources you have used.

32b Organizing notes

Taking thorough and organized notes (on screen or on paper) is critical when you are preparing to write a research paper in which you attribute specific words and ideas to others while taking credit for your own ideas.

(1) Taking notes on photocopies and printouts

An easy way to take notes is to use photocopies of articles and excerpts from books or printouts of sources from the Web, marking quotable material while also jotting down your own ideas in the margins. This method reduces the risk of including inaccurate quotations in your paper, because you have eliminated the step of copying quotations exactly as they appear in the original source. Make sure to record the source on a photocopy if this information is not shown on the original page(s). Printouts from the Web almost always indicate the source and the date of access, but you should also note the date on which the site was posted or last updated.

(2) Organizing notes in computer files

You may find it efficient to use a computer for taking notes—recording them quickly and storing them safely. Then, later, you can easily copy and paste information into various files and ultimately into a draft of your paper. Given the ease of computer use, though, it is important to remember to identify which records are direct quotations, which are paraphrases, and which are your own thoughts. Always provide complete bibliographic information so that you will not have trouble finding the source later.

> **TIPS ON USING A COMPUTER TO ORGANIZE NOTES**
>
> - Create a separate master folder (or directory) for the paper.
> - Create folders within the master folder for your bibliography, notes, and drafts.
> - Keep all the notes for each source in a separate file.
> - Use a distinctive font or a different color to distinguish your own thoughts from the ideas of others.
> - Place direct quotations in quotation marks.
> - When taking notes, record exactly where the information came from.
> - When you discover new sources, add them to your working bibliography.
> - Consider using the Annotation or Comment feature of your word-processing program to make notes on documents you have downloaded.

(3) Arranging notes on note cards

Taking notes on index cards can be useful if you are working in a library without a laptop or if you prefer handwritten notes that you can rearrange as your research proceeds. Each index card should show the author's name (and a short title if the bibliography contains more than one work by that author), the exact page number(s) from which the information is drawn, and a brief comment on how you intend to use the information or a reflection on what you think about it. By putting a heading of two or three key words at the top of each card, you can easily arrange your cards as you prepare to draft your paper.

TIPS FOR TAKING NOTES

- Identify the source, including page number(s), for every note.
- Put the full bibliographic citation on the first page of every photocopy.
- Copy verbatim any useful passage you think you may quote. Put quotation marks around quoted words. In computer files, you can also use different fonts or different colors to identify quoted text.
- When a source has stimulated your thinking, identify both the source and your own idea based on that source.

32c Working bibliography and annotated bibliography

A **working bibliography,** or preliminary bibliography, contains information (titles, authors' names, publication dates, and so on) about the materials you think you might use. Creating a working bibliography can help you evaluate the quality of your research.

It is a good idea to follow the bibliographical format you have been instructed to use in your paper right from the start, such as that of the Modern Language Association (MLA) or that of the American Psychological Association (APA). The examples given in the rest of this chapter follow the MLA's bibliographical and documentation style.

If you are asked to prepare an **annotated bibliography,** you should list all your sources alphabetically according to the last name of the author. Then, at the end of each entry, summarize the content of the source in one or two sentences.

Zimmer, Carl. *Soul Made Flesh: The Discovery of the Brain—and How It Changed the World*. New York: Free, 2004. Print. This book is a historical account of how knowledge of the brain developed and influenced ideas about the soul. It covers a span of time and place, beginning four thousand years ago in ancient Egypt and ending in Oxford, England, in the seventeenth century.

32d Integrating sources

You can integrate sources into your own writing in a number of ways: quoting exact words, paraphrasing sentences, and summarizing longer pieces of text or even entire texts. Remember to be careful to integrate the material—properly cited—into your own sentences and paragraphs.

(1) Introducing sources

When you borrow textual material, introduce it to readers by establishing the source, usually an author's name. You may also need to include additional information about the author, especially if the author is unfamiliar to your audience. For example, in a paper on medications given to children, the following statement becomes more credible if the audience is given the added information about Jerome Groopman's background.

According to Jerome Groopman, ^*professor of medicine at Harvard University,* "Pediatricians sometimes adopt extraordinary measures to insure that their patients are not harmed by treatments that have not been adequately studied in children" (33).

Phrases such as *According to Jerome Groopman* and *from the author's perspective* are called **attributive tags** because they attribute, or ascribe, information to a source. Most attributive tags consist of the name of an author (or a related noun or pronoun) and a verb in order to report what that author has said or written.

VERBS USED IN ATTRIBUTIVE TAGS

argue	conclude	find	point out
believe	disagree	imply	reject
claim	discuss	note	state
concede	explain	observe	suggest

If you decide to integrate graphics as source material, you must label them as figures and assign them arabic numbers. You can then refer to them within the text of your paper in a parenthetical comment, as in this example: "The red and black bands of the Western coral snake are bordered by narrower bands of yellow or white (fig. 32.1)." You may also want to include a title or caption with the figure number.

Figure 32.1. Western coral snake.

(2) Using direct quotations

Include a direct quotation in a paper only if

- you want to retain the beauty or clarity of someone's words,
- you need to reveal how the reasoning in a specific passage is flawed or insightful, or
- you plan to discuss the implications of the quoted material.

Keep quotations as short as possible, and make them an integral part of your text.

Quote *accurately.* Any quotation of another person's words should be placed in quotation marks or, if longer than four lines, set off as an indented block. If you need to clarify a quotation by changing it in any way, place square brackets around the added or changed words.

"In this role, he [Robin Williams] successfully conveys a diverse range of emotion."

If you want to omit part of a quotation, replace the deleted words with ellipsis points.

"Overseas markets . . . are critical to the financial success of Hollywood films."

When modifying a quotation, never alter its essential meaning.

> **CHECKLIST for Using Direct Quotations**
>
> - Have you copied all the words and punctuation accurately?
> - Have you attributed the quotation to a specific source?
> - Have you used square brackets around anything you added to or changed in a direct quotation?
> - Have you used ellipsis points to indicate anything you omitted?
> - Have you used quotations sparingly? If not, consider paraphrasing or summarizing the information instead.

(3) Paraphrasing another person's ideas

A **paraphrase** is a restatement of someone else's ideas in approximately the same number of words. Paraphrasing allows you to demonstrate that you have understood what you have read; it also enables you to help your audience understand it. Paraphrase when you want to

- clarify difficult material by using simpler language,
- use another writer's idea but not his or her exact words,

- create a consistent tone for your paper as a whole, or
- interact with a point that your source has made.

Your paraphrase should be almost entirely in your *own* words and should accurately convey the content of the original passage.

(a) Using your own words and sentence structure

As you compare the source below with the paraphrases that follow, note the similarities and differences in both sentence structure and word choice.

Source

Zimmer, Carl. *Soul Made Flesh: The Discovery of the Brain—and How It Changed the World.* New York: Free, 2004. 7. Print.

> The maps that neuroscientists make today are like the early charts of the New World with grotesque coastlines and blank interiors. And what little we do know about how the brain works raises disturbing questions about the nature of our selves.

Inadequate paraphrase

The maps used by neuroscientists today resemble the rough maps of the New World. Because we know so little about how the brain works, we must ask questions about the nature of our selves (Zimmer 7).

If you simply change a few words in a passage, you have not adequately restated it. You may be committing plagiarism if the wording of your version follows the original too closely, even if you provide a page reference for the source.

Adequate paraphrase

Carl Zimmer compares today's maps of the brain to the rough maps made of the New World. He believes that the lack of knowledge about the workings of the brain makes us ask serious questions about our nature (7).

In the second paraphrase, both vocabulary and sentence structure differ from those in the original. This paraphrase also includes an attributive tag ("Carl Zimmer compares").

(b) Maintaining accuracy

Any paraphrase must accurately and ethically maintain the sense of the original. Compare the original statement below with the paraphrases.

Source

Hanlon, Michael. "Climate Apocalypse When?" *New Scientist* 17 Nov. 2007: 20. Print.

> Disastrous images of climate change are everywhere. An alarming graphic recently appeared in the UK media showing the British Isles reduced to a scattered archipelago by a 60-metre rise in sea level. Evocative scenes of melting glaciers, all-at-sea polar bears and forest fires are routinely attributed to global warming. And of course Al Gore has just won a Nobel prize for his doomsday flick *An Inconvenient Truth,* starring hurricane Katrina.
> . . . There is a big problem here, though it isn't with the science. The evidence that human activities are dramatically modifying the planet's climate is now overwhelming—even to a former paid-up sceptic like me. The consensus is established, the fear real and justified. The problem is that the effects of climate change mostly haven't happened yet, and for journalists and their editors that presents a dilemma. Talking about what the weather may be like in the 2100s, never mind the 3100s, doesn't sell.

Inaccurate or unethical paraphrase

Evocative scenes of melting glaciers, landless polar bears, and forest fires are attributed to global warming in Al Gore's *An Inconvenient Truth.* The trouble is that Gore cannot predict what will happen (Hanlon 20).

Accurate paraphrase

According to Michael Hanlon, the disastrous images of climate change that permeate the media are distorting our understanding of what is actually happening now globally and what might happen in the future (20).

Although both paraphrases include a reference to an author and a page number, the first focuses misleadingly on Al Gore, whereas the second paraphrase notes the much broader problem, which can be blamed on the media's focus on selling a story.

(4) Summarizing an idea

A **summary** reports a writer's main idea and the most important support given for it. Whereas the length of a paraphrase is usually close to that of the original material, a summary conveys the gist of the author's ideas, in fewer words. Summaries can include short quotations of key phrases or ideas, but you must always enclose another writer's exact words in quotation marks when you blend them with your own.

Source

Marshall, Joseph M., III. "Tasunke Witko (His Crazy Horse)." *Native Peoples* Jan.-Feb. 2007: 76-79. Print.

> The world knows him as Crazy Horse, which is not a precise translation of his name from Lakota to English. *Tasunke Witko* means "his crazy horse," or "his horse is crazy." This slight mistranslation of his name seems to reflect the fact that Crazy Horse the man is obscured by Crazy Horse the legendary warrior. He was both, but the fascination with the legendary warrior hides the reality of the man. And it was as the man, shaped by his family, community and culture—as well as the events in his life—that he became legend.

Summary

The Lakota warrior English speakers refer to as "Crazy Horse" was actually called "his crazy horse." That mistranslation may distort what Crazy Horse was like as a man.

This example reduces five sentences to two, retaining the key idea but eliminating the source author's analysis and speculation.

32e Avoiding plagiarism

To use the work of other writers responsibly, you need to ensure that your audience can distinguish between those writers' ideas and your own contributions and that you give credit for all information you gather through research. It is not necessary to credit information that is **common knowledge,** which includes well-known facts. If you have been scrupulous about recording your own thoughts as you took notes, you should have little difficulty distinguishing between what you knew to begin with and what you learned through your research. If you take even part of someone else's work and present it as your own, you leave yourself open to charges of **plagiarism.** Plagiarism is illegal, and penalties range from failing a paper or course to being expelled from school. Never compromise your integrity or risk your future by submitting someone else's work as your own.

To review how to draw responsibly on the words and ideas of others, consider the following examples.

Source

McConnell, Patricia B. *The Other End of the Leash*. New York: Ballantine, 2002. 142. Print.

> Status in male chimpanzees is particularly interesting because it is based on the formation of coalitions, in which no single male can achieve and maintain power without a cadre of supporting males.

Paraphrase with documentation

Patricia B. McConnell, an authority on animal training, notes that by forming alliances with other male chimpanzees, a specific male can enjoy status and power (142).

This example includes not only the original author's name but also a parenthetical citation, which marks the end of the paraphrase and provides the page number where the source can be found. Paraphrases must include citations.

Quotation with documentation

Patricia B. McConnell, an authority on animal training, argues that male chimpanzees achieve status "based on the formation of coalitions, in which no single male can achieve and maintain power without a cadre of supporting males" (142).

Quotation marks show where the copied words begin and end; the number in parentheses indicates the exact page on which those words appear. Again, the author is identified in the sentence, although her name could have been omitted at the beginning of the sentence and noted within the parenthetical reference instead:

An authority on animal training argues that male chimpanzees achieve status "based on the formation of coalitions, in which no single male can achieve and maintain power without a cadre of supporting males" (McConnell 142).

CHECKLIST of Sources That Should Be Cited

- Writings, both published and unpublished
- Opinions and judgments that are not your own
- Statistics and other facts that are not widely known
- Images and graphics, such as works of art, drawings, charts, graphs, tables, photographs, maps, and advertisements
- Personal communications, such as interviews, letters, and e-mail messages
- Electronic communications, including television and radio broadcasts, motion pictures and videos, sound recordings, Web sites, and online discussion groups or forums

32f Responding to sources

When incorporating sources, not only will you summarize, paraphrase, quote, and document them, you will respond to them as well. To prepare for interacting with your sources, make notes in the margins of whatever you are reading. Next to relevant passages, jot down your agreement, disagreement, questions, and so on.

As you read and work with published research, you will want to know whether facts are accurate or erroneous, whether logic is strong or weak, whether the information is well or poorly organized, and whether conclusions are valid or doubtful. You will also evaluate the strengths and weaknesses of sources in order to motivate your own line of research. Overall, consider responding to your sources by examining their timeliness, coverage, reliability, and reasoning.

(1) Considering the currency of sources

Using up-to-date sources is crucial when researching most topics. Even a source published in the same year that you are doing research may include data that are several years old and thus possibly irrelevant.

(2) Noting the thoroughness of research

Coverage refers to the comprehensiveness of research. The more comprehensive a study is, the more convincing are its findings. Similarly, the more examples an author provides, the more compelling are his or her conclusions.

(3) Checking the reliability of findings

Research, especially when derived from experiments or surveys, must be reliable. Experimental results are considered **reliable** if they can be reproduced by researchers using a similar methodology. Results that cannot be replicated in this way are not reliable because they are supported by only one experiment.

Reliability is also a requirement for reported data. Researchers are expected to report their findings accurately and honestly, not distorting them to support their own beliefs or claiming others' ideas as their own. To ensure the reliability of their work, researchers must also report all relevant information, not intentionally excluding any that weakens their conclusions.

(4) Examining the author's reasoning

When a source is logical, its reasoning is sound. Lapses in logic may be the result of using evidence that does not directly support a claim, appealing to the reader's emotions, or encouraging belief in false authority.

D

DOCUMENTATION

CHAPTER 33
MLA Documentation 280

- **33a** MLA-style in-text citations 280
- **33b** MLA list of works cited 290
- **33c** Sample MLA-style paper 323

CHAPTER 34
APA Documentation 337

- **34a** APA-style in-text citations 337
- **34b** APA-style reference list 340
- **34c** Sample APA-style paper 355

CHAPTER 35
CMS Documentation 366

- **35a** CMS note and bibliographic forms 366
- **35b** Sample CMS-style paper 379

CHAPTER 36
CSE Documentation 384

- **36a** CSE citation-sequence, name-year, and citation-name systems 384
- **36b** Sample CSE-style paper 392

33 MLA Documentation

The Modern Language Association (MLA) provides guidelines for documenting research in literature, languages, linguistics, and composition studies. The *MLA Handbook for Writers of Research Papers* is published specifically for undergraduates.

33a MLA-style in-text citations

(1) Citing material from other sources

The citations you use within the text of a research paper refer your readers to the list of works cited at the end of the paper, tell them where to find the borrowed material in the original source, and indicate the boundaries between your ideas and those you have borrowed. In the following example, the parenthetical citation guides the reader to page 88 of the book by Pollan in the works-cited list.

In-text citation

Since the 1980s virtually all the sodas and most of the fruit drinks sold in the supermarkets have been sweetened with high-fructose corn syrup (HFCS)—after water, corn sweetener is their principal ingredient (Pollan 88).

Works-cited entry

Pollan, Michael. *The Omnivore's Dilemma: A Natural History of Four Meals.* New York: Penguin, 2006. Print.

The MLA suggests reserving numbered notes for supplementary comments—for example, when you wish to explain a point further but the subject matter is tangential to your topic. When numbered notes are used, superscript numbers are inserted in the appropriate places in the text, and the notes are gathered at the end of the paper on a separate page titled "Notes." Each note begins with an indent.

In-text note number

Most food found in American supermarkets is ultimately derived from corn.[1]

Notes entry

1. Nearly all farm animals—from cows and chickens to various kinds of farmed fish—are fed a diet of corn.

An in-text citation usually provides two pieces of information about borrowed material: (1) information that directs the reader to the relevant source on the works-cited list and (2) information that directs the reader to a specific page or section within that source. An author's last name and a page number generally suffice. To create an in-text citation, either place both the author's last name and the page number in parentheses or introduce the author's name in the sentence and supply just the page number in parentheses.

A "remarkably narrow biological foundation" supports the variety of America's supermarkets (Pollan 18).

Pollan explains the way corn products "feed" the familiar meats, beverages, and dairy products that we find on our supermarket shelves (18).

When referring to information from a range of pages, separate the first and last pages with a hyphen: (34-42). If the page numbers have the same hundreds or thousands digit, do not repeat it when listing the final page in the range: (234-42) or (1350-55) but (290-301) or (1395-1402). If you refer to an entire work or a work with only one page, no page numbers are necessary.

Directory of MLA Parenthetical Citations

1. Work by one author   282
2. More than one work by the same author(s)   282
3. Work by two or three authors   283
4. Work by more than three authors   283
5. Works by different authors with the same last name   283
6. Work by a corporate author   284
7. Two or more works in the same citation   284
8. Multivolume work   284
9. Anonymous work   285
10. Indirect source   285
11. Poetry, drama, and sacred texts   285
12. Constitution   286
13. Works with numbered paragraphs or sections   287

The following examples are representative of the types of in-text citations you might be expected to use.

1. Work by one author

Set on the frontier and focused on characters who use language sparingly, Westerns often reveal a "pattern of linguistic regression" (Rosowski 170).

OR

Susan J. Rosowski argues that Westerns often reveal a "pattern of linguistic regression" (170).

2. More than one work by the same author(s)

When your works-cited list includes more than one work by the same author(s), provide a shortened title in your in-text citation that identifies the relevant work. Use a comma to separate the name (or names) from the shortened title when both are in parentheses. For example, if you listed two works by Antonio Damasio on your works-cited page, then you would cite one of those within your text as follows:

According to one neurological hypothesis, "feelings are the expression of human flourishing or human distress" (Damasio, *Looking for Spinoza* 6).

OR

Antonio Damasio believes that "feelings are the expression of human flourishing or human distress" (*Looking for Spinoza* 6).

3. Work by two or three authors

Some environmentalists seek to protect wilderness areas from further development so that they can both preserve the past and learn from it (Katcher and Wilkins 174).

Use commas to separate the names of three authors: (Bellamy, O'Brien, and Nichols 59).

4. Work by more than three authors

Use either the first author's last name followed by the abbreviation *et al.* (from the Latin *et alii,* meaning "and others") or all the last names. (Do not italicize the abbreviated Latin phrase, which ends with a period.)

In one important study, women graduates complained more frequently about "excessive control than about lack of structure" (Belenky et al. 205).

OR

In one important study, women graduates complained more frequently about "excessive control than about lack of structure" (Belenky, Clinchy, Goldberger, and Tarule 205).

5. Works by different authors with the same last name

When your works-cited list includes works by different authors with the same last name, provide a first initial, along with the last name, in parenthetical citations, or use the author's first and last name in the text. For example, if your works-cited list included entries for works by both Richard Enos and Theresa Enos, you would cite the work of Theresa Enos as follows:

Pre-Aristotelian rhetoric still has an impact today (T. Enos 331-43).

OR

Theresa Enos mentions the considerable contemporary reliance on pre-Aristotelian rhetoric (331-43).

If two authors have the same last name and first initial, spell out each author's first name in a parenthetical citation.

6. Work by a corporate author

A work has a corporate author when individual members of the group that created it are not identified. If the corporate author's name is long, you may use common abbreviations for parts of it—for example, *Assn.* for "Association" and *Natl.* for "National." Do not italicize the abbreviations.

Strawbale constructions are now popular across the nation (Natl. Ecobuilders Group 2).

7. Two or more works in the same citation

When two sources provide similar information or when you combine information from two sources in the same sentence, cite both sources, separating them with a semicolon.

Agricultural scientists believe that crop productivity will be adversely affected by solar dimming (Beck and Watts 90; Harris-Green 153-54).

8. Multivolume work

When you cite material from more than one volume of a multivolume work, include the volume number (followed by a colon and a space) before the page number.

Katherine Raine claims that "true poetry begins where human personality ends" (2: 247).

You do not need to include the volume number in a parenthetical citation if your list of works cited includes only one volume of a multivolume work.

9. Anonymous work

The Tehuelche people left their handprints on the walls of a cave, now called Cave of the Hands ("Hands of Time" 124).

Use the title of an anonymous work in place of an author's name. If the title is long, provide a shortened version. For example, the shortened title for "Chasing Down the Phrasal Verb in the Discourse of Adolescents" is "Chasing Down."

10. Indirect source

If you need to include material that one of your sources quoted from another work because you cannot obtain the original source, use the following format (*qtd.* is the abbreviation for "quoted").

The critic Susan Hardy Aikens has argued on behalf of what she calls "canonical multiplicity" (qtd. in Mayers 677).

A reader turning to the list of works cited should find a bibliographic entry for Mayers, the source consulted, but not for Aikens.

11. Poetry, drama, and sacred texts

When you refer to poetry, drama, or sacred texts, you should give the numbers of lines, acts, and scenes or of chapters and verses, rather than page numbers. This practice enables readers to consult an edition other than the one you have used. Act, scene, and line numbers (all arabic numerals) are separated by periods with no space before or after them. The MLA suggests that biblical chapters and verses be treated similarly, although some writers prefer to use colons instead of periods in such citations. In all cases, the progression is from larger to smaller units.

The following example illustrates a citation referring to lines of poetry.

> Emily Dickinson alludes to her dislike of public appearance in "I'm Nobody! Who Are You?" (5-8).

The following citation shows that the famous "To be, or not to be" soliloquy appears in act 3, scene 1, lines 56-89 of *Hamlet*.

> In *Hamlet*, Shakespeare presents the most famous soliloquy in the history of the English theater: "To be, or not to be . . ." (3.1.56-89).

Citations of biblical material identify the book of the Bible, the chapter, and the pertinent verses. In the following example, the writer refers to the creation story in Genesis, which begins in chapter 1 with verse 1 and ends in chapter 2 with verse 22.

> The Old Testament creation story, told with remarkable economy, culminates in the arrival of Eve (*New American Standard Bible*, Gen. 1.1-2.22).

Mention in your first citation which version of the Bible you are using; list only book, chapter, and verse in subsequent citations. Note that the names of biblical books are neither italicized nor enclosed in quotation marks.

The MLA provides standard abbreviations for the parts of the Bible, as well as for the works of Shakespeare and Chaucer and certain other literary works.

12. Constitution

When referring to the U.S. Constitution, use in-text citations only. You do not need to include a works-cited entry. The following are common abbreviations for in-text citations:

United States Constitution	US Const.
article	art.
section	sec.

The testimony of two witnesses is needed to convict someone of treason (US Const., art. 3, sec. 3).

13. Works with numbered paragraphs or sections

If paragraphs in an electronic source are numbered, cite the number(s) of the paragraph(s) after the abbreviation *par.* (for one paragraph) or *pars.* (for more than one). If a section number is provided, cite that number after the abbreviation *sec.* (or *secs.* for more than one).

Alston describes three types of rubrics for evaluating customer service (pars. 2-15).

Hilton and Merrill provide examples of effective hyperlinks (sec. 1).

If an electronic source includes no numbers distinguishing one part from another, you should cite the entire source. In this case, to establish that you have not accidentally omitted a number, avoid using a parenthetical citation by providing what information you have within the sentence that introduces the material.

Raymond Lucero's *Shopping Online* offers useful advice for consumers who are concerned about transmitting credit card information over the Internet.

(2) Guidelines for in-text citations and quotations

(a) Placement of in-text citations

When you acknowledge your use of a source by placing the author's name and a relevant page number in parentheses, insert this parenthetical citation directly after the information you used, generally at the end of a sentence but *before* the final punctuation mark (a period, question mark, or exclamation point).

Oceans store almost half the carbon dioxide released by humans into the atmosphere (Wall 28).

However, you may need to place a parenthetical citation earlier in a sentence to indicate that only the first part of the sentence contains borrowed material. Place the citation after the clause containing the material but before a punctuation mark (a comma, semicolon, or colon).

Oceans store almost half the carbon dioxide released by humans into the atmosphere (Wall 28), a fact that provides hope for scientists studying global warming but alarms scientists studying organisms living in the oceans.

If you cite the same source more than once in a paragraph, with no intervening citations of another source, you can place one parenthetical citation at the end of the last sentence in which the source is used: (Wall 28, 32).

(b) Lengthy quotations

When a quotation is more than four lines long, set it off from the surrounding text by indenting all lines one inch from the left margin. The first line should not be indented further than the others. The right margin should remain the same. Double-space the entire quotation and do not begin and end it with quotation marks.

In *Nickel and Dimed*, Barbara Ehrenreich describes the dire living conditions of the working poor:

> The lunch that consists of Doritos or hot dog rolls, leading to faintness before the end of the shift. The "home" that is also a car or a van. The illness or injury that must be "worked through," with gritted teeth, because there's no sick pay or health insurance and the loss of one day's pay will mean no groceries for the next. These experiences are not part of a sustainable lifestyle, even a lifestyle of chronic deprivation and relentless low-level punishment. They are, by almost any standard of subsistence, emergency situations. And that

> is how we should see the poverty of millions of low-wage Americans—as a state of emergency. (214)

A problem of this magnitude cannot be fixed simply by raising the minimum wage.

Note that the period precedes the parenthetical citation at the end of an indented (block) quotation. Note, too, how the writer introduces and then comments on the block quotation from Ehrenreich, explaining the signficance of the quotation to the larger essay.

Rarely will you need to quote more than a paragraph, but if you do, indent the first line of each paragraph an extra quarter of an inch.

(c) Punctuation within citations and quotations

Punctuation marks clarify meaning in quotations and citations. The following list summarizes their common uses.

- A colon separates volume numbers from page numbers in a parenthetical citation.

  (Raine 2: 247)

- A comma separates the author's name from the title when it is necessary to list both in a parenthetical citation.

  (Kingsolver, *Animal Dreams*)

  A comma also indicates that page or line numbers are not sequential.

  (44, 47)

- Ellipsis points indicate an omission within a quotation.

  "They lived in an age of increasing complexity and great hope; we in an age of . . . growing despair" (Krutch 2).

- A hyphen indicates a continuous sequence of pages or lines.

  (44-47)

- A period separates acts, scenes, and lines of dramatic works.

  (3.1.56)

  A period also distinguishes chapters from verses in biblical citations.

  (Gen. 1.1)

- A question mark placed inside the final quotation marks indicates that the quotation is a question. Notice that the period after the parenthetical citation marks the end of the sentence.

  Peter Elbow asks, "What could be more wonderful than the pleasure of creating or appreciating forms that are different, amazing, outlandish, useless—the opposite of ordinary, everyday, pragmatic?" (542).

  When placed outside the final quotation marks, a question mark indicates that the quotation has been incorporated into a question posed by the writer of the paper.

  What does Kabat-Zinn mean when he advises people to practice mindfulness "as if their lives depended on it" (305)?

- Square brackets enclose words that have been added to the quotation as clarification and are not part of the original material.

  "The publication of this novel [*Beloved*] establishes Morrison as one of the most important writers of our time" (Boyle 17).

33b MLA list of works cited

All of the works you cite should be listed at the end of your paper, beginning on a separate page with the heading "Works Cited." Use the following tips as you prepare your list.

TIPS FOR PREPARING A LIST OF WORKS CITED

- Center the heading "Works Cited" (not enclosed in quotation marks) one inch from the top of the page.
- Arrange the list of works alphabetically by the author's last name.
- If a source has more than one author, alphabetize the entry according to the last name of the first author.
- If you use more than one work by the same author, alphabetize the works by the first major word in each title. For the first entry, provide the author's complete name (last name given first), but substitute three hyphens (---) for the author's name in subsequent entries. If that author is also the first author in a collaboration, write out the author's name in full.
- For a work without an author or editor, alphabetize the entry according to the first important word in the title.
- Type the first line of each entry flush with the left margin and indent subsequent lines one-half inch (a hanging indent).
- Double-space equally throughout—between lines of an entry and between entries.

Directory of MLA-Style Entries for a Works-Cited List

PRINT PUBLICATIONS

Print Articles

1. Article in a journal   298
2. Article in a monthly magazine   298
3. Article in a weekly magazine or newspaper   298
4. Article in a daily newspaper   298
5. Unsigned article or wire service article   298
6. Editorial in a newspaper or magazine   299
7. Book or film review in a magazine   299
8. Book or film review in a journal   299

Print Books

9. Book by one author 299
10. Book by two authors 301
11. Book by three authors 301
12. Book by more than three authors 302
13. Book by a corporate author 302
14. Book by an anonymous author 302
15. Book with an author and an editor 302
16. Book with an editor instead of an author 302
17. Edition after the first 302
18. Introduction, preface, foreword, or afterword to a book 302
19. Anthology 303
20. A work originally published in an anthology 303
21. A work from a journal reprinted in a textbook or an anthology 304
22. A work from an edited collection reprinted in a textbook or an anthology 304
23. Translated book 304
24. Republished book 304
25. Multivolume work 305
26. Article in a multivolume work 305
27. Book in a series 306

Other Print Texts

28. Dictionary entry 306
29. Sacred text 306
30. Government publication 306
31. Law case 307
32. Public law 307
33. Pamphlet or bulletin 307
34. Published dissertation 308
35. Published letter 308

Print Cartoons, Maps, and Other Visuals

36. Cartoon or comic strip 308
37. Map or chart 308
38. Advertisement 309

ONLINE PUBLICATIONS

Online Articles

39. Scholarly journal article 310
40. Popular magazine article 311
41. Newspaper article 311

Online Books

42. Book available only online 311
43. Book available online and in print 312
44. Part of an online book 312

Online Databases

45. ERIC 313
46. EBSCO 313
47. LexisNexis 314
48. ProQuest 314
49. InfoTrac 314
50. JSTOR 314
51. Project MUSE 314
52. Abstract from a subscription database 314

Online Communications and Web Sites

53. Web site 315
54. Web site with incomplete information 315
55. Section of a Web site 315
56. Discussion group or forum 315
57. Newsgroup 316
58. Web log (blog) 316

Other Online Documents

59. Online encyclopedia entry 316
60. Online congressional document 316
61. Online document from a government office 317
62. Online law case 317
63. Online public law 317
64. Online sacred text 317

Online Recordings and Images

65. Online music 317
66. Online speech 318
67. Online video 318
68. Online television or radio program 318
69. Online interview 318
70. Online work of art 318
71. Online photograph 319
72. Online map or chart 319
73. Online advertisement 319
74. Online cartoon or comic strip 319

OTHER COMMON SOURCES

Live and Recorded Performances

75. Play performance 319
76. Lecture or presentation 319
77. Interview 320
78. Film 320
79. Radio or television program 320

Works of Visual Art

80. Painting 321
81. Photograph 321

Digital Sources
82. CD-ROM 321
83. Work from a periodically published database on CD-ROM 322
84. DVD 322
85. Sound recording on CD 322

When writing down source information for your bibliography, be sure to copy the information directly from the source.

PRINT PUBLICATIONS

Print Articles

A **journal** is a publication written for a specific discipline or profession. **Magazines** and **newspapers** are written for the general public. You can find most of the information required for a works-cited entry for a journal article on the first page of the journal (fig. 33.1) or at the bottom of the first page of the article you are citing.

Title of article and name of periodical

Put the article title in quotation marks with a period inside the closing quotation marks. Italicize the name of the periodical; do not add any punctuation following the name. Capitalize all major words (nouns, pronouns, verbs, adjectives, adverbs, and subordinating conjunctions). Omit the word *A*, *An*, or *The* from the beginning of the name of a periodical.

"Into the Void." *New Scientist*

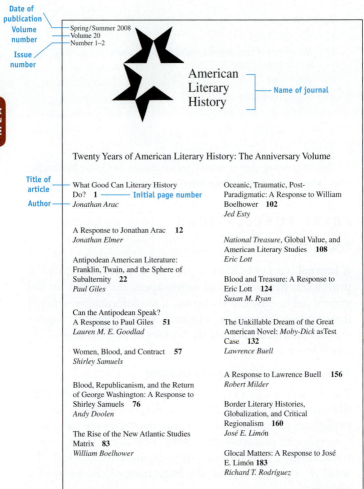

Figure 33.1. First page of a journal.

Volume and issue numbers

In an entry for an article from a journal, provide the volume number. If the issue number is available, put a period after the volume number and add the issue number.

Contemporary Review 194   *Studies in the Literary Imagination* 26.3

Date

For journals, place the year of publication in parentheses after the volume or issue number. For magazines and newspapers, provide the date of issue after the name of the periodical. Note the day first (if provided), followed by the month (abbreviated except for May, June, and July) and year.

Journal	*American Literary History* 20.1-2 (2008)
Magazine	*Economist* 13 Aug. 2005
Newspaper	*Chicago Tribune* 24 July 2002

Page numbers

Use a colon to separate the date from the page number(s). Note all the pages on which the article appears, separating the first and last page with a hyphen: 21-39. If the page numbers have the same hundreds or thousands digit, do not repeat it when listing the final page in the range: 131-42 or 1680-99. Magazine and newspaper articles are often interrupted by advertisements or other articles. If the first part of an article appears on pages 45 through 47 and the rest on pages 92 through 94, give only the first page number followed by a plus sign: 45+.

Medium of publication

Be sure to include the medium of publication (*Print*) at the end of the entry. Do not italicize the medium of publication.

1. Article in a journal

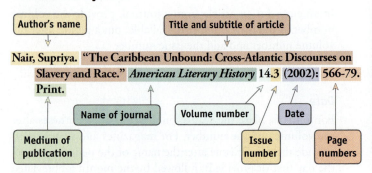

2. Article in a monthly magazine

Keizer, Garret. "How the Devil Falls in Love." *Harper's* Aug. 2002: 43-51. Print.

3. Article in a weekly magazine or newspaper

Chown, Marcus. "Into the Void." *New Scientist* 24 Nov. 2007: 34-37. Print.

4. Article in a daily newspaper

Moberg, David. "The Accidental Environmentalist." *Chicago Tribune* 24 Sept. 2002, final ed., sec. 2: 1+. Print.

When the name of the city is not part of a locally published newspaper's name, it should be given in brackets after the title: *Star Telegram* [Fort Worth]. If a specific edition is not identifed on the masthead, put a colon after the date and then provide the page reference. Specify the section by inserting the letter and/or number as it appears in the newspaper (A7 or 7A, for example).

5. Unsigned article or wire service article

"View from the Top." *National Geographic* July 2001: 140. Print.

6. Editorial in a newspaper or magazine

Beefs, Anne. "Ending Bias in the Human Rights System." Editorial.
New York Times 22 May 2002, natl. ed.: A27. Print.

7. Book or film review in a magazine

Denby, David. "Horse Power." Rev. of *Seabiscuit*, dir. Gary Ross.
New Yorker 4 Aug. 2003: 84-85. Print.

Include the name of the reviewer, the title of the review (if any), the phrase *Rev. of* (for "Review of"), the title of the work being reviewed, and the name of the editor, author, or director.

8. Book or film review in a journal

Graham, Catherine. Rev. of *Questionable Activities: The Best*, ed. Judith
Rudakoff. *Canadian Theatre Review* 113 (2003): 74-76. Print.

Print Books
9. Book by one author

The title page and copyright page of a book (see figs. 33.2 and 33.3) provide the information needed to create a bibliographic entry. If more than one city is listed on the title page, mention only the first. Place a colon after the name of

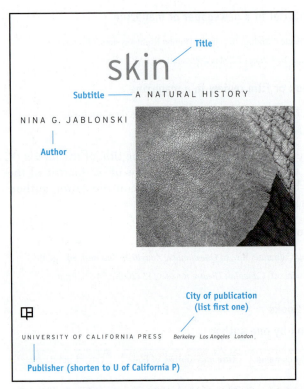

Figure 33.2. A title page includes most, if not all, of the information needed for a bibliographic entry. In this case, the title page omits the publication date.

the city, followed by a shortened form of the publisher's name with a comma after it and then the copyright date. Place a period after the date. Be sure to include the medium of publication at the end of the entry, followed by a period.

> University of California Press, one of the most distinguished
> university presses in the United States, enriches lives around the
> world by advancing scholarship in the humanities, social sciences,
> and natural sciences. Its activities are supported by the UC Press
> Foundation and by philanthropic contributions from individuals
> and institutions. For more information, visit www.ucpress.edu.
>
> University of California Press
> Berkeley and Los Angeles, California
>
> University of California Press, Ltd.
> London, England
>
> ────────────── Copyright year
> ©2006 by Nina G. Jablonski

Figure 33.3. If the title page does not give the book's date of publication, turn to the copyright page, which is usually the page following the title page.

10. Book by two authors

West, Nigel, and Oleg Tsarev. *The Crown Jewels: The British Secrets at the Heart of the KGB Archives*. New Haven: Yale UP, 1999. Print.

Type the first author's name in inverted order, followed by a comma, the word *and*, and the name of the second author in normal order. The title and subtitle (if any) are italicized with all major words capitalized.

11. Book by three authors

Spinosa, Charles, Ferdinand Flores, and Hubert L. Dreyfus. *Disclosing New Worlds: Entrepreneurship, Democratic Action, and the Cultivation of Solidarity*. Cambridge: MIT P, 1997. Print.

12. Book by more than three authors

Bullock, Jane A., George D. Haddow, Damon Cappola, Erdem Ergin, Lissa
 Westerman, and Sarp Yeletaysi. *Introduction to Homeland Security*.
 Boston: Elsevier, 2005. Print.

OR

Bullock, Jane A., et al. *Introduction to Homeland Security*. Boston: Elsevier,
 2005. Print.

13. Book by a corporate author

Institute of Medicine. *Blood Banking and Regulation: Procedures, Problems,
 and Alternatives*. Washington: Natl. Acad., 1996. Print.

14. Book by an anonymous author

Primary Colors: A Novel of Politics. New York: Warner, 1996. Print.

Begin the entry with the title. Do not use *Anonymous* or *Anon*.

15. Book with an author and an editor

Stoker, Bram. *Dracula*. Ed. Glennis Byron. Peterborough: Broadview,
 1998. Print.

Include both the name of the author and the name of the editor (preceded by *Ed.*).

16. Book with an editor instead of an author

Kachuba, John B., ed. *How to Write Funny*. Cincinnati: Writer's Digest, 2000. Print.

17. Edition after the first

Murray, Donald. *The Craft of Revision*. 4th ed. Boston: Heinle, 2001. Print.

18. Introduction, preface, foreword, or afterword to a book

Olmos, Edward James. Foreword. *Vietnam Veteranos: Chicanos Recall the
 War*. By Lea Ybarra. Austin: U of Texas P, 2004. ix-x. Print.

The name that begins the entry is that of the author of the section of the book, not of the entire book. The name is followed by the title of the section (Introduction, Preface, Foreword, or Afterword).

19. Anthology (a collection of works by different authors)

Buranen, Lisa, and Alice M. Roy, eds. *Perspectives on Plagiarism and Intellectual Property in a Postmodern World*. New York: State U of New York P, 1999. Print.

If an editor or editors are listed instead of an author or authors, include the abbreviation *ed.* or *eds.* (not italicized) following the name(s). For individual works within an anthology, consult the following two models.

20. A work originally published in an anthology

Rowe, David. "No Gain, No Game? Media and Sport." *Mass Media and Society*. Ed. James Curran and Michael Gurevitch. 3rd ed. New York: Oxford UP, 2000. 346-61. Print.

Use this form for an article, essay, story, poem, or play that was published for the first time in the anthology you are citing. Place the title of the anthology after the title of the individual work. Provide the name(s) of the editor(s) after the abbreviation *Ed.* for "edited by," and note the edition if it is not the first. List the publication data for the anthology and the range of pages on which the work appears.

If you cite more than one work from an anthology, provide only the name(s) of the author(s), the title of the work, the name(s) of the editor(s), and the inclusive page numbers in an entry for each work. Also include an entry for the entire anthology, which presents the publication data.

Clark, Irene L. "Writing Centers and Plagiarism." Buranen and Roy 155-67.

Howard, Rebecca Moore. "The New Abolitionism Comes to Plagiarism." Buranen and Roy 87-95.

21. A work from a journal reprinted in a textbook or an anthology

Selfe, Cynthia L. "Technology and Literacy: A Story about the Perils of Not Paying Attention." *College Composition and Communication* 50.3 (1999): 411-37. Rpt. in *Views from the Center: The CCCC Chairs' Addresses 1977-2005*. Ed. Duane Roen. Boston: Bedford; Urbana: NCTE, 2006. 323-51. Print.

Use the abbreviation *Rpt.* (not italicized) for "Reprinted." Two cities and publishers are listed in the sample entry because the collection was copublished.

22. A work from an edited collection reprinted in a textbook or an anthology

Brownmiller, Susan. "Let's Put Pornography Back in the Closet." *Take Back the Night: Women on Pornography*. Ed. Laura Lederer. New York: Morrow, 1980. 252-55. Rpt. in *Conversations: Readings for Writing*. By Jack Selzer. 4th ed. New York: Allyn, 2000. 578-81. Print.

See item 20 for information on citing more than one work from the same anthology.

23. Translated book

Garrigues, Eduardo. *West of Babylon*. Trans. Nasario Garcia. Albuquerque: U of New Mexico P, 2002. Print.

Place the abbreviation *Trans.* (not italicized) for "Translated by" before the translator's name.

24. Republished book

Alcott, Louisa May. *Work: A Story of Experience*. 1873. Harmondsworth: Penguin, 1995. Print.

After the title of the book, provide the original publication date, followed by a period.

25. Multivolume work

Young, Ralph F., ed. *Dissent in America*. 2 vols. New York: Longman-Pearson,

2005. Print.

Cite the total number of volumes in a work when you have used material from more than one volume. Include the year the volumes were published. If the volumes were published over a span of time, provide inclusive dates: 1997-99 or 1998-2004.

If you have used only one volume, include that volume's number (preceded by the abbreviation *Vol.*) in place of the total number of volumes.

Young, Ralph F., ed. *Dissent in America*. Vol. 1. New York: Longman-Pearson,

2005. Print.

Note that the publisher's name in this entry is hyphenated: the first name is the imprint; the second is the publisher.

26. Article in a multivolume work

To indicate a specific article in a multivolume work, provide the author's name and the title of the article in quotation marks. Note the page numbers for the article after the date of publication.

Baxby, Derrick. "Jenner, Edward." *Oxford Dictionary of National Biography*.

Ed. H. C. G. Matthew and Brian Harrison. Vol. 30. Oxford: Oxford UP,

2004. 4-8. Print.

If required by your instructor, include the number of volumes and the inclusive publication dates after the medium of publication: Print. 23 vols. 1962-97.

27. Book in a series

Sumner, Colin, ed. *Blackwell Companion to Criminology*. Malden: Blackwell,
    2004. Print. Blackwell Companions to Sociology 8.

When citing a book that is part of a series, add the name of the series and, if one is listed, the number designating the work's place in it. The series name is not italicized. Abbreviate words in the series name according to the MLA guidelines; for example, the word *Series* is abbreviated *Ser.* (not italicized).

Other Print Texts

28. Dictionary entry

When citing a specific dictionary definition for a word, use the abbreviation *Def.* (for "Definition") and indicate which one you used if the entry has two or more.

"Reactive." Def. 2a. *Merriam-Webster's Collegiate Dictionary*. 10th ed. 2001. Print.

29. Sacred text

Begin your works-cited entry for a sacred text with the title of the work, rather than information about editors or translators.

New American Standard Bible. Anaheim: Foundation, 1997. Print.

The Qur'an. Trans. Muhammad A. S. Abdel Haleem. Oxford: Oxford UP,
    2004. Print.

30. Government publication

United States. Office of Management and Budget. *A Citizen's Guide to the*
    Federal Budget. Washington: GPO, 1999. Print.

When citing a government publication, list the name of the government (e.g., United States or Minnesota) and the agency that issued the work. Italicize the title of a book or pamphlet. Indicate the city of publication. Federal publications are usually printed by the Government Printing Office (GPO) in Washington DC, but be alert for exceptions.

When the name of an author, editor, or compiler appears on a government publication, you can begin the entry with that name, followed by the abbreviation *ed.* or *comp.* if the person is not the author. Alternatively, insert that name after the publication's title and introduce it with the word *By* or the abbreviation *Ed.* or *Comp.*

31. Law case

Chavez v. Martinez. 538 US 760. Supreme Court of the US. 2003. *United States Reports.* Washington: GPO, 2004. Print.

Include the last name of the first plaintiff, the abbreviation *v.* for "versus," the last name of the first defendant, data on the law report (volume, abbreviated name, and page or reference number), the name of the deciding court, and the year of the decision. Although law cases are italicized in the text of a paper, they are *not* italicized in works-cited entries.

32. Public law

No Child Left Behind Act of 2001. Pub. L. 107-10. 115 Stat. 1425-2094. 8 Jan. 2002. Print.

Include the name of the act, its public law number, its Statutes at Large cataloging number and page numbers, the date it was enacted, and the medium of publication. Notice the use of abbreviations in the example. Although no works-cited entry is needed for familiar sources such as the U.S. Constitution, an in-text citation should still be included.

33. Pamphlet or bulletin

Stucco in Residential Construction. St. Paul: Lath & Plaster Bureau, 2000. Print.

If the pamphlet has an author, begin with the author's name, as you would for a book.

34. Published dissertation

Fukuda, Kay Louise. *Differing Perceptions and Constructions of the Meaning of Assessment in Education.* Diss. Ohio State U, 2001. Ann Arbor: UMI, 2002. Print.

After the title of the dissertation, include the abbreviation *Diss.,* the name of the university granting the degree, the date of completion, and the publication information. In the example, *UMI* stands for "University Microfilms International," which publishes many dissertations.

35. Published letter

In general, treat a published letter like a work in an anthology, adding the date of the letter and the number (if the editor assigned one).

Jackson, Helen Hunt. "To Thomas Bailey Aldrich." 4 May 1883. *The Indian Reform Letters of Helen Hunt Jackson, 1879-1885.* Ed. Valerie Sherer Mathes. Norman: U of Oklahoma P, 1998. 258-59. Print.

Print Cartoons, Maps, and Other Visuals

36. Cartoon or comic strip

Cheney, Tom. Cartoon. *New Yorker* 9 June 2003: 93. Print.

Trudeau, Garry. "Doonesbury." Comic strip. *Daily Record* [Ellensburg] 21 Apr. 2005: A4. Print.

After the creator's name, place the title of the work (if given) in quotation marks and include the descriptor *Cartoon* or *Comic strip.*

37. Map or chart

Cincinnati and Vicinity. Map. Chicago: Rand, 2008. Print.

Include the title and the appropriate descriptor, *Map* or *Chart.*

38. Advertisement

Nu by Yves Saint Laurent. Advertisement. *Allure* June 2003: 40. Print.

The name of the product and/or that of the company being advertised is followed by the designation *Advertisement*.

ONLINE PUBLICATIONS

Many of the guidelines for documenting online sources are similar to those for print sources. For sources found online, provide electronic publication information and access information.

Electronic publication information

Indicate the author's name, the title of the work, the title of the Web site, the site's sponsoring organization (usually found at the bottom of the site's home page; see fig. 33.4), the date of publication, and the medium of publication (*Web*). All of this information precedes the access information.

Access information

When you document an online source, you must include the date of access: the day, month, and year on which you consulted the source. Either keep track of the date of access or print out the source so that you have a record.

You are not required to include the URL if your readers can easily locate the online source by searching for the author's name and the title of the work. For cases in which your readers cannot easily locate a source, you should provide the complete URL (between angle brackets), including the protocol (http, ftp, telnet, or news). When the URL does not fit on a single line, break it only after a slash. Make sure that the URL is accurate. Take care to distinguish between uppercase and lowercase letters and to include hyphens and

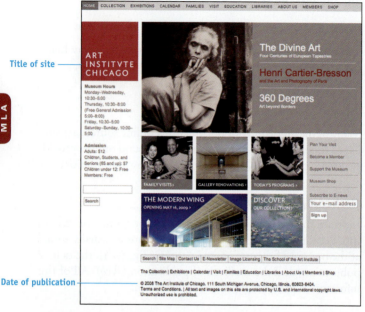

Figure 33.4. The home page for the Art Institute of Chicago indicates the title of the site (which is also the name of the sponsoring organization) and the date of publication.

underscores. The URL follows the date of access, appearing after a period and a space. The closing angle bracket should also be followed by a period.

Online Articles

The following formats apply to articles available only online.

39. Scholarly journal article

Harnack, Andrea, and Gene Kleppinger. "Beyond the MLA Handbook: Documenting Sources on the Internet." *Kairos* 1.2 (1996): n. pag. Web. 14 Aug. 1997.

Page numbers may not be provided for online journals; if this is the case, write *n. pag.* (for "no pagination"). If they are provided, place them after the colon that follows the year of publication. The access date ends the entry.

40. Popular magazine article

Plotz, David. "The Cure for Sinophobia." *Slate.com*. Newsweek Interactive, 4 June 1999. Web. 15 June 1999.

41. Newspaper article

"Tornadoes Touch Down in S. Illinois." *New York Times*. New York Times, 16 Apr. 1998. Web. 20 May 1998.

When no author is identified, begin with the title of the article. If the article is an editorial, include *Editorial* (not italicized) after the title: "America's Promises." Editorial. (In the sample entry, the first mention of *New York Times* is the title of the Web site, and the second, which is not italicized, is the name of the site's sponsor.)

Online Books

42. Book available only online

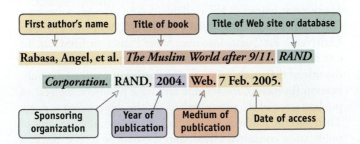

Because there are more than three authors, the abbreviation *et al.* has been used in the example, but listing all names is also acceptable: Rabasa, Angel, Cheryl Benard, Peter Chalk, C. Christine Fair, Theodore W. Karasik, Rollie Lal, Ian O. Lesser, and David E. Thaler. Note that in this example the name of the sponsoring organization is in the title of the Web site.

43. Book available online and in print

Rohrbough, Malcolm J. *Days of Gold: The California Gold Rush and the American Nation.* Berkeley: U of California P, 1997. *History E-book Project.* Web. 17 Feb. 2005.

Begin the citation with print citation information: the author's name, the title of the work, city of publication, publisher, and date. Follow this information with the title of the database or Web site (italicized), the medium of publication (*Web*), and the date of access.

44. Part of an online book

Strunk, William, Jr. "Elementary Rules of Usage." *The Elements of Style.* Ithaca: Humphrey, 1918. N. pag. *Bartleby.com.* Web. 6 June 2003.

Online Databases

Many print materials are available online through a database (JSTOR, Project MUSE, ERIC, PsycINFO, Academic Universe, LexisNexis, ProQuest, InfoTrac, Silver Platter, or EBSCO). To cite material from an online database, begin with the author, the title of the article (in quotation marks), the title of the publication (in italics), the volume and issue numbers, the year of publication, and the page numbers (or the abbreviation *n. pag.*). Then add the name of the database (in italics), the medium of publication consulted (*Web*), and the date of access. You can find most of the information you need for a works-cited entry on the abstract page of the article you select (see fig. 33.5).

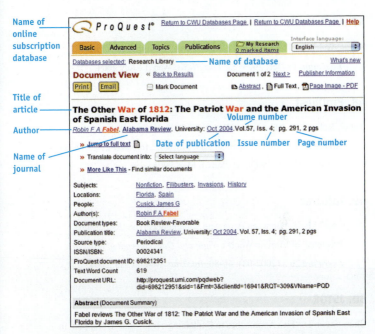

Figure 33.5. Abstract page from an online subscription database.

45. ERIC

Taylor, Steven J. "Caught in the Continuum: A Critical Analysis of the Principle of the Least Restrictive Environment." *Research and Practice for Persons with Severe Disabilities* 29.4 (2004): 218-30. *ERIC*. Web. 3 Mar. 2009.

46. EBSCO

Folks, Jeffrey J. "Crowd and Self: William Faulkner's Sources of Agency in *The Sound and the Fury*." *Southern Literary Journal* 34.2 (2002): 30+. *EBSCO*. Web. 6 June 2003.

For sources that list only the page number on which a work begins, include that number followed by a plus sign.

47. LexisNexis

Suggs, Welch. "A Hard Year in College Sports." *Chronicle of Higher Education* 19 Dec. 2003: 37. *LexisNexis*. Web. 17 July 2004.

48. ProQuest

Fabel, Robin F. A. "The Other War of 1812: The Patriot War and the American Invasion of Spanish East Florida." *Alabama Review* 57.4 (2004): 291-92. *ProQuest*. Web. 8 Mar. 2005.

49. InfoTrac

Priest, Ann-Marie. "Between Being and Nothingness: The 'Astonishing Precipice' of Virginia Woolf's *Night and Day*." *Journal of Modern Literature* 26.2 (2002-03): 66-80. *InfoTrac*. Web. 12 Jan. 2004.

50. JSTOR

Blum, Susan D. "Five Approaches to Explaining 'Truth' and 'Deception' in Human Communication." *Journal of Anthropological Research* 61.3 (2005): 289-315. *JSTOR*. Web. 3 Mar. 2009.

51. Project MUSE

Muñoz, Alejandro Anaya. "Transnational and Domestic Processes in the Definition of Human Rights Policies in Mexico." *Human Rights Quarterly* 31.1 (2009): 35-58. *Project MUSE*. Web. 3 Mar. 2009.

52. Abstract from a subscription database

Landers, Susan J. "FDA Panel Findings Intensify Struggles with Prescribing of Antidepressants." *American Medical News* 47.37 (2004): 1-2. *ProQuest Direct*. Web. 7 Feb. 2005.

Online Communications and Web Sites

53. Web site

McGann, Jerome, ed. *The Complete Writings and Pictures of Dante Gabriel Rossetti*. Inst. for Advanced Technology in the Humanities, U of Virginia, n.d. Web. 16 Mar. 2009.

Include the name of the author, editor, compiler, director, or translator, followed by the title of the site (italicized), the version or edition (if given), the publisher or sponsor (if not available, use *N.p.*), the date of publication (if not available, use *n.d.*), the medium of publication (*Web*), and the date of access.

54. Web site with incomplete information

Breastcancer.org. N.p., 2 Feb. 2008. Web. 5 Feb. 2008.

If a Web site does not provide all the information usually included in a works-cited entry, list as much as is available.

55. Section of a Web site

Altman, Andrew. "Civil Rights." *Stanford Encyclopedia of Philosophy*. Ed. Edward N. Zalta. Center for the Study of Lang. and Information, Stanford U, 3 Feb. 2003. Web. 12 June 2003.

Mozart, Wolfgang Amadeus. "Concerto No. 3 for Horn, K. 447." *Essentials of Music*. Sony Music Entertainment, 2001. Web. 3 Mar. 2009.

56. Discussion group or forum

Schipper, William. "Re: Quirk and Wrenn Grammar." *Ansaxnet*. N.p., 5 Jan. 1995. Web. 12 Sept. 1996.

Provide the name of the forum (in this case, *Ansaxnet*) after the title of the work. If the posting is untitled, identify the genre (e.g., *Online posting*) instead of providing the title.

57. Newsgroup

May, Michaela. "Questions about RYAs." *Generation X*. N.p., 19 June 1996.
   Web. 29 June 1996.

The name of a newsgroup (*Generation X*) takes the place of the title of the Web site.

58. Web log (blog)

Cuthbertson, Peter. "Are Left and Right Still Alright?" *Conservative
   Commentary*. N.p., 7 Feb. 2005. Web. 18 Feb. 2005.

Other Online Documents

59. Online encyclopedia entry

"Iran." *Encyclopaedia Britannica Online*. Encyclopaedia Britannica, 2002.
   Web. 6 Mar. 2004.

60. Online congressional document

United States. Cong. Senate. Special Committee on Aging. *Global Aging:
   Opportunity or Threat for the U.S. Economy?* 108th Cong., 1st sess. S.
   Hrg. 108-30. Washington: GPO, 2003. *GPO Access*. Web. 7 Jan. 2005.

Provide the number and session of Congress and the type and number of publication. (*S* stands for "Senate"; *H* or *HR* stands for "House of Representatives.")

Bills	S 41, HR 82
Reports	S. Rept. 14, H. Rept. 18
Hearings	S. Hrg. 23, H. Hrg. 25
Resolutions	S. Res. 32, H. Res. 52
Documents	S. Doc. 213, H. Doc. 123

61. Online document from a government office

United States. Dept. of State. Bur. of Democracy, Human Rights, and Labor.
Guatemala Country Report on Human Rights Practices for 1998. Feb.
1999. Web. 1 May 1999.

Begin with the name of the country, state, or city whose government is responsible for the document and the department or agency that issued it. If a subdivision of the larger organization is responsible, name the subdivision. If an author is identified, provide the name, preceded by the word *By*, between the title and the date of issue of the document.

62. Online law case

Tennessee v. Lane. 541 US 509. Supreme Court of the US. 2004. *Supreme
Court Collection*. Legal Information Inst., Cornell U Law School, n.d.
Web. 28 Jan. 2005.

63. Online public law

Individuals with Disabilities Education Act. Pub. L. 105-17. 104 Stat.
587-698. *Thomas*. Lib. of Cong., 4 June 1997. Web. 29 Jan. 2005.

64. Online sacred text

Sama Veda. Trans. Ralph T. H. Griffith. 1895. *Sacred-Texts.com*. Ed. John B.
Hare. N.p., 2008. Web. 6 Mar. 2008.

Online Recordings and Images
65. Online music

Moran, Jason. "Jump Up." *Same Mother*. Blue Note, 2005. *Blue Note*. Blue
Note Records. Web. 7 Mar. 2005.

In this entry, "Blue Note" is the manufacturer of the CD, *Blue Note* is the title of the Web site where the song was accessed, and "Blue Note Records" is the sponsor of that site.

66. Online speech

Malcolm X. "The Ballot or the Bullet." Detroit. 12 Apr. 1964. *American Rhetoric: Top One Hundred Speeches*. Ed. Michael E. Eidenmuller. N.p., 2005. Web. 14 Jan. 2005.

"12 Apr. 1964" is the date the speech was delivered, "2005" is the year of the speech's electronic publication, and "14 Jan. 2005" is the date of access.

67. Online video

Riefenstahl, Leni, dir. *Triumph of the Will*. Reichsparteitag-Film, 1935. *Movieflix.com*. MovieFlix, 2005. Web. 17 Feb. 2005.

"1935" is the year in which the movie was originally released, "2005" is the year in which it was made available online, and "17 Feb. 2005" is the date of access.

68. Online television or radio program

"Religion and the American Election." Narr. Tony Hassan. *The Religion Report*. ABC Radio National, 3 Nov. 2004. Web. 18 Feb. 2005.

69. Online interview

McLaughlin, John. Interview by Wolf Blitzer. *CNN.com*. Cable News Network, 14 July 2004. Web. 21 Dec. 2004.

70. Online work of art

Vermeer, Johannes. *Young Woman with a Water Pitcher*. c. 1660. Metropolitan Museum of Art, New York. *The Metropolitan Museum of Art*. Web. 2 Oct. 2002.

71. Online photograph

Marmon, Lee. *Engine Rock*. 1985. *Lee Marmon Gallery*. Web. 9 Feb. 2009.

72. Online map or chart

"Virginia 1624." Map. *Map Collections 1544-1996*. Lib. of Cong. Web. 26 Apr. 1999.

United States. Dept. of Health and Human Services. Centers for Disease Control and Prevention. "Daily Cigarette Smoking among High School Seniors." Chart. 27 Jan. 2005. *National Center for Health Statistics*. Web. 25 Feb. 2005.

73. Online advertisement

Milk Processor Education Program. "Got Milk?" Advertisement. *MilkPEP*. MilkPEP, n.d. Web. 16 Feb. 2005.

74. Online cartoon or comic strip

Cagle, Daryl. "Social Security Pays 3 to 2." Cartoon. *Slate.com*. Newsweek Interactive, 4 Feb. 2005. Web. 5 Feb. 2005.

OTHER COMMON SOURCES

Live and Recorded Performances

75. Play performance

Proof. By David Auburn. Dir. Daniel Sullivan. Walter Kerr Theater, New York. 8 Oct. 2002. Performance.

Cite the date of the performance you attended.

76. Lecture or presentation

Guinier, Lani. Barbara Jordan Lecture Ser. Schwab Auditorium, Pennsylvania State U, University Park. 4 Oct. 2004. Address.

Scharnhorst, Gary. English 296.003. Dane Smith Hall, U of New Mexico,

    Albuquerque. 30 Apr. 2008. Class lecture.

Identify the site and the date of the lecture or presentation. Use the title if available; otherwise, provide a descriptive label.

77. Interview

Furstenheim, Ursula. Personal interview. 16 Jan. 2003.

Sugo, Misuzu. Telephone interview. 20 Feb. 2003.

For an interview you conducted, give only the name of the person you interviewed, the type of interview, and the date of the interview. If the interview was conducted by someone else, add the name of the interviewer, a title or a descriptive label, and the name of the source.

Harryhausen, Ray. Interview by Terry Gross. *Fresh Air*. Natl. Public Radio.

    WHYY, Philadelphia, 6 Jan. 2003. Radio.

78. Film

My Big Fat Greek Wedding. Dir. Joel Zwick. IFC, 2002. Film.

The name of the company that produced or distributed the film (IFC, in this case) appears before the year of release. It is not necessary to cite the city in which the production or distribution company is based.

When you want to highlight the contribution of a specific person, list the contributor's name first. Other supplementary information may be included after the title.

Gomez, Ian, perf. *My Big Fat Greek Wedding*. Screenplay by Nia Vardalos.

    Dir. Joel Zwick. IFC, 2002. Film.

79. Radio or television program

When referring to a specific episode, place quotation marks around its title. Italicize the title of the program.

"'Barbarian' Forces." *Ancient Warriors*. Narr. Colgate Salsbury. Dir. Phil

   Grabsky. Learning Channel. 1 Jan. 1996. Television.

To highlight a specific contributor or contributors, begin the entry with the name or names and note the nature of the contribution.

Abumrad, Jad, and Robert Kulwich, narrs. "Choice." *Radiolab*. New York

   Public Radio. WNYC, New York, 14 Nov. 2008. Radio.

Works of Visual Art
80. Painting

Gauguin, Paul. *Ancestors of Tehamana*. 1893. Oil on canvas. Art Inst. of

   Chicago, Chicago.

Identify the artist's name, the title of the work (italicized), the date of composition (if known; otherwise, write *N.d.*), the medium of composition, the organization or individual holding the work, and the city in which the work is located. For a photograph or reproduction of a work of art, provide the preceding information followed by complete publication information for the source, including medium of publication.

81. Photograph

Marmon, Lee. *White Man's Moccasins*. 1954. Photograph. Native American

   Cultural Center, Albuquerque.

Digital Sources
82. CD-ROM

"About *Richard III*." *Cinemania 96*. Redmond: Microsoft, 1996. CD-ROM.

Indicate which part of the CD-ROM you are using, and then provide the title of the CD-ROM. Begin the entry with the name of the author if one has been provided.

Jordan, June. "Moving towards Home." *Database of Twentieth-Century African American Poetry on CD-ROM*. Alexandria: Chadwyck-Healey, 1999. CD-ROM.

83. Work from a periodically published database on CD-ROM

Parachini, John V. *Combating Terrorism: The 9/11 Commission Recommendations and the National Strategies*. CD-ROM. *RAND Electronically Distributed Documents*. RAND. 2004. Disc 8.

84. DVD

A River Runs through It. Screenplay by Richard Friedenberg. Dir. Robert Redford. 1992. Columbia, 1999. DVD.

Cite relevant information about the title and director as you would for a film. Note the original release date of the film and the release date for the DVD. If the original company producing the film did not release the DVD, list the company that released the DVD instead.

85. Sound recording on CD

Franklin, Aretha. *Amazing Grace: The Complete Recordings*. Atlantic, 1999. CD.

For a sound recording on another medium, identify the type (*Audiocassette* or *LP*).

Raitt, Bonnie. *Nick of Time*. Capitol, 1989. Audiocassette.

When citing a recording of a specific song, begin with the name of the performer and place the song title in quotation marks. Identify the author(s) after the song title. If the performance is a reissue from an earlier recording, provide the original date of recording (preceded by *Rec.* for "Recorded").

Horne, Lena. "The Man I Love." By George Gershwin and Ira Gershwin. Rec. 15 Dec. 1941. *Stormy Weather*. BMG, 1990. CD.

33c Sample MLA-style paper

(1) Submit a title page if your instructor requires one

The MLA recommends omitting a title page and instead providing identifying information on the first page of the paper. However, if your instructor requires a title page, type the title of the paper, your name, the instructor's name, the name of the course with its section number, and the date—all centered on the page.

(2) Sample MLA-style paper

Interested in the controversy surrounding genetically modified foods, Marianna Suslin explores both sides of the debate as she comes to her conclusion in the MLA-documented paper that follows.

TIPS FOR PREPARING AN MLA-STYLE PAPER

- Number all pages (including the first one) with an arabic numeral in the upper-right corner, one-half inch from the top. Put your last name before the page number.
- On the left side of the first page, one inch from the top, type a heading that includes your name, the name of your professor, the course number, and the date of submission.
- Double-space between the heading and the title of your paper, which should be centered on the page. If your title consists of two or more lines, double-space them and center each.
- Double-space between your title and the first line of text.
- Indent the first paragraph, and every subsequent paragraph, one-half inch.
- Double-space throughout.

Marianna Suslin

Professor Squier

Sociology 299, Section 1

27 November 2007

Genetically Modified Foods and Developing Countries

Since the 1960s, thousands of genetically modified plants, also referred to as "genetically modified organisms" (GMOs) and "transgenic crops," have been introduced to global markets. Those who argue for the support of genetic modification claim that the crops have higher yield, grow in harsher conditions, benefit the ecology, and hold great potential for benefiting poor farmers in developing countries. Despite these claims, the practice of genetic engineering—of inserting genetic material into the DNA of a plant—continues to be controversial, with no clear answers as to whether genetically engineered foods can be the answer for developing countries.

One of the most important potential benefits of the technology to both proponents and opponents of genetic engineering is its potential to improve the economies of developing countries. According to Sakiko Fukuda-Parr, "Investing in agricultural technology increasingly turns up these days on the lists of the top ten practical actions the rich world could take to contribute to reducing global poverty." Agriculture is the source of income for the world's poorest—70 percent of those living on less than a dollar a day support themselves through agriculture. These farmers could benefit greatly from higher yield crops that could grow in nutrient poor soil. Genetic modification "has shown how high-yielding varieties developed at international centers can be adapted to local conditions, dramatically increasing yields and farm incomes" (Fukuda-Parr 3).

Theoretically, genetic engineering can bring about an increase in farm productivity that would give people in developing countries the chance to enter the global market on better terms. Developing countries are often resource poor and thus have little more than labor to contribute to the world economy. Farming tends to be subsistence level, as farmers can grow only enough on the land—which tends to be nutrient poor—to feed themselves. But the higher yield of genetically modified crops, along with their resistance to pests and ability to thrive in nutrient poor soil, can enable the farmers to produce more crops, maybe to the point of exporting extra crops not needed for subsistence (Fukuda-Parr 1). Genetic modification can also help poor farmers by using genetics to delay the ripening process and thereby allowing the farmer to store the crops longer, have more time in which to sell the crops without fear of spoilage, and avoid the heavy losses caused by "uncontrolled ripening and spoiling of fruits and vegetables" (Royal Society et al. 238).

Today, eighteen percent of people living in developing countries do not have enough food to meet their needs (Royal Society et al. 235). "Malnutrition plays a significant role in half of the nearly 12 million deaths each year of children under five in developing countries" (UNICEF, qtd. in Royal Society et al. 235). Genetically modified foods producing large yields in nutrient poor soils could help feed the world's increasing population and combat malnutrition, since scientists are working on ways to make the genetically modified foods more nutritious than unmodified crops. Genetically modified rice, for example, has already been created that "exhibits an increased production of beta-carotene," which is a precursor to vitamin A (Royal Society et al. 240). Because vitamin A deficiencies are common in developing countries and contribute to half a million children becoming partially or totally blind each year, advances in genetic engineering offer hope for millions of people who live with nutrient deficiencies (Royal Society et al. 239).

Proponents of genetic engineering have also argued that genetically modified crops have the potential to decrease the amount of damage modern farming technologies have on ecology at the same time that they improve the economy. For example, genetically modified plants with resistance to certain insects would decrease the amount of pesticides that farmers have to use. Genes for insect resistance have already been introduced into cotton, making possible a huge decrease in insecticide use (Royal Society et al. 238). A decrease in the amount of pesticides used is good from an ecological perspective.[1] Pesticides not only can be washed into streams and be harmful to wildlife but have also been known to appear in groundwater, thus potentially causing harm to humans.

Scientists have argued that genetic engineering is only the latest step in the human involvement in plant modification that has been going on for thousands of years.[2] Since the dawn of the agricultural revolution, people have been breeding plants for desirable traits and thus altering the genetic makeup of plant populations. Genetic engineering, however, produces plants with the desirable trait much faster (Fukuda-Parr 5).

While there are many potential benefits that can come from genetic engineering for farmers in developing countries and even in the United States, many people remain skeptical about this new technology. Many Americans are uneasy about consuming foods that have been genetically enhanced, citing the potential risks of consuming GMOs, which outweigh the benefits

Suslin 5

> The writer describes disadvantages of eating genetically modified foods.

of this new technology (Brossard, Shanahan, and Nesbitt 10). Considering the risks of genetically modified foods, people in developing countries are likely to feel the same way: that the risks outweigh the benefits. No matter how many potential benefits genetically modified crops may bring, if they are not safe for consumption, they will not help but hurt the economies of developing countries.

In "Genetically Modified Food Threatens Human Health," Jeffrey Smith argues that inserting foreign genetic material into food is extremely dangerous because it may create unknown toxins or allergens. Smith points to the fact that gene insertion could also damage a plant's DNA in unpredictable ways. For example, when scientists were working with the soybean plant, the process of inserting the foreign gene damaged a section of the plant's own DNA, "scrambling its genetic code" (105). The sequence of the gene that was inserted had inexplicably rearranged itself over time. The protein the gene creates as a result of this rearrangement is likely to be different, and since this new protein has not been evaluated for safety, it could be harmful or toxic (105).

> Direct quotation of a phrase from a cited work

In *Genetically Modified Food: A Short Guide for the Confused*, Andy Rees argues a similar point: genetically modified foods carry unpredictable health risks. He cites the 1989 incident in which bacteria genetically modified to produce large amounts of the food supplement L-tryptophan "yielded impressively toxic contaminants that killed 37 people, partially paralyzed 1,500 and temporarily disabled 5,000 in the US" (75). Rees also argues that genetically modified foods have possible carcinogenic effects: "Given the huge complexity of genetic coding, even in very simple organisms such as bacteria, no one can possibly predict the overall, long-term effects of GM [genetically modified] foods on the health of those who eat them" (78). Rees cites the 1999 study on male rats fed genetically modified potatoes, explaining that the genetically modified potatoes had "a powerful effect on the lining of the gut (stomach, small bowel, and colon)" leading to a proliferation of cells, which according to histopathologist Stanley Ewen, is then likely to "act on any polyp present in the colon . . . and drastically accelerate the development of cancer in susceptible persons" (qtd. in Rees 78).

    In addition to the health risks involved in consuming genetically modified foods, some experts also argue that such foods will not benefit farmers in developing countries but will aid big corporations here in the United States. In "The Emperor's New Crops," Brian Halweil brings up the fact that global sales for genetically modified crops grew from seventy-five million dollars

Three ellipsis points mark an omission in quoted material.

in 1995 to one and a half billion dollars in 1998. Genetically modified crops are obviously lucrative for large companies. In addition, of the fifty-six transgenic products approved for commercial planting in 1998, thirty-three belonged to just four corporations (Halweil 256).

The spread of genetic engineering can change power relations between nations (Cook 3). The big American corporations that sell genetically modified seeds can hold power over the governments of developing countries, hindering their further economic development. Because all transgenic seeds are patented, it is illegal for farmers to practice "seed saving" (reserving a certain amount of seeds from the harvest to plant in the next growing season). Farmers thus have to depend entirely on the big corporations for their seeds. Since these corporations have a monopoly on genetically modified seeds, the prices for these seeds are likely to remain high, and poor farmers are unlikely to be able to afford them. Genetically altered seeds can then become just one more way that rich countries and their corporations exploit the people of developing countries. Thus, genetic engineering could become one more way of hindering the development of poor countries—not the opportunity for economic improvement and increased social equality that its proponents claim it is. Unscrupulous companies could also use the economic vulnerability of developing countries to develop and test genetically modified products that have been rejected in the United States or Europe (Newell 68), thereby rendering harm to people in developing countries.

With many concerned about the health risks associated with GMOs, international organizations such as Greenpeace and Friends of the Earth have advocated food labeling, believing that consumers should have the right to choose whether or not to buy and expose themselves to the risks associated with consuming GMOs (Huffman 3). The FDA, however, contends that scientific studies "detect no substantial difference between food from traditional crops and GM crops" (*Federal Register*) and regards genetic modification as not altering the product enough to require labeling. Interestingly, one of the reasons for not labeling genetically modified food is the concern that consumers will shun the products with the GMO label, and thus the industry producing genetic modifications will suffer (Weirich 17). The interests of corporate giants, therefore, appear to be able to influence decision making in the United States, where the government and economy are comparatively strong. The impact of corporations on the governments of poorer countries, then, is likely to be much more pronounced, and poorer countries are likely to be victimized by big corporations.

Moreover, there is some evidence that genetically modified foods do not live up to their promise and, therefore, lack the

The writer continues to explore both sides of the controversy.

benefits that could help farmers in poor countries. Rees argues that genetically modified crops will not be able to ameliorate world hunger. Rather, he believes that more than enough food is produced to feed everyone in the world without these crops and that people go hungry because they cannot afford to buy from the plenty around them for socioeconomic reasons (49). Rees also argues that genetically modified crops have not increased farmers' incomes, regardless of what proponents of genetic engineering may claim. He points to a 2003 study by Professor Caroline Saunders at Lincoln University, New Zealand, which found that "GM food releases have not benefited producers anywhere in the world" and that "the soil association's 2002 'Seeds of Doubt' report, created with feedback from farmers and data from six years of commercial farming in North America, shows that GM soy and maize crops deliver less income to farmers (on average) than non-GM crops" (50-51). The potential benefit of genetically modified crops thus remains uncertain.

While proponents of genetic engineering insist that genetically modified crops can increase yield and help feed the hungry, opponents point to health risks and challenge the research that appears to prove that genetically modified foods are beneficial. However, even if genetically modified crops do prove to be as beneficial as proponents claim, there is nothing to ensure that this technology would benefit poor farmers in developing countries. Since large corporations hold patents on all genetically modified seeds, there is nothing to guarantee that poor farmers would have access to these seeds, no matter how advanced or beneficial the technology turns out to be. As of now, developing countries continue to be at a disadvantage despite the creation and wide distribution of genetically modified crops. Therefore, it is far from certain whether this new technology will benefit developing nations in the dramatic way that proponents of genetic engineering assert.

The writer's conclusion is drawn from research reported on the previous pages.

Notes

1. There is some concern, however, about the long-term effects of crops genetically engineered for pest resistance. Since these plants are engineered to continually produce a form of the pesticide used to combat the pest problem, insects are constantly exposed to the chemical used to kill them. Such exposure increases the likelihood that the insects will develop a tolerance for this chemical, making the pesticide ineffective.

2. The main difference between genetic engineering and the breeding of plants for desired traits that people have practiced for thousands of years is that genetic engineering actually alters the DNA of a particular plant. Traditional breeding cannot alter the DNA of an individual plant but instead seeks to increase the number of plants that have a trait that occurs naturally. While the end product of both genetic engineering and selective breeding is similar in that both produce plants with desirable traits, the actual processes are radically different.

Works Cited

Brossard, Dominique, James Shanahan, and T. Clint Nesbitt, eds. *The Public, the Media, and Agricultural Biotechnology*. Cambridge: CABI, 2007. Print.

Cook, Guy. *Genetically Modified Language: The Discourse of Arguments for GM Crops and Food*. New York: Routledge, 2005. Print.

Easton, Thomas A., ed. *Taking Sides: Clashing Views on Controversial Environmental Issues*. 11th ed. Dubuque: McGraw, 2005. Print.

Federal Register 54.104 (1992): 22991. Print.

Fukuda-Parr, Sakiko, ed. *The Gene Revolution: GM Crops and Unequal Development*. Sterling: Earthscan, 2007. Print.

Halweil, Brian. "The Emperor's New Crops." Easton 249-59.

Huffman, W. E. "Production, Identity Preservation, and Labeling in a Marketplace with Genetically Modified and Non-Genetically Modified Foods." *Plant Physiology* 134 (2004): 3-10. Web. 5 Nov. 2007.

Newell, Peter. "Corporate Power and 'Bounded Autonomy' in the Global Politics of Biotechnology." *The International Politics of Genetically Modified Food: Diplomacy, Trade, and Law*. Ed. Robert Falkner. Hampshire: Palgrave, 2007. 67-84. Print.

Rees, Andy. *Genetically Modified Food: A Short Guide for the Confused*. Ann Arbor: Pluto, 2006. Print.

Royal Society et al. "Transgenic Plants and World Agriculture." Easton 234-45.

Smith, Jeffrey M. "Genetically Modified Food Threatens Human Health." *Humanity's Future*. Ed. Louise I. Gerdes. Detroit: Gale, 2006. 103-08. Print.

Weirich, Paul, ed. *Labeling Genetically Modified Food: The Philosophical and Legal Debate*. New York: Oxford UP, 2007. Print.

34 APA Documentation

The American Psychological Association (APA) publishes a style guide entitled *Publication Manual of the American Psychological Association.* Its documentation system (called an *author-date system*) is used in psychology and many other disciplines, including education, economics, and sociology.

34a APA-style in-text citations

APA-style in-text citations usually include just the last name(s) of the author(s) of the work and the year of publication. However, be sure to specify the page number(s) for any quotations you use in your paper. The abbreviation *p.* (for "page") or *pp.* (for "pages") should precede the number(s). If you do not know the author's name, use a shortened version of the source's title instead. The following examples are representative of the types of in-text citations you can expect to use.

Directory of APA-Style Parenthetical Citations

1. Work by one author 338
2. Work by two authors 338
3. Work by more than two authors 338
4. Anonymous work 339
5. Two or more works by different authors in the same parenthetical citation 339
6. Two or more works by the same author in the same parenthetical citation 339
7. Personal communication 340
8. Indirect source 340

1. Work by one author

Yang (2006) admits that speech, when examined closely, is a "remarkably messy means of communication" (p. 13).

OR

When examined closely, speech is "a remarkably messy means of communication" (Yang, 2006, p. 13).

Use commas to separate the author's name from the date and the date from the page number. Include page numbers only when quoting from the source.

2. Work by two authors

Darvas and Walsh (2002) claim that, regardless of whether children spend time in day care, their development in early childhood is determined primarily by the nature of the care they receive from parents.

OR

Regardless of whether children spend time in day care, their development in early childhood is determined primarily by the nature of the care they receive from parents (Darvas & Walsh, 2002).

When the authors' names are in parentheses, use an ampersand (&) to separate them.

3. Work by more than two authors

The speech of Pittsburgh, Pennsylvania, is called *Pittsburghese* (Johnstone, Bhasin, & Wittkofski, 2002).

For works with three to five authors, cite all the authors the first time the work is referred to, but in subsequent references give only the last name of the first author followed by *et al.* (meaning "and others").

According to Johnstone et al. (2002), newspapers published in Pittsburgh frequently use nonstandard spelling to represent the pronunciation of /aw/.

For works with six or more authors, provide only the last name of the first author followed by *et al.* in both the first and subsequent citations.

4. Anonymous work

Use a shortened version of the title to identify an anonymous work.

Chronic insomnia often requires medical intervention ("Sleep," 2009).

This citation refers to an article identified in the bibliography as "Sleep disorders: Standard methods of treatment."
If the word *Anonymous* is used in the source itself to designate the author, it appears in place of an author's name.

The documents could damage the governor's reputation (Anonymous, 2009).

5. Two or more works by different authors in the same parenthetical citation

Smokers frequently underestimate the long-term effects of smoking (O'Conner, 2005; Polson & Truss, 2007).

Arrange the citations in alphabetical order, using a semicolon to separate them.

6. Two or more works by the same author in the same parenthetical citation

The amygdala is active when a person experiences fear or anger (Carey, 2001, 2002).

Jameson (2007a, 2007b) has proposed an anxiety index for use by counselors.

Order the publication dates of works by the same author from earliest to most recent; however, if the works have the same publication date, distinguish the dates with lowercase letters (a, b, c, and so on) assigned according to the order in which the entries for the works are listed in your bibliography.

7. Personal communication

State educational outcomes are often interpreted differently by teachers in the same school (J. K. Jurgensen, personal communication, May 4, 2009).

Letters, memos, e-mail messages, interviews, and telephone conversations are cited in the text only, not in the reference list.

8. Indirect source

Korovessis (2002, p. 63) points out Toqueville's description of the "strange melancholy" exhibited by citizens living amid abundance.

Toqueville (as cited in Korovessis, 2002, p. 63) observed the "strange melancholy" exhibited by citizens living amid abundance.

In the reference list, include a bibliographic entry for the source read, not for the original source. Use an indirect source only when you are unable to obtain the original.

34b APA-style reference list

All of the works you cite should be listed at the end of your paper, beginning on a separate page with the heading "References." The following tips will help you prepare your list.

TIPS FOR PREPARING A REFERENCE LIST

- Center the heading "References" one inch from the top of the page.
- Include entries for only those sources you explicitly cite in your paper but not for personal communications or original works cited in indirect sources.
- Arrange the list of works alphabetically by the author's last name or by the last name of the first author.
- If you use more than one work by the same author(s), arrange the entries according to the date of publication, placing the entry with the earliest date first. If two or more works by the same author(s) have the same publication date, the entries are arranged so that the titles of the works are in alphabetical order, according to the first important word in each title; lowercase letters are then added to the date (e.g., 2008a, 2008b) to distinguish the works.
- When an author's name appears both in a single-author entry and as the first name in a multiple-author entry, place the single-author entry first.
- For a work without an author, alphabetize the entry according to the first important word in the title.
- Type the first line of each entry flush with the left margin and indent subsequent lines one-half inch or five spaces (a hanging indent).
- Double-space between lines of each entry and between entries.

Directory of APA-Style Entries for the Reference List

BOOKS

1. Book by one author 343
2. Book by two or more authors 345
3. Book with editor(s) 345
4. Book with a corporate or group author 345
5. Edition after the first 346
6. Translation 346
7. Multivolume work 346
8. Government report 346
9. Selection from an edited book 347
10. Selection from a reference book 347

ARTICLES IN PRINT

11. Article with one author in a journal with continuous pagination 348
12. Article with two authors in a journal with each issue paginated separately 349
13. Article with three to seven authors 349
14. Article with more than seven authors 349
15. Article in a monthly, biweekly, or weekly magazine 349
16. Article in a newspaper 349
17. Letter to the editor 350
18. Book review 350

SOURCES PRODUCED FOR ACCESS BY COMPUTER

19. Online journal article with a Digital Object Identifier (DOI) 352
20. Online journal article without a DOI 352
21. Online magazine article based on a print source 352
22. Online magazine article not found in print 352
23. Article in an online newspaper 352

24. Online book 353
25. Online book chapter 353
26. Web log posting 353
27. Lecture notes posted online 353
28. Authored document from a Web site 354
29. Online document with no identified author 354
30. Personal communication 354
31. Online encyclopedia 354
32. Online consumer brochure 354
33. Online report from a professional organization 355

OTHER SOURCES

34. Motion picture 355
35. Television program 355

BOOKS

When preparing an entry for the reference list, be sure to copy the bibliographic information directly from the title page of a book (see fig. 34.1).

1. Book by one author

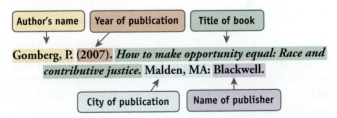

Invert the author's last name and his or her initials; place a comma after the last name. Capitalize only the first word

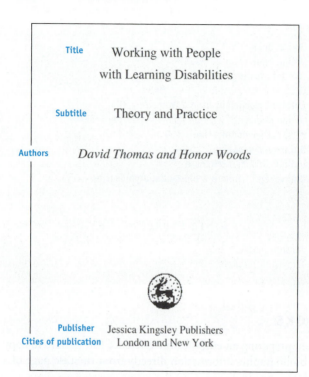

Figure 34.1. The title page of a book provides most of the information necessary for creating a bibliographic entry for a research paper.

and any proper nouns in the title and subtitle (if there is one). Italicize both title and subtitle. Include the city of publication and the United States Postal Service two-letter state abbreviation.

2. Book by two or more authors

Thomas, D., & Woods, H. (2003). *Working with people with disabilities: Theory and practice*. London, England: Jessica Kingsley.

Invert the last names and initials of all authors. Use a comma after each last name and after each set of initials except the last. Use an ampersand (in addition to the comma) before the last author's name. If there are more than seven authors, list the first six names followed by a comma and three ellipsis points and then the last author's name. When a work has been published in a city outside the United States, include the name of the country.

3. Book with editor(s)

Wolfe, D. A., & Mash, E. J. (Eds.). (2005). *Behavioral and emotional disorders in adolescents: Nature, assessment, and treatment*. New York, NY: Guilford Press.

Provide only enough of the publisher's name so that it can be identified clearly. Omit words such as *Publishers* and abbreviations such as *Inc.* However, include *Books* and *Press* when they are part of the publisher's name.

4. Book with a corporate or group author

U.S. War Department. (2003). *Official military atlas of the Civil War*. New York, NY: Barnes & Noble.

When the author and the publisher of a book are the same, use the publisher's name at the beginning of the entry and *Author* at the end.

American Psychiatric Association. (1995). *American Psychiatric Association capitation handbook*. Washington, DC: Author.

5. Edition after the first

Lycan, W., & Prinz, J. (Eds.). (2008). *Mind and cognition* (3rd ed.). Malden, MA: Blackwell.

If a work has an editor or editors, include the abbreviation *Ed.* for "editor" or *Eds.* for "editors." Identify the edition in parentheses immediately after the title. Use abbreviations: *2nd, 3rd,* and so on for the edition number and *ed.* for "edition."

6. Translation

Rank, O. (2002). *Psychology and the soul: A study of the origin, conceptual evolution, and nature of the soul* (G. C. Richter & E. J. Lieberman, Trans.). Baltimore, MD: Johns Hopkins University Press. (Original work published 1930)

A period follows the name of the publisher but not the parenthetical note about the original publication date.

7. Multivolume work

Doyle, A. C. (2003). *The complete Sherlock Holmes* (Vols. 1–2). New York, NY: Barnes & Noble.

If the multivolume work was published over a period of more than one year, use the range of years for the publication date.

Hawthorne, N. (1962–1997). *The centenary edition of the works of Nathaniel Hawthorne* (Vols. 1–23). Columbus: Ohio University Press.

If the publisher is a university press whose name mentions a state, do not include the state abbreviation.

8. Government report

Executive Office of the President. (2003). *Economic report of the President, 2003* (GPO Publication No. 040-000-0760-1). Washington, DC: U.S. Government Printing Office.

9. Selection from an edited book

Empson, R. (2007). Enlivened memories: Recalling absence and loss in Mongolia. In J. Carsten (Ed.), *Ghosts of memory: Essays on remembrance and relatedness* (pp. 58–82). Malden, MA: Blackwell.

Italicize the book title but not the title of the selection.

10. Selection from a reference book

Wickens, D. (2001). Classical conditioning. In *The Corsini encyclopedia of psychology and behavioral science* (Vol. 1, pp. 293–298). New York, NY: John Wiley.

ARTICLES IN PRINT

11. Article with one author in a journal with continuous pagination

Italicize the name of the journal; capitalize all major words, as well as any other words consisting of four or more letters. Do not italicize the title of the article; capitalize only the first word of the title and subtitle (if there is one) and any proper nouns. Figure 34.2 shows where the information for this type of entry is found on the first page of an article.

Title — Tricksters and the Marketing of Breakfast Cereals

Author — THOMAS GREEN

BREAKFAST CEREALS ARE SOLD BY TRICKSTERS. FROM LUCKY THE Leprechaun to the Cookie Crook to the mischievous live-action squirrels who vend General Mills Honey Nut Clusters, an astounding number of Saturday morning television commercials feature 30-second dramatizations of trickster tales that are designed to promote breakfast cereals. True, breakfast cereals are not the only products sold by tricksters, and not all cereals are sold by tricksters—especially in the last decade. But the association is common enough to persist as an unexamined assumption that seems obvious to most Americans once it is pointed out. Naturally, breakfast cereals are often sold by animated tricksterish mascot characters, and naturally such commercials feature motifs and narrative patterns that are common in trickster tales. But the perception of an inherent internal logic in this scheme overlooks a couple of key questions. Why, for example, are tricksters considered a particularly appropriate or effective means of marketing breakfast cereals? And why breakfast cereals in particular (and a few other breakfast products), almost to the exclusion of tricksters in other types of marketing campaigns? The answers to these questions, it turns out, may lie back in the semi-mystical, pseudoreligious origins of prepared breakfast foods and the mating of the mythology of those foods with the imperatives of the competitive, prepared-foods marketplace.

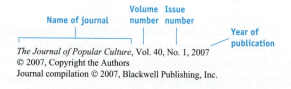

The Journal of Popular Culture, Vol. 40, No. 1, 2007
© 2007, Copyright the Authors
Journal compilation © 2007, Blackwell Publishing, Inc.

Figure 34.2. The first page of a journal article provides the information needed to complete a bibliographic entry for that source.

12. Article with two authors in a journal with each issue paginated separately

Rudisill, J. R., & Edwards, J. M. (2002). Coping with job transitions. *Consulting Psychology Journal, 54*(1), 55–62.

When you use an article from a journal paginated separately (that is, a journal whose every issue begins on page 1), provide the issue number (placed in parentheses) directly after the volume number (italicized). Do not insert a space between the volume and issue numbers.

13. Article with three to seven authors

Frost, R. O., Steketee, G., & Williams, L. (2002). Compulsive buying, compulsive hoarding, and obsessive-compulsive disorder. *Behavior Therapy, 33*(2), 201–213.

14. Article with more than seven authors

Reddy, S. K., Arora, M., Perry, C. L., Nair, B., Kohli, A., Lytle, L. A., … Stigler, M. (2002). Tobacco and alcohol use outcomes of a school-based intervention in New Delhi. *American Journal of Health Behavior, 26,* 173–181.

15. Article in a monthly, biweekly, or weekly magazine

Winson, J. (2002, June). The meaning of dreams. *Scientific American, 12,* 54–61.

For monthly publications, provide both the year and the month, separated by a comma. For magazines published weekly or biweekly, add the day of the issue: (2003, May 8).

16. Article in a newspaper

Simon, S. (2007, October 14). Winning hearts, minds, homes. *Los Angeles Times,* p. A1.

Include both the section letter and the page number.

17. Letter to the editor

Mancall, M. (2002, June 17). Answer to cynicism [Letter to the editor]. *The New York Times,* p. A20.

Indicate within brackets that the work is a letter to the editor.

18. Book review

Orford, J. (2007). Drug addiction and families [Review of the book *Drug addiction and families*]. *Addiction, 102,* 1841–1842.

If the review has its own title, use that instead of the title of the book. Retain the bracketed information.

SOURCES PRODUCED FOR ACCESS BY COMPUTER

The APA guidelines for electronic sources are similar to those for print sources. Exceptions are explained after the sample entries that follow. Information about when and/or how a source was retrieved appears at the end of the entry. The period that normally ends an entry is omitted after a URL because it could cause difficulty in retrieving a file. If a URL has to continue on a new line, break it before a punctuation mark or other special character. Note that many scholarly journals now use a Digital Object Identifier (DOI) to simplify searching for an article. Whenever possible, use a DOI (without a period following it) instead of a URL at the end of an entry. The DOI will appear on the first page of the article, which usually contains the abstract. Figure 34.3 shows the location of a DOI and other pertinent bibliographic information on the first page of an online journal article.

Journal of Experimental Psychology: Applied
2001, Vol. 7, No. 1, 27–50

Copyright 2001 by the American Psychological Association, Inc.
1076-898X/01/S5.00 DOI: 10.1037//1076-898X.7.1.27

Children's Eyewitness Reports After Exposure to Misinformation From Parents

Debra Ann Poole
Central Michigan University

D. Stephen Lindsay
University of Victoria

> This study examined how misleading suggestions from parents influenced children's eyewitness reports. Children (3 to 8 years old) participated in science demonstrations, listened to their parents read a story that described experienced and nonexperienced events, and subsequently discussed the science experience in two follow-up interviews. Many children described fictitious events in response to open-ended prompts, and there were no age differences in suggestibility during this phase of the interview. Accuracy declined markedly in response to direct questions, especially for the younger children. Although the older children retracted many of their false reports after receiving source-monitoring instructions, the younger children did not. Path analyses indicated that acquiescence, free recall, and source monitoring all contribute to mediating patterns of suggestibility across age. Results indicate that judgments about the accuracy of children's testimony must consider the possibility of exposure to misinformation prior to formal interviews.

During the past decade, there has been keen interest in young children's performance when interviewed about autobiographical events. This interest was sharpened by broad social changes that led the public to be more concerned about crimes to which child victims are often the sole witnesses (e.g., child sexual abuse), but it also reflected a movement in psychology away from relatively artificial research paradigms (e.g., studies of memory for word lists) and toward more naturalistic and multifaceted approaches to research. Although the field of eyewitness testimony receives considerable attention for its forensic implications, researchers increasingly view eyewitness paradigms as tools for studying basic issues in memory and cognition.

There have been several recent reviews of the literature on interviewing children for forensic purposes (e.g., Ceci & Bruck, 1995; Poole & Lamb, 1998), and we do not offer an exhaustive recapitulation here. In its broadest outlines, the literature can be crudely summarized by saying that even very young children (i.e., 3- to 4-year-olds) can provide quite detailed and accurate accounts of past autobiographical events under some conditions but that even older children and adults often provide impoverished and inaccurate accounts under others. The aim of the current research was to provide additional insight into factors that compromise or enhance the amount and accuracy of the information interviewers gain from young children. Borrowing terms from Wells's (1993) analysis of eyewitness suspect identification, our research examined both "system variables" (i.e., factors that are under the control of investigators in forensic cases, such as the way questions are phrased) and "estimator variables" (i.e., factors that may affect the amount or accuracy of information children report but that cannot be

Figure 34.3. First page of an online journal article.

19. Online journal article with a Digital Object Identifier (DOI)

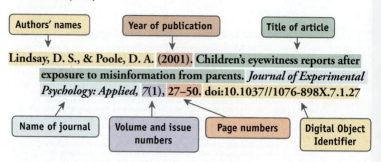

20. Online journal article without a DOI

Tuladhar-Douglas, W. (2007). Leaf blowers and antibiotics: A Buddhist stance for science and technology. *Journal of Buddhist Ethics, 14,* 200–238. Retrieved from http://www.buddhistethics.org

If there is no DOI, use the URL for the journal's home page instead of the URL for the article.

21. Online magazine article based on a print source

Acocella, J. (2008, May 26). A few too many. *The New Yorker, 84*(15), 32–37. Retrieved from http://www.newyorker.com

22. Online magazine article not found in print

Saletan, W. (2008, August 27). Unfinished race: Race, genes, and the future of medicine. *Slate.* Retrieved from http://www.slate.com

23. Article in an online newspaper

McGrath, C. (2002, June 15). Father time. *The New York Times.* Retrieved from http://nytimes.com

24. Online book

Stevens, K. (n.d.). *The dreamer and the beast*. Available from http://www
.onlineoriginals.com/showitem.asp?itemID=321&action=setvar&vartype
=history&varname=bookmark&v1=1&v2=46&v3=1

If access to an online book is not free, use "Available from" instead of "Retrieved from."

25. Online book chapter

Wallner, F., & Durnwalder, K. (1994). Sciences, psychology and realism. In
V. Shen, R. Knowles, & T. Van Doan (Eds.), *Psychology, phenomenology
and Chinese philosophy. Chinese philosophical studies: Vol. 6.* Retrieved
from http://www.crvp.org/book/Series03/III-6/chapter_i__science.htm

If a DOI has been provided, use the DOI instead of the URL.

26. Web log posting

Chatham, C. (2008, August 29). Action without intention: Parietal damage
alters attention awareness. [Web log message]. Retrieved from
http://scienceblogs.com/developingintelligence/2008/08/action
_without_intention_parie.php

27. Lecture notes posted online

Wolfe, J. (2004). *Lecture 18: Freud and fairy tales* [Lecture notes]. Retrieved
from http://ocw.mit.edu/OcwWeb/Brain-and-Cognitive-Sciences
/9-00Fall-2004/LectureNotes/index.htm

28. Authored document from a Web site

Darling, C. (2002). *Guide to grammar and writing*. Retrieved from Capital
 Community College Web site: http://cctc2.commnet.edu/grammar
 /modifiers.htm

Provide the name of the host organization before the URL only when the document is from a large Web site, such as one sponsored by a university or government body.

29. Online document with no identified author

American School Counselor Association. (2006). *Position statement:
 Equity for all students*. Retrieved from http://asca2.timberlakepublishing
 .com/content.asp?contentid=503

Use the name of the organization hosting the Web site as the author of the document. If a date for the document is provided, place it in parentheses. If no date is listed, use the abbreviation *n.d.* The URL is located at either the top or the bottom of a printout.

30. Personal communication

Personal communications such as e-mail messages, letters, interviews, and telephone conversations are not included in the reference list but should be cited in the text as follows: (S. L. Johnson, personal communication, September 3, 2003).

31. Online encyclopedia

Dowe, P. (2007). Causal processes. In E. N. Zalta (Ed.), *The Stanford
 encyclopedia of philosophy* (Fall 2008 ed.). Retrieved from
 http://plato.stanford.edu/archives/sum2007/entries/cognitive-science/

32. Online consumer brochure

American Psychological Association. (2008). Elder abuse and neglect: In search
 of solutions. Retrieved from http://www.apa.org/pi/aging/eldabuse.html

33. Online report from a professional organization

Yones, M. (n.d.). Psychology of happiness and unhappiness. Retrieved
 from International Institute of Management: http://www.iim-edu
 .org/executivejournal/index.htm

OTHER SOURCES

34. Motion picture

Smith, M. (Producer/Writer), & Gaviria, M. (Producer/Director). (2001).
 Medicating kids [Motion picture]. United States: Public Broadcasting
 Service.

Begin with the primary contributor(s), identifying the nature of the contribution. Then provide the release date, the title, and the descriptive label in square brackets. End by indicating the country where the movie was produced and the name of the studio.

35. Television program

Holt, S. (Producer). (2002, October 1). *The mysterious lives of caves*
 [Television broadcast]. Alexandria, VA: Public Broadcasting Service.

Give the title of the program in italics. If citing an entire series (e.g., *Nova*), cite the producer for the series as a whole. Use the descriptive label *Television series* in the square brackets.

34c Sample APA-style paper

The APA recognizes that a paper may have to be modified so that it adheres to an instructor's requirements. The following boxes offer tips for preparing a title page, an abstract page, and the body of a typical student paper. For tips on preparing a reference list, see 34b.

TIPS FOR PREPARING THE TITLE PAGE OF AN APA-STYLE PAPER

- The title page includes both the full title of the paper and a shortened version of it. The shortened version, along with a page number, is placed in the header. On the left side of the header, include the words "Running head:" (note the colon) and a version of your title that consists of no more than fifty characters. Use all uppercase letters for this title. On the right side of the header, insert the page number. The title page is page 1 of your paper.
- Place the full title in the upper half of the page, with your name below it. You may include your affiliation or a course name or number if your instructor requests one. Double-space these lines.

TIPS FOR PREPARING THE ABSTRACT AND THE BODY OF AN APA-STYLE PAPER

- The header for the remaining parts of the paper (including the abstract page) is similar to the header on the title page. It should have the shortened title on the left and the page number on the right; the body of the paper begins on page 3.
- Center the word "Abstract" one inch from the top of the page.
- Be sure that the abstract is no more than 250 words. For advice on summarizing, see page 273.
- Double-space throughout the body of the abstract. Do not indent the first line of the abstract.
- Center the title of the paper one inch from the top of the page.
- Use one-inch margins on both the left and right sides of all pages.
- Double-space throughout the body of the paper, indenting each paragraph one-half inch or five to seven spaces.

Running head: THE SCIENCE BEHIND AN ART   1

The Science Behind an Art:

Historical and Current Trends in Tattooing

Rachel L. Pinter and Sarah M. Cronin

Central Washington University

Abstract

Current research demonstrates that the social practice of tattooing has changed greatly over the years. Not only have the images chosen for tattoos and the demographic of people getting tattoos changed, but the ideology behind tattooing itself has evolved. This paper first briefly describes the cross-cultural history of the practice. It then examines current social trends in the United States and related ideological issues.

The Science Behind an Art: Historical and Current Trends in Tattooing

    Tattoos have existed throughout history in countless cultures. Currently, tattoos are considered popular art forms. They can be seen on men and women from all walks of life in the United States, ranging from a trainer at the local gym to a character on a television show. Due to an increase in the popularity of tattooing, studies of tattooing behavior have proliferated as researchers attempt to identify trends. This paper seeks to explore both the history of tattooing and its current practice in the United States.

    Tattooing can be found in the histories of people worldwide, though its origin is currently unknown. Krcmarik (2003) provides a helpful geographical overview. In Asia, tattooing has existed for thousands of years in Chinese, Japanese, Middle Eastern, and Indian cultures. In Europe, tattooing flourished during the 19th century, most notably in England. Many of the sailors traveling with Captain James Cook returned with tales of exotic tattooing practices and sometimes with tattoos themselves. The Samoans in the South Pacific are famous for their centuries old tattooing practice, known as *tatau*—the word from which *tattoo* is said to have originated. The Maori of New Zealand

THE SCIENCE BEHIND AN ART 4

are also well known for their hand-carved facial tattoos, known as *Moko* (see Figure 1).

In Africa, tattoos can be found on Egyptian and Nubian mummies, which date back to approximately 2000 BCE. The tattooing history of South America is noted in the written accounts of Spanish explorers' encounters with tattooed Mayans. Finally, in North America, tattooing became popular during the 1900s and has experienced advances and retreats in social acceptance since then. Starting in the 1960s, its popularity rose dramatically and continues to rise.

Figure 1. A Maori man with a facial tattoo. *Note.* Photo © Tim Graham/Getty Images.

The practice of tattooing has gained and lost popularity, often as a result of rather extreme changes in the ideologies supporting or discouraging it. This rollercoaster pattern of acceptance is well demonstrated in the United States.

Since the 19th century, the wearing of tattoos has allowed for subculture identification by such persons as sailors, bikers, circus "freak" performers, and prison inmates (DeMello, 1995). As a collective group behavior indicating deviant subculture membership, tattooing flourished during this time but remained plagued by negative associations. In the last 10 years, however, the practice has represented a more individualistic yet mainstream means of body adornment (Kosut, 2006).

> The writers discuss changing perspectives on the appropriateness of tattoos.

> Citation of a work by one author

The trend toward acceptance of tattoos may be a result of how American society views the people who wear them. Earlier, tattoos were depicted in mainstream media as worn by people with marginal status; now, they are considered to be an artful expression among celebrities as well as educated middle and upper classes, as Figure 2 illustrates (Kosut, 2006). This shift in the symbolic status of tattoos—self-expression among the social elite rather than deviant expression among the working class—has allowed tattoos to be obtained in greater numbers. Even in the workplace, where employees were often forbidden to display tattoos, employers now "take advantage of the open-mindedness and innovation that younger [tattooed] employees bring into the workplace" (Org, 2003, p. D1).

> To clarify a direct quotation from a source, the writers insert a word in square brackets.

Figure 2. Tattoos are becoming more common among middle-class professionals. *Note.* Photo © Eric Anthony Photography/Monsoon Images/PhotoLibrary.

As the acceptability of tattoos has increased, tattooing has undergone the process of commercialization that frequently occurs in American society. Tattoos are now acquired as embodied status symbols and are used to sell tattoo maintenance products, skateboards, and fashion items (Kosut, 2006). This introduction into the consumer culture allows tattoos to gain even more popularity.

Researchers have been tracking the popularity of tattoos, though no one seems able to agree on a number. In 2000, MSNBC aired a documentary called "Skin Deep," which cited the tattooing rate at 20% of the population (Rosenbaum, 2000). In 2003, citing a lower number, Harris Interactive reported that 16% of all adults in the United States have at least one tattoo (Sever, 2003). The actual number of individuals with tattoos is unknown, but most researchers believe the trend has been consistently gaining ground since the 1960s. Within the context of the larger population, statistics on the frequency of tattooing among specific age groups show a similar increase (Armstrong, Owen, Roberts, & Koch, 2002). However, due to the limitations of the various research designs, more research on a national level is needed to obtain truly representative figures.

The increase in acquisition of tattoos has resulted in trends concerning the images and locations of tattoos, which appear to be divided down lines of gender. Many of the tattoo images commonly found on men include, but are not limited to, death themes, military insignia, tribal armbands, and family crests. During the 1980s, cartoon images such as Bugs Bunny and the Tasmanian Devil were also popular for males. Males choose various locations for tattoos, but the most popular male sites are the upper back, back of the calves, and the upper arm, according to tattoo artist Ben Reames (personal communication, July 12, 2007). Conversely, females often obtain tattoos that symbolize traditional femininity, such as flowers, stars, and butterflies. A noticeable trend for females in the 1980s was the rose tattoo. Stars and butterflies now rival the rose in popularity. Popular spots for tattoos include the hip, foot (see Figure 3), and lower back.

The art of tattooing has existed in many culturally determined forms throughout human history, and its current manifestations are as varied as the cultures themselves. However, based on the current literature, the social behavior of tattooing is experiencing unparalleled growth in the United States. In fact, Kosut (2006) argues, "New generations of American children are growing up in a cultural landscape that is more tattoo-friendly and tattoo-flooded than any other time in history" (p. 1037). Because today's children see tattoos and tattoo-related products everywhere, usually in neutral or positive situations, they will likely be more accepting of tattoos than earlier generations were. Certainly, the tattooing trend shows no signs of leveling off.

Figure 3. Many females who get a tattoo choose to have it on the foot. *Note.* Photo © Color-Blind Images/Blend Images/Corbis.

References

Armstrong, M. L., Owen, D. C., Roberts, A. E., & Koch, J. R. (2002). College students and tattoos: Influence of image, identity, and family. *Journal of Psychosocial Nursing, 40*(10), 20–30.

DeMello, M. (1995). Not just for bikers anymore: Popular representations of American tattooing. *Journal of Popular Culture, 29*(3), 37–53.

Kosut, M. (2006). An ironic fad: The commodification and consumption of tattoos. *Journal of Popular Culture, 39*(6), 1035–1049.

Krcmarik, K. L. (2003). *History of tattooing*. Retrieved from Michigan State University: http://www.msu.edu/~krcmari1/individual/history.html

Org, M. (2003, August 28). The tattooed executive. *The Wall Street Journal*. Retrieved from http://online.wsj.com

Rosenbaum, S. (Executive Producer). (2000, August 20). *MSNBC investigates: Tattoos—skin deep* [Television broadcast]. New York, NY: MSNBC.

Sever, J. (2003, October 8). *A third of Americans with tattoos say they make them feel more sexy*. Retrieved from http://www.harrisinteractive.com/harris_poll/index.asp?PID=868

35 CMS Documentation

The Chicago Manual of Style (CMS), published by the University of Chicago Press, provides guidelines for writers in history and other subject areas in the humanities. Its humanities style documents sources by using either footnotes or endnotes and, for most assignments, a bibliography. CMS also has an author-date citation style used in the sciences and social sciences.

35a CMS note and bibliographic forms

According to CMS humanities style, in-text citations take the form of sequential numbers that refer to **footnotes** (notes at the bottom of each page) or **endnotes** (notes at the end of the paper). The information in these notes may be condensed if a bibliography lists all the sources used in the paper. The condensed, or short, form for a note includes only the author's last name, the title (shortened if longer than four words), and the relevant page number(s): Eggers, *Court Reporters,* 312–15.

When a paper has no bibliography, the full note form is used for the first citation of each source. For either footnotes or endnotes, place a superscript number in the text wherever documentation of a source is necessary. The number should be as close as possible to whatever it refers to, following most punctuation that appears at the end of the direct quotation or paraphrase but preceding a dash.

TIPS FOR PREPARING FOOTNOTES

- Most word-processing programs will footnote your paper automatically. In Microsoft Word, pull down the Insert menu and choose Footnote. A superscript number will appear in the cursor's position. A box will also appear at the bottom of your page, in which you can insert the requisite information.
- Each note begins with a full-size number followed by a period and a space.
- Indent the first line of a note five spaces.
- Single-space lines within a footnote.
- Double-space between footnotes when more than one appears on a page.
- Use the abbreviation *Ibid.* (not italicized) to indicate that the source cited in an entry is identical to the one in the preceding entry. Include page numbers if they differ from those in the preceding entry: Ibid., 331–32.
- No bibliography is necessary when the footnotes provide complete bibliographic information for all sources.

TIPS FOR PREPARING ENDNOTES

- Place endnotes on a separate page, following the last page of the body of the paper and preceding the bibliography (if one is included).
- Center the word *Notes* (not italicized) at the top of the page.
- Use the abbreviation *Ibid.* (not italicized) to indicate that a source cited in an entry is identical to the one in the preceding entry. Include page numbers if they differ from those in the preceding entry: Ibid., 331–32.

- Indent the first line of a note five spaces.
- Single-space within an endnote and leave one blank line between endnotes.
- No bibliography is necessary when the endnotes provide complete bibliographic information for all sources used in the paper.

TIPS FOR PREPARING A BIBLIOGRAPHY

- Start the bibliography on a separate page, following the last page of the body of the paper if footnotes are used or following the last page of endnotes.
- Center the word *Bibliography* (not italicized) at the top of your paper.
- Alphabetize entries in the bibliography according to the author's last name.
- If a source has more than one author, alphabetize by the last name of the first author.
- For a work without an author, alphabetize the entry according to the first important word in the title.
- To indicate that a source has the same author(s) as in the preceding entry, begin an entry with a three-em dash (———) instead of the name(s) of the author(s). (If you do not know how to create this mark, search for *em dash,* using the Help function of your word processor.)
- Indent the second and subsequent lines of an entry five spaces (that is, use a hanging indent).
- Single-space within an entry and leave one blank line between entries.

Directory of CMS Note and Bibliographic Forms

BOOKS

1. Book with one author   370
2. Book with two authors   371
3. Book with three authors   371
4. Book with more than three authors   372
5. Book with an editor   372
6. Book with an author and an editor   372
7. Translated book   373
8. Edition after the first   373
9. One volume in a multivolume work   373
10. Government document   374
11. Selection from an anthology   374
12. Published letter   375
13. Indirect source   375

ARTICLES

14. Article in a journal   376
15. Article in a popular (general-circulation) magazine   376
16. Article from an online journal   376
17. Article from a journal database   377
18. Article from an online magazine   377
19. Newspaper article   378

OTHER SOURCES

20. Interview   379
21. Videocassette or DVD   379

BOOKS

1. Book with one author

Full note form

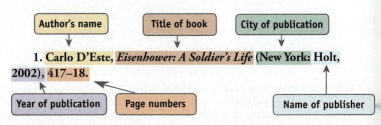

1. Carlo D'Este, *Eisenhower: A Soldier's Life* (New York: Holt, 2002), 417–18.

Provide the author's full name, in normal order, followed by a comma. The city of publication, publisher, and date of publication are all within parentheses. Italicize the titles of books, magazines, journals, and films. Capitalize all major words.

Short note form

1. D'Este, *Eisenhower*, 417–18.

Bibliographic form

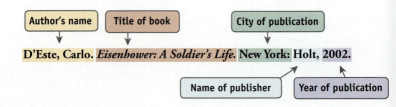

D'Este, Carlo. *Eisenhower: A Soldier's Life*. New York: Holt, 2002.

Provide the author's full name, last name first, followed by a comma and the first name. Provide either the full name of the publisher or an abbreviated version. The style chosen must be used consistently throughout the notes and the bibliography. End the entry with a period.

2. Book with two authors

Full note form

2. Cathy Scott-Clark and Adrian Levy, *The Stone of Heaven* (Boston: Little, Brown, 2001), 28.

Use the word *and* between the authors' names.

Bibliographic form

Scott-Clark, Cathy, and Adrian Levy. *The Stone of Heaven.* Boston: Little, Brown, 2001.

Invert the first author's name and follow it with a comma, the word *and* (not italicized), and the second author's name in normal order. The second and subsequent lines of an entry are indented five spaces.

3. Book with three authors

Full note form

3. Karen A. Foss, Sonja K. Foss, and Cindy L. Griffin, *Feminist Rhetorical Theories* (Thousand Oaks, CA: Sage, 1999).

Bibliographic form

Foss, Karen A., Sonja K. Foss, and Cindy L. Griffin. *Feminist Rhetorical Theories.* Thousand Oaks, CA: Sage, 1999.

Only the first author's name is inverted. If the city of publication is not widely known, include a two-letter state abbreviation.

4. Book with more than three authors

Full note form

4. Mike Palmquist et al., *Transitions: Teaching Writing in Computer-Supported and Traditional Classrooms* (Greenwich, CT: Ablex, 1998), 153.

In a note use the first person's name followed by the Latin phrase *et al.* or *and others,* its English translation. Neither phrase is italicized. Include all authors' names in the bibliographic form.

Bibliographic form

Palmquist, Mike, Kate Kiefer, James Hartvigsen, and Barbara Goodlew. *Transitions: Teaching Writing in Computer-Supported and Traditional Classrooms.* Greenwich, CT: Ablex, 1998.

5. Book with an editor

Full note form

5. Hanna Schissler, ed., *The Miracle Years* (Princeton, NJ: Princeton Univ. Press, 2001).

Place the abbreviation *ed.* after the editor's name.

Bibliographic form

Schissler, Hanna, ed. *The Miracle Years.* Princeton, NJ: Princeton Univ. Press, 2001.

6. Book with an author and an editor

Full note form

6. Ayn Rand, *The Art of Fiction,* ed. Tore Boeckmann (New York: Plume, 2000).

Use the abbreviation *ed.* for "edited by."

Bibliographic form

Rand, Ayn. *The Art of Fiction.* Edited by Tore Boeckmann. New York: Plume, 2000.

Write out the words *Edited by.*

7. Translated book

Full note form

7. Murasaki Shikibu, *The Tale of Genji,* trans. Royall Tyler (New York: Viking, 2001).

Use the abbreviation *trans.* for "translated by."

Bibliographic form

Shikibu, Murasaki. *The Tale of Genji.* Translated by Royall Tyler. New York: Viking, 2001.

Write out the words *Translated by.*

8. Edition after the first

Full note form

8. Edward O. Wilson, *On Human Nature,* 14th ed. (Cambridge: Harvard Univ. Press, 2001).

Bibliographic form

Wilson, Edward O. *On Human Nature.* 14th ed. Cambridge: Harvard Univ. Press, 2001.

9. One volume in a multivolume work

Full note form

9. Thomas Cleary, *Classics of Buddhism and Zen,* vol. 3 (Boston: Shambhala Publications, 2001), 116.

Bibliographic form

Cleary, Thomas. *Classics of Buddhism and Zen.* Vol. 3. Boston: Shambhala Publications, 2001.

10. Government document

Full note form

10. US Bureau of the Census, *Statistical Abstract of the United States,* 120th ed. (Washington, DC, 2001), 16.

Bibliographic form

US Bureau of the Census. *Statistical Abstract of the United States.* 120th ed. Washington, DC, 2001.

11. Selection from an anthology

Full note form

11. Elizabeth Spencer, "The Everlasting Light," in *The Cry of an Occasion,* ed. Richard Bausch (Baton Rouge: Louisiana State Univ. Press, 2001), 171–82.

If you are citing information from a specific page or pages of a book or an article, place the page number(s) at the end of the note.

Bibliographic form

Spencer, Elizabeth. "The Everlasting Light." In *The Cry of an Occasion,* edited by Richard Bausch, 171–82. Baton Rouge: Louisiana State Univ. Press, 2001.

Use quotation marks to enclose the titles of selections from anthologies. The title is followed by a comma in the note form or by a period in the bibliographic form.

When only one selection from an anthology is used, inclusive page numbers precede the publication data in the bibliographic entry.

12. Published letter

Full note form

12. Lincoln to George McClellan, Washington, DC, 13 October 1862, in *This Fiery Trial: The Speeches and Writings of Abraham Lincoln,* ed. William E. Gienapp (New York: Oxford Univ. Press, 2002), 178.

Bibliographic form

Lincoln, Abraham. Abraham Lincoln to George McClellan, Washington DC, 13 October 1862. In *This Fiery Trial: The Speeches and Writings of Abraham Lincoln,* ed. William E. Gienapp, 178. New York: Oxford Univ. Press, 2002.

13. Indirect source

Full note form

13. Toni Morrison, *Playing in the Dark* (New York: Vintage, 1992), 26, quoted in Jonathan Goldberg, *Willa Cather and Others* (Durham, NC: Duke Univ. Press, 2001), 37.

Bibliographic form

Goldberg, Jonathan. *Willa Cather and Others*. Durham, NC: Duke Univ. Press, 2001.

Morrison, Toni. *Playing in the Dark.* New York: Vintage, 1992, 26. Quoted in Goldberg, *Willa Cather and Others*, 37.

In the note cite both the original work and the secondary source in which it is quoted. In the bibliography cite the secondary source in full and the original work in a separate citation with a cross-reference.

ARTICLES

14. Article in a journal

Full note form

14. A. Schedler, "The Menu of Manipulation," *Journal of Democracy* 13, no. 2 (2002): 48.

Use initials for an author's first and middle names only when they are used in the original publication.

Bibliographic form

Schedler, A. "The Menu of Manipulation." *Journal of Democracy* 13,
   no. 2 (2002): 36–50.

15. Article in a popular (general-circulation) magazine

Full note form

15. John O'Sullivan, "The Overskeptics," *National Review,* June 17, 2002, 23.

Bibliographic form

O'Sullivan, John. "The Overskeptics." *National Review,* June 17,
   2002, 22–26.

For a magazine published monthly, include only the month and the year, with no comma inserted between them.

16. Article from an online journal

Full note form

16. Zina Peterson, "Teaching Margery and Julian in Anthropology-Based Survey Courses," *College English* 68, no. 5 (2006): 481–501, accessed May 5, 2010, doi:10.2307/25472167.

Give the DOI (digital object identifier), a permanent identifying number, when citing electronic sources you used online.

If the source does not have a DOI, list the URL (see page 378). If the material is time-sensitive or if your discipline or instructor requires it, include the access date before the DOI or URL.

Bibliographic form

Peterson, Zina. "Teaching Margery and Julian in Anthropology-Based Survey Courses." *College English* 68, no. 5 (2006): 481–501. Accessed May 5, 2010. doi:10.2307/25472167.

17. Article from a journal database

Full note form

17. Samuel Guy Inman, "The Monroe Doctrine and Hispanic America," *Hispanic America Historical Review* 4, no. 4 (1921): 635, http://www.jstor.org/stable/2505682.

If there is no DOI, give the stable URL for the article on the online database.

Bibliographic form

Inman, Samuel Guy. "The Monroe Doctrine and Hispanic America." *Hispanic America Historical Review* 4, no. 4 (1921): 635–76. http://www.jstor.org/stable/2505682.

18. Article from an online magazine

Full note form

18. Mark Frank, "Judge for Themselves: Why a Supreme Court Ruling on Sentencing Guidelines Puts More Power Back on the Bench," *Time*, January 24, 2005, http://www.time.com/time/magazine/printout/0,8816,1018063,00.html.

Bibliographic form

Frank, Mark. "Judge for Themselves: Why a Supreme Court Ruling on
   Sentencing Guidelines Puts More Power Back on the Bench."
   Time, January 24, 2005. http://www.time.com/time/magazine
   /printout/0,8816,1018063,00.html.

If the source has no DOI, cite the URL. A URL or DOI continued on a second line may be broken *after* a colon or double slash or *before* a single slash, a comma, a period, a hyphen, a question mark, a percent symbol, a number sign (#), a tilde (~), or an underscore (_). It can be broken either before or after an ampersand (&) or equals sign.

19. Newspaper article

Full note form

   19. Rick Bragg, "An Oyster and a Way of Life, Both at Risk," *New York Times,* June 15, 2002, national edition, sec. A.

Omit the initial *The* in the newspaper's name. If the city of publication is not part of the name, add it at the beginning (italicized) as part of the name: *St. Paul Pioneer Press.* If the city is not well known or could be confused with another city of the same name, add the state name or abbreviation in parentheses after the city's name. If the paper is a well-known national one, such as the *Wall Street Journal,* it is not necessary to add the city.

Bibliographic form

Bragg, Rick. "An Oyster and a Way of Life, Both at Risk." *New York Times.*
   June 15, 2002, national edition, sec. A.

If the name of the newspaper and the date of publication are mentioned in the text of the paper, no bibliographic entry is needed.

OTHER SOURCES

20. Interview

Full note form

20. Yoko Ono, "Multimedia Player: An Interview with Yoko Ono," interview by Carolyn Burriss-Krimsky, *Ruminator Review,* no. 10 (Summer 2002): 28.

Bibliographic form

Ono, Yoko. "Multimedia Player: An Interview with Yoko Ono." By Carolyn Burriss-Krimsky. *Ruminator Review,* no. 10 (Summer 2002): 26–29.

If you are required to list interviews, each entry should include the name of the person being interviewed, the title of the interview, the name of the person who conducted it, and any available publication data, online identifier, or audiovisual medium information.

21. Videocassette or DVD

Full note form

21. *Araby,* produced and directed by Dennis J. Courtney (Los Angeles: American Street Productions, 1999), videocassette (VHS).

Bibliographic form

Araby. Produced and directed by Dennis J. Courtney. Los Angeles: American Street Productions, 1999. Videocassette (VHS).

Place *Videocassette (VHS)* or *DVD* at the end of the entry.

35b Sample CMS-style paper

The following student paper by Nicole Hester addresses an important development in the civil rights movement. Because it includes a full bibliography, the endnotes are written in short form. Only the first pages of her paper, notes, and bibliography appear here. The entire paper is available on this handbook's Web site.

1

Race in the U.S. Army: An Executive

Order for Hope

While students of the civil rights movement are often familiar with the Supreme Court decision *Brown v. Board of Education,* which acknowledged the inherent inequality in separate but equal practices, that decision would not happen until 1955, nearly eight years after President Harry S. Truman issued an executive order to integrate the federal government and, in particular, the United States military. Although the earlier Thirteenth (1865), Fourteenth (1868), and Fifteenth (1870) Amendments redefined freedom, citizenship, and voting, these amendments were diluted by Supreme Court decisions in the nineteenth and early twentieth centuries. In cases like *Plessy v. Ferguson,* the court established the precedent of "separate but equal," which legally allowed the separation of races in public facilities.[1] Thus, Truman's executive order in 1948 became an important step in the long-term struggle for civil rights.

Like American schools, the United States Army was segregated, and this segregation remained in place until after the Second World War (1941–45). In July of 1948, by executive order, President Truman demanded equal treatment and equal opportunity in the armed forces, setting into motion a series of events that would force change, however slow it might be:

> It is hereby declared to be the policy of the President that there shall be equality of treatment and opportunity for all persons in the armed services without regard to race, color, religion or national origin. This policy shall be put into effect as rapidly as possible, having due regard to the time required to effectuate any necessary changes without impairing efficiency or morale.[2]

[Paper continues online.]

11

Notes

1. Plessy v. Ferguson, 163 U.S. 537 (1896).

2. Merrill, *Documentary History,* 11:741.

3. It is beyond the scope of my paper to discuss all the non-Whites who were affected by Truman's order. In this essay, I focus on the effect of Truman's order on people whom I refer to as Black.

4. Lee, *Employment of Negro Troops*, 4.

5. Ibid., 73–74.

6. Mershon and Schlossman, *Foxholes and Color Lines*, 44–45.

7. Ibid., 73–77.

8. Nalty and MacGregor, *Blacks in the Military*, 108.

9. Ibid.

10. Lee, *Employment of Negro Troops,* 141.

11. Reddick, "Negro Policy," 12.

12. Gallup, *Public Opinion 1935–1971,* 2:782–83.

13. Nalty and MacGregor, *Blacks in the Military,* 114–15.

14. Merrill, *Documentary History,* 11:741.

15. Gardner, *Truman and Civil Rights*, 114.

16. Billington, "Freedom to Serve," 273.

17. Mershon and Schlossman, *Foxholes and Color Lines,* 209.

18. Nalty and MacGregor, *Blacks in the Military,* 289.

19. Ibid., 269.

20. Mershon and Schlossman, *Foxholes and Color Lines,* 217.

[Notes continue online.]

13

Bibliography

Billington, Monroe. "Freedom to Serve: The President's Committee on Equality of Treatment and Opportunity in the Armed Forces, 1949–1950." *Journal of Negro History* (1966): 262–74. doi:10.2307/2716101.

Gallup, George H. *The Gallup Poll: Public Opinion 1935–1971.* Vol. 2. New York: Random House, 1972.

Gardner, Michael R. *Harry Truman and Civil Rights: Moral Courage and Political Risks.* Carbondale: Southern Illinois Univ. Press, 2002.

Humphrey, Hubert H. *Beyond Civil Rights: A New Day of Equality.* New York: Random House, 1968.

Lee, Ulysses. *The Employment of Negro Troops.* Washington, DC: Center of Military History, 1963.

Mayer, Kenneth. *With the Stroke of a Pen: Executive Orders and Presidential Power.* Princeton: Princeton Univ. Press, 2001.

McCullough, David. *Truman.* New York: Simon & Schuster, 1992.

Merrill, Dennis, ed. *Documentary History of the Truman Presidency.* Vol. 11. Bethesda, MD: University Publishers of America, 1996.

Mershon, Sherie, and Steven Schlossman. *Foxholes and Color Lines.* Baltimore: Johns Hopkins Univ. Press, 1998.

Nalty, Bernard C., and Morris J. MacGregor. *Blacks in the Military.* Wilmington, DE: Scholarly Resources, 1981.

[Bibliography continues online.]

36 CSE Documentation

The Council of Science Editors (CSE) has established guidelines for writers in the life and physical sciences: *Scientific Style and Format: The CSE Manual for Authors, Editors, and Publishers*, seventh edition, presents three systems for citing and documenting research sources: the citation-sequence system, the name-year system, and the citation-name system.

36a CSE citation-sequence, name-year, and citation-name systems

The citation-sequence system, the name-year system, and the citation-name system differ significantly, so be sure to know which you will be expected to use before you get started. Once you know your instructor's preference, follow the guidelines in one of the following boxes as you prepare your in-text references and end references.

TIPS FOR PREPARING CITATION-SEQUENCE IN-TEXT REFERENCES

- Place a superscript number after each mention of a source or each use of material from it. This number corresponds to the number assigned to the source in the end references.
- Be sure to place the number immediately after the material used or the word or phrase indicating the source: Herbert's original method[1] was used.
- Use the same number each time you refer to a source.
- Order the numbers according to the sequence in which sources are introduced: Both Li[1] and Holst[2] have shown. . . .
- When referring to more than one source, use commas to separate the numbers corresponding to the sources; note that there is no space after each comma. Use an en dash between two numbers to indicate a sequence of sources: The early studies[1,2,4–7]. . . .

TIPS FOR PREPARING NAME-YEAR IN-TEXT REFERENCES

- Place the author's last name and the year of publication in parentheses after the mention of a source: In a more recent study (Karr 2009), these findings were not replicated. Using the author's last name, the reader will be able to find the corresponding entry in the alphabetized reference list.
- Omit the author's name from the parenthetical citation if it appears in the text preceding it: In Karr's study (2009), these findings were not replicated.
- If the source has two authors, use both of their last names: (Phill and Richardson 2009). If there are three or more authors, use the first author's last name and the abbreviation *et al.*: (Drake et al. 2008).
- Use semicolons to separate multiple citations. Order these citations chronologically when the years differ but alphabetically when the years are the same: (Li 2008; Holst 2009) but (Lamont 2008; Li 2008).

TIPS FOR PREPARING CITATION-NAME IN-TEXT REFERENCES

- Arrange your end references alphabetically. Then assign each reference a number. Use the superscript form of this number in the text immediately after the material used or the word or phrase indicating the source: Stress-related illnesses are common among college students.[1]
- Use the same number each time you refer to a source.
- When referring to more than one source, use commas to separate the numbers corresponding to the sources; note that there is no space after each comma. Use an en dash between two numbers to indicate a sequence of sources: Recent studies of posttraumatic stress disorder[1,2,4–7]. . . .

TIPS FOR PREPARING END REFERENCES

- Place the heading "References" or "Cited References" next to the left margin.
- If you are using the citation-sequence system, list the sources in the order in which they were introduced in the text. If your paper employs the citation-name system, your end references should be ordered alphabetically according to the first author's last name and then numbered.
- If your paper employs the name-year system, your end references should be ordered alphabetically. See pages 395–396 for an example of end references in alphabetical order.
- Entries on citation-sequence and citation-name reference lists differ only in overall organization: citation-sequence references are listed according to the order of occurrence within the text; citation-name references are listed alphabetically. The name-year system differs from both the citation-sequence and citation-name systems only in the placement of the date of publication: the name-year system calls for the date to be placed after the author's name; the citation-sequence and the citation-name systems call for the date to be placed after the publisher's name in entries for books and after the name of the periodical in entries for articles.

Use the following directory to find sample end references for the citation-sequence or citation-name system.

> **Directory of CSE Citation-Sequence or Citation-Name Bibliographic Entries**

BOOKS

1. Book with one author   388
2. Book with two or more authors   389
3. Book with an organization (or organizations) listed as author   389
4. Book with editor(s)   389
5. Chapter or part of an edited book   389

ARTICLES

6. Article in a scholarly journal or popular magazine   390
7. Article in a newspaper   390

ELECTRONIC SOURCES

8. Online book   390
9. Article in an online journal or magazine   391
10. Article in an online newspaper   391
11. Web site   391
12. Database   391

BOOKS

1. Book with one author

Citation-sequence or citation-name system

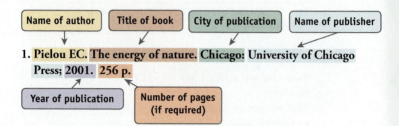

Begin the entry with the author's last name and his or her first initial and middle initial (if given). Capitalize only the first word of the title and any proper nouns or adjectives. Include the place of publication, the publisher's name, and the year of publication. Provide the total page count if required, using the abbreviation *p* for "pages."

Name-year system

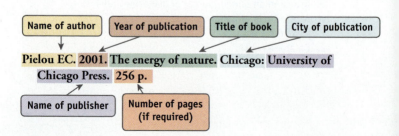

The following entries are formatted according to the citation-sequence or citation-name system. For a list of entries reflecting the name-year system, see page 392.

2. Book with two or more authors

2. McPherson GR, DeStefano S. Applied ecology and natural resource management. Cambridge (GB): Cambridge University Press; 2002.

Invert the name and initials of all authors, using commas to separate the names. If the city is not well known or could be confused with another city, include an abbreviation for the state or country in parentheses after the name of the city.

3. Book with an organization (or organizations) listed as author

3. Seattle Times. Natural wonders: the flora, fauna & formations of Washington. Seattle (WA): Seattle Times; 2003.

The first word of a subtitle is not capitalized unless it is a proper noun.

4. Book with editor(s)

4. Lund B, Hunter P, editors. The microbiological safety of food in healthcare settings. Malden (MA): Blackwell; 2007.

Include the word *editor* or *editors* after the last name.

5. Chapter or part of an edited book

5. Martin DJ. Social data. In: Wilson J, Fotheringham AS, editors. The handbook of geographic information science. Malden (MA): Blackwell; 2008. p. 35–48.

ARTICLES

6. Article in a scholarly journal or popular magazine

6. Milad MR, Quirk GJ. Neurons in medial prefrontal cortex signal memory for fear extinction. Nature. 2002;420(6911):70–73.

Place a period after the name of the journal or magazine; then list the year of publication, the volume number, and the issue number. Place a semicolon between the year of publication and the volume number. Put the issue number in parentheses. Note that there are no spaces separating the year, the volume number, and the issue number. Page numbers should be expressed as a range.

7. Article in a newspaper

7. O'Connor A. Heart attack risk linked to time spent in traffic. New York Times. 2004 Oct 26;Sect. F:9 (col. 4).

Place the year, month, and day of publication after the name of the newspaper. Include the section letter, the page number, and the column number.

ELECTRONIC SOURCES

8. Online book

8. Committee on Planetary and Lunar Exploration. National Research Council. The quarantine and certification of Martian samples [Internet]. Washington (DC): National Academy Press; 2002 [cited 2007 Oct 31]. Available from: http://www.nap.edu/openbook.php?isbn=0309075718

Place the word *Internet* (not italicized) in brackets after the title of the book or journal. Give the date of access in brackets after the date of publication. Provide the full URL unless it is excessively long, in which case, give the URL for the home page only.

9. Article in an online journal or magazine

9. Miller MR, White A, Boots M. Host life span and the evolution of resistance characteristics. Evol [Internet]. 2007 [cited 2007 Oct 31]; 61(1):2–14. Available from: http://www.blackwell-synergy.com/doi/full/10.1111/j.1558–5646.2007.00001.x

10. Article in an online newspaper

10. Forero J. As Andean glaciers shrink, water worries grow. New York Times on the Web [Internet]. 2002 Nov 23 [cited 2002 Dec 7]; [2 p.]. Available from: http://www.nytimes.com/2002/11/24/international/americas/24BOLI.html?pagewanted51

11. Web site

11. Corvus corax [Internet]. Bay Shore (NY): Long Island Ravens MC; c2000–2002 [updated 2001 Dec 3; cited 2003 Jan 3]. Available from: http://www.liravensmc.org/About/about_ravens.htm

12. Database

12. Honey Bee Genome Project [Internet]. Houston (TX): Baylor College of Medicine. [date unknown] -   [updated 2005 Jan 27; cited 2007 Nov 1]. Available from: http://www.hgsc.bcm.tmc.edu/projects/honeybee/

If you do not know the date of publication, place the words *date unknown* (not italicized) in square brackets; then add a space, a hyphen, and three more spaces.

Name-year system

The following sample entries for a reference list in the name-year format correspond to those listed in the section on the citation-sequence or citation-name system. The individual entries for books and articles differ from those in the citation-sequence and citation-name formats only in the placement of the date. In the name-year system, the date follows the author's name. Because the CSE manual provides only one format for online sources, the entries for these sources are not repeated in this list. For more samples of end references, see pages 395–396.

References

Lund B, Hunter P, editors. 2007. The microbiological safety of food in healthcare settings. Malden (MA): Blackwell.

Martin DJ. 2008. Social data. In: Wilson J, Fotheringham AS, editors. The handbook of geographic information science. Malden (MA): Blackwell. p. 35–48.

McPherson GR, DeStefano S. 2002. Applied ecology and natural resource management. Cambridge (GB): Cambridge University Press.

Milad MR, Quirk GJ. 2002. Neurons in medial prefrontal cortex signal memory for fear extinction. Nature. 420(6911):70–73.

O'Connor A. 2004 Oct 26. Heart attack risk linked to time spent in traffic. New York Times. Sect. F:9 (col. 4).

Pielou EC. 2001. The energy of nature. Chicago: University of Chicago Press.

Seattle Times. 2003. Natural wonders: the flora, fauna & formations of Washington. Seattle: Seattle Times.

36b Sample CSE-style paper

Papers written for courses in the natural sciences often report the results of a study. They are generally divided into six main sections: **abstract, introduction, methods and materials, results, discussion,** and **references.** The following excerpts from Michelle Tebbe's report, "Trace Element Distribution in Agate: Open- Versus Closed-System Formation," will help you understand how to format an abstract, an introduction, and a bibliography according to the name-year system.

Trace Element Distribution in Agate:

Open- Versus Closed-System Formation

Michelle Tebbe

Geology 481: Advanced Mineralogy

January 14, 2008

Abstract

Agate is a silica-rich rock that preserves a record of ancient hydrology and water/rock interaction. However, there is little consensus on how agate forms. Two end-member formation models exist for agate hosted by basalt and are tested here by trace element investigation of agate samples from Brazil, Germany, and Washington, US.

[The abstract continues.]

Introduction

Agate is a semiprecious gemstone prized for millennia for its colors and complex patterns (Figure 1). The mining of agate has historically been a thriving industry in countries such as Germany and Scotland and continues to be so today in Brazil and Mexico, where agate is fashioned into objects of art and jewelry (Figure 2). Agate is also of interest to the geologist because it preserves a record of rock formation and may be one of the most striking examples of self-organization in geology.

Figure 1. Agate from Scurdie Ness, Scotland, illustrating the typical concentrically banded texture of most agate worldwide. Width of sample is 8 cm. Photo by Brian Jackson, Natural History Museum, Edinburgh.

Figure 2. Agate forms part of the base of these candlesticks by Julian Cross, which are displayed in the Small Dining Room of the residence of the Prime Minister of Great Britain. Photo by Alf Barnes, Courtesy of The Silver Trust.

9

References

Abruzzese MJ, Waldbauer JR, Chamberlain, CP. 2005. Oxygen and hydrogen isotope ratios in freshwater chert as indicators of ancient climate and hydrologic regime. Geochim Cosmochim. 69(6):1377–1390.

Bryxina NA, Halden NM, Ripinen OI. 2002. Oscillatory zoning in an agate from Kazakhstan: autocorrelation function and fractal statistics of trace element distributions. Math Geol. 34(8):915–927.

Friedman I, O'Neil JR. 1977. Compilation of stable isotope fractionation factors of geochemical interest. In: Fleischer M, editor. Data of geochemistry. 6th ed. Reston (VA): United States Geological Survey.

Gilg HA, Morteani G, Kostitsyn Y, Preinfalk C, Gatter I, Strieder AJ. 2003. Genesis of amethyst geodes in basaltic rocks of the Serra Geral Formation (Ametista do Sul, Rio Grande do Sul, Brazil): a fluid inclusion, REE, oxygen, carbon, and Sr isotope study on basalt, quartz, and calcite. Miner Deposita. 38(8):1009–1025.

Götze J, Tichomirowa M, Fuchs H, Pilot J, Sharp, ZD. 2001. Geochemistry of agates: a trace element and stable isotope study. Chem Geol. 175(3–4):523–541.

Hamilton A. 2002. Relative ages and timing of deformation of the Manastash and Taneum formations in Kittitas County, Central Washington [senior thesis]. [Ellensburg (WA)]: Central Washington University.

Merino E, Wang Y. 2001. Geochemical self-organization in rocks: occurrences, observations, modeling, testing—with emphasis on agate genesis. In: Krug HJ, Kruhl, JH, editors. Nonequilibrium processes and dissipative structures in geoscience. Berlin (GR): Drucker & Humboldt. p. 13–45.

[The reference list continues.]

A
ADVICE for MULTILINGUAL WRITERS

CHAPTER 37
Determiners, Nouns, and Adjectives 398

- **37a** Determiners and proper nouns 398
- **37b** Determiners and count nouns 399
- **37c** Determiners and noncount nouns 400
- **37d** Determiners and adjectives 403
- **37e** Shifting from nonspecific to specific references 404

CHAPTER 38
Verbs and Verb Forms 406

- **38a** Verb tenses 406
- **38b** Auxiliary verbs 414
- **38c** Prepositional verbs and phrasal verbs 417
- **38d** Participles used as adjectives 419

CHAPTER 39
Word Order 420

- **39a** Ordering adjectives 420
- **39b** Placing adverbs of frequency 420
- **39c** Placing adverbs and direct objects 421
- **39d** Ordering words within clauses 421

37 Determiners, Nouns, and Adjectives

Studying the unique system of English determiners will help you overcome typical challenges faced by multilingual writers.

37a Determiners and proper nouns

A **proper noun** is the specific name of someone or something (for example, *Benito*, *Mexico*, or *Museum of Popular Art*). Proper nouns are capitalized (21a). A **determiner** is a noun marker—a word that comes *before* a noun. The most common determiners are **articles** (*a*, *an*, and *the*), **demonstratives** (*this*, *that*, *these*, and *those*), **possessives** (*my*, *your*, *his*, *her*, *its*, *our*, and *their*), and **quantifiers** (*many*, *few*, *much*, and *less*).

Proper nouns are preceded either by *the* or by no article at all. To decide whether to use *the* with a proper noun, first ask yourself this question: **Is the proper noun singular or plural?** If the proper noun is plural, use *the* (*the Browns*, *the United States*). If the proper noun is singular, you can usually omit the article (*Jeff*, *Mr. Brown*, *Atlanta*, *China*). However, there are some singular proper nouns that *are* preceded by *the*.

SINGULAR PROPER NOUNS PRECEDED BY *THE*

- **Historical documents, periods, and events:** *the* Magna Carta, *the* Renaissance, *the* Velvet Revolution
- **Buildings, hotels, museums, and some bridges:** *the* Burj Khalifa, *the* Sheraton, *the* Prado, *the* Brooklyn Bridge

- **Oceans, seas, rivers, and deserts:** *the* Pacific Ocean, *the* Aegean Sea, *the* Amazon River, *the* Sahara Desert
- **Names that include *of*:** *the* Gulf of Mexico, *the* Statue of Liberty, *the* University of Tennessee, *the* Fourth of July

37b Determiners and count nouns

A **common noun** is a general label (such as *president, country, museum*). Common nouns are not capitalized. A common noun may or may not be preceded by a determiner (37a). To decide whether to use a determiner with a common noun, begin by asking yourself this question: **Is the noun a count noun or a noncount noun?** A **count noun** names something that can be counted and has a singular and a plural form (one *car*, two *cars*). If the common noun is a count noun, ask yourself another question: **Is the count noun referring to someone or something specific?** If so, the following guidelines indicate appropriate determiners to use with the noun.

DETERMINERS WITH COUNT NOUNS: SPECIFIC REFERENCES

- A singular count noun is preceded by *the, this, that,* or a possessive.

    The/This/That/My book is heavy.

- A plural count noun is preceded by *the, these, those,* or a possessive.

    The/These/Those/My books are heavy.

- Count nouns that refer to unique individuals or entities (that have only one possible referent) are preceded by *the*.

    The president of the organization will arrive soon.

    The sun sets in the west.

Determiners, Nouns, and Adjectives

If a count noun does not refer to someone or something specific, but instead to a type of individual or entity, use the following guidelines.

DETERMINERS WITH COUNT NOUNS: NONSPECIFIC REFERENCES

- The article *a* is used before a singular count noun or an adjective beginning with a consonant *sound* (not necessarily the letter representing the sound).

    We went to *a* **c**afe.

    He lived in *a* **s**mall apartment.

- The article *an* is used before a singular count noun or an adjective beginning with a vowel *sound*.

    They had *an* **a**rgument.

    It had *an* **e**asy solution.

- Plural count nouns are preceded by *some, many,* or *few* when the quantity is a consideration.

    Some/Many/Few students have volunteered.

- Plural count nouns take no determiner at all when quantity is not a consideration.

    Potatoes are grown in Idaho.

37c Determiners and noncount nouns

A **noncount noun** names something that cannot be counted; it has neither a singular nor a plural form. Some noncount nouns never take determiners.

TYPES OF NONCOUNT NOUNS THAT TAKE NO DETERMINERS

- **Games and sports:** baseball, chess, football, poker, tennis

    Soccer is my favorite sport.
- **Subjects of study:** biology, chemistry, economics, English, history

    English is my favorite subject.

Other types of noncount nouns may or may not take determiners.

TYPES OF NONCOUNT NOUNS THAT MAY OR MAY NOT TAKE DETERMINERS

- **Abstractions:** confidence, democracy, education, happiness, health, honesty, importance, knowledge, love, news, wisdom
- **Groups of things:** clothing, equipment, garbage, homework, money, scenery, traffic, transportation, vocabulary
- **Substances:** air, blood, coffee, ice, rice, tea, water, wood

To decide which determiner to use with a noun referring to an abstraction, a group, or a substance, begin with the question you asked about count nouns: **Is the noncount noun referring to something specific?** If it is, use the determiners in the following list.

DETERMINERS WITH NONCOUNT NOUNS THAT REFER TO SPECIFIC ABSTRACTIONS, GROUPS OF THINGS, OR SUBSTANCES

Use *the, this, that,* or a possessive before a noncount noun making a specific reference.

The/This/That/Our information is important.

If the noncount noun is *not* referring to something specific, use the following guidelines.

> **DETERMINERS WITH NONCOUNT NOUNS THAT DO NOT REFER TO SPECIFIC ABSTRACTIONS, GROUPS OF THINGS, OR SUBSTANCES**
>
> A noncount noun is preceded by the determiner *some*, *much*, or *little* when quantity is a consideration.
>
> We drank *some/little* water.
>
> We didn't drink *much* water.
>
> A noncount noun takes no determiner at all when quantity is not a consideration.
>
> We drank only water.

Because noncount nouns do not have singular and plural forms, sentences like the following should be edited:

We used a lot of equipments. [An *s* is not added to a noncount noun.]

I finished two homeworks *assignments* today. [Numbers are not used with noncount nouns.]

The job requires ~~a~~ special machinery. [*A* and *an* are not used with noncount nouns.]

The vocabulary ~~are~~ *is* difficult. [Use a singular verb with a noncount noun.]

Some words can be used as either a count noun or a noncount noun.

They believed **life** was sacred. [noncount noun]

He led *an* interesting **life.** [count noun]

37d Determiners and adjectives

Some adjectives add specificity to nouns. Use *the* before the following types of adjectives.

ADJECTIVES AND DETERMINERS: SPECIFIC REFERENCES

- Adjectives indicating sequence, such as *first, next, last,* and so forth

    The **first/next/last** person in line will win a prize.

- Adjectives indicating a single person or item, such as *right, only,* and so forth

    She had *the* **right/only** answer.

When describing how one of two individuals or entities differs from or surpasses the other, use the comparative form of an adjective (**26b**). The comparative form has the suffix *-er* or the word *more* or *less*:

Cars are cheap*er* here. Cars are *more* expensive there.

Use the article *the* before the comparative form in this phrase: *the* [comparative form] *of the two* [plural noun].

The older *of the two* sons is now a doctor.

When describing how one of three or more individuals or entities surpasses all the others, use the superlative form of an adjective (**6b**). There are two superlative forms: (1) the adjective has the suffix *-est* and is preceded by the article *the*, or (2) the adjective does not have that suffix and is preceded by *the most* or *the least*.

Cars are *the* cheap*est* here. Cars are *the most* expensive there.

GUIDELINES FOR FORMING COMPARATIVES AND SUPERLATIVES

- One-syllable words generally take the ending *-er* or *-est*: *fast, faster, fastest*.

- Two-syllable words ending in a consonant and *-y* also generally take the ending *-er* or *-est*, with the *y* changed to an *i*: *noisy, noisier, noisiest*.

- Two-syllable adjectives ending in *-ct, -nt,* or *-st* are preceded by *more/less* or *most/least*: *less exact, least exact; more recent, most recent*. Two-syllable adjectives with a suffix such as *-ous, -ish, -ful, -ing,* or *-ed* are also preceded by *more/less* or *most/least*: *more/most famous; less/least careful*.

- Two-syllable adjectives ending in *-er, -ow,* or *-some* either take the ending *-er* or *-est* or are preceded by *more/less* or *most/least*: *narrower, more narrow, less narrow, narrowest, most narrow, least narrow*.

- Words of three or more syllables are preceded by *more/less* or *most/least*: *less/least fortunate; more/most intelligent*.

- Some modifiers have irregular comparative and superlative forms:

  little, less, least   good/well, better, best   bad, worse, worst

37e Shifting from nonspecific to specific references

When introduced, an individual or an entity is usually nonspecific. After the introduction, the individual or entity is considered specific.

First mention

A tsunami <u>warning</u> was issued last night.

Subsequent mention

This <u>warning</u> affected all low-lying areas.

A subsequent mention does not have to repeat the word used in the first mention. However, the word chosen must be closely related to the one introduced first.

The weather service <u>warned</u> people about possible flooding.

The <u>warning</u> included possible evacuation routes.

EXERCISE 1

Edit the following common sayings so that determiners are used correctly.

1. The absence makes a heart grow fonder.
2. The actions speak louder than the words.
3. The bad news travels fast.
4. Best things come in the small packages.
5. The blood is thicker than the water.
6. Don't cry over the spilled milk.

38 Verbs and Verb Forms

Building on the discussion in chapter 4, this chapter gives more information about how the *form* of a verb affects its meaning.

38a Verb tenses

English verbs are either regular verbs or irregular verbs (4a). This distinction is based on the forms of a verb. The forms of irregular verbs do not follow the set pattern that the forms of regular verbs do. If you have trouble choosing the right verb forms, study the charts on pages 34 and 35–36. As you become more familiar with English verb forms, you will understand how they provide information about time. Keep in mind that, although the words *present, past,* and *future* may lead you to think that these tenses refer to actions or events occurring now, in the past, and in the future, respectively, this strict separation is not always the case.

(1) Simple tenses

Simple tenses have many uses, which are not limited to indicating specific times. The conjugation of the **simple present tense** of a regular verb includes two forms of the verb: the base form and the *-s* form. Notice that the third-person singular form is the only form with the *-s* ending.

Simple Present Tense		
	Singular	Plural
First person	I **use**	We **use**
Second person	You **use**	You **use**
Third person	He, she, it **uses**	They **use**

Use the simple present tense for the following purposes.

USES OF THE SIMPLE PRESENT TENSE

- To indicate a current state: The application **is** complete.
- To report a general fact: Earth **revolves** around the sun.
- To describe a habitual action: The group **meets** on Mondays.
- To add a sense of immediacy to a description of a historical event: On November 9, 1989, people **begin** to demolish the Berlin Wall.
- To discuss literary and artistic works: In his paintings of water lilies, Monet **offers** the viewer glimpses into his garden at Giverny.
- To refer to future events: The president **departs** for the campaign trail next week.

The simple past tense of a regular verb has only one form: the base form with the *-ed* ending. The past tense forms of irregular verbs vary (see 4a).

Simple Past Tense
I, you, he, she, it, we, they **used**

The simple past tense is used to refer to completed actions or past events.

USES OF THE SIMPLE PAST TENSE

- To indicate a completed action: He **worked** in the mines for ten years.
- To report a past event: Post-hurricane problems **lasted** for weeks.

The simple future tense of a regular verb also has only one form: the base form accompanied by the auxiliary *will*.

Simple Future Tense
I, you, he, she, it, we, they **will use**

The simple future tense refers to future actions or states.

USES OF THE SIMPLE FUTURE TENSE

- To promise to perform an action: I **will send** you a hard copy.
- To predict a future action: The president **will veto** the bill.
- To predict a future state of being: Someone **will be** upset.

It is also possible to use a form of *be going to* when referring to the future (**38b(2)**).

I **am going to** do fieldwork in Mexico next year.

(2) Progressive tenses

Progressive tenses indicate that actions or events are repetitive, ongoing, or temporary. The present progressive tense consists of a present-tense form of the auxiliary verb *be* and the present participle (*-ing* form) of the main verb, whether that verb is regular or irregular.

Present Progressive Tense		
	Singular	Plural
First person	I **am using**	We **are using**
Second person	You **are using**	You **are using**
Third person	He, she, it **is using**	They **are using**

The present progressive tense signals an activity in progress or a temporary situation.

USES OF THE PRESENT PROGRESSIVE TENSE

- To show that an activity is in progress: The diplomats **are discussing** the treaty.
- To indicate that a situation is temporary: They **are living** in a dormitory.
- To refer to an action that will occur at a specific time in the future: They **are voting** on the bill next week.

Like the present progressive, the past progressive tense is a combination of the auxiliary verb *be* and the present participle (*-ing* form) of the main verb. However, the auxiliary verb is in the past tense, rather than in the present tense.

Past Progressive Tense		
	Singular	Plural
First person	I **was using**	We **were using**
Second person	You **were using**	You **were using**
Third person	He, she, it **was using**	They **were using**

The past progressive tense signals that an action or event occurred in the past and was repeated or ongoing.

USES OF THE PAST PROGRESSIVE TENSE

- To indicate that a past action was repetitive: She **was** always **asking** for volunteers.
- To signal that a past action was occurring when something else happened: He **was checking** his e-mail when his roommate returned.

A verb in the future progressive tense has only one form. Two auxiliaries, *will* and *be,* are used with the *-ing* form of the main verb.

Future Progressive Tense

I, you, he, she, it, we, they **will be using**

The future progressive tense indicates that actions will occur over some period of time in the future.

USE OF THE FUTURE PROGRESSIVE TENSE

- To indicate that an action will occur over a span of time in the future: They **will be using** the projector during their presentation.

CAUTION

Some verbs do not express actions but rather mental states, emotions, conditions, or relationships. These verbs are not used in progressive forms: *believe, belong, contain, cost, know, like, own, prefer,* and *want.*

The book ~~is containing~~ contains many Central American folktales.

(3) Perfect tenses

Perfect tenses indicate actions that were performed or events that occurred before a particular time. The present perfect tense is formed by combining the auxiliary *have* with the past participle of the main verb. The participle remains the same regardless of person and number; however, the auxiliary has two forms: *has* for third-person singular and *have* for the other person-number combinations.

	Present Perfect Tense	
	Singular	Plural
First person	I **have used**	We **have used**
Second person	You **have used**	You **have used**
Third person	He, she, it **has used**	They **have used**

The present perfect tense is used for the following purposes.

USES OF THE PRESENT PERFECT TENSE

- To signal that a situation originating in the past is continuing into the present: She **has taught** sign language for five years.
- To refer to a past action that has current relevance: They **have reviewed** his application but still need to call his references.

The past perfect tense is also formed by combining the auxiliary *have* with the past participle. However, the auxiliary is in the past tense. There is only one form of the past perfect.

Past Perfect Tense
I, you, he, she, it, we, they **had used**

The past perfect tense specifies that an action was completed at a time in the past prior to another time or before another past action.

USES OF THE PAST PERFECT TENSE

- To indicate that a past action occurred prior to a given time in the past: By the age of twenty, he **had gained** national attention.
- To indicate that a past action occurred prior to another past action: I **had** already **completed** college when I joined the army.
- To emphasize the point of preceding discourse: The protestors completed a peaceful march, sat quietly in front of the courthouse, and chatted amiably with journalists. Their plan **had succeeded**.

The future perfect tense consists of two auxiliaries, *will* and *have*, along with the past participle of the main verb. There is only one form of the future perfect tense.

Future Perfect Tense

I, you, he, she, it, we, they **will have used**

The future perfect tense refers to an action that is to be completed prior to a future time.

USE OF THE FUTURE PERFECT TENSE

- To refer to future completion of an action: When I turn twenty-two, I **will have lived** in the United States for ten years.

(4) Perfect progressive tenses

Perfect progressive tenses combine the forms and meanings of the progressive and the perfect tenses. The present perfect progressive form consists of two auxiliaries, *have* and *be*, plus the present participle (*-ing* form) of the main verb. The form of the auxiliary *have* varies with person and number. The auxiliary *be* appears as the past participle, *been*.

Present Perfect Progressive Tense

	Singular	Plural
First person	I **have been using**	We **have been using**
Second person	You **have been using**	You **have been using**
Third person	He, she, it **has been using**	They **have been using**

The present perfect progressive signals that an action, state, or event originating in the past is ongoing or incomplete.

USES OF THE PRESENT PERFECT PROGRESSIVE TENSE

- To signal that a state of being is ongoing: They **have been leading** expeditions for a long time.
- To indicate that an action is incomplete: They **have been rehearsing** since May.

The past perfect progressive tense follows the pattern *had* + *been* + present participle (*-ing* form) of the main verb. (The auxiliary *have* is in the past tense.)

Past Perfect Progressive Tense

I, you, he, she, it, we, they **had been using**

The past perfect progressive tense refers to a situation or an action occurring over a period of time in the past and prior to another past action.

USE OF THE PAST PERFECT PROGRESSIVE TENSE

- To indicate that an ongoing action occurred prior to a past action: The band **had been touring** for so long that its fan base was enormous.

The future perfect progressive form has the pattern *will* + *have* + *been* + present participle (*-ing* form) of the main verb.

Future Perfect Progressive Tense

I, you, he, she, it, we, they **will have been using**

The future perfect progressive tense refers to an action that is occurring in the present and will continue to occur for a specific amount of time.

USE OF THE FUTURE PERFECT PROGRESSIVE TENSE

- To indicate that an action will continue until a specified time: By the end of next month, we **will have been developing** the new business model for a full year.

EXERCISE 1

Explain how the meaning of each sentence changes when the verb tense changes.

1. In "Fiji's Rainbow Reef," Les Kaufman (describes/described) the coral reefs of Fiji and (discusses/discussed) the factors affecting their health.
2. Rising water temperatures (damaged/have damaged/did damage) the reefs.
3. The lack of algae (has left/had left) the coral "bleached."
4. Strangely, though, new life (is flourishing/was flourishing/has been flourishing) in some of these areas.
5. Scientists (study/will study) this area to understand its resilience.

38b Auxiliary Verbs

Auxiliary verbs add nuances of meaning to main verbs. Some provide information about time, while others are used to provide emphasis, to form questions, or to indicate ability, certainty, obligation, and so on.

(1) The auxiliary verb *do*

Unlike *be* and *have,* the auxiliary verb *do* does not occur with other verbs to indicate tense. Instead, it is used in questions, negations, and emphatic sentences.

Do you have any questions? [question]

I **do** not have any questions. [negation]

I **do** have a few comments. [emphatic sentence]

The auxiliary *do* is used only in the simple present (*do, does*) and the simple past (*did*).

(2) Modal verbs

The modal auxiliary verbs in English are *can, could, may, might, must, shall, should, will,* and *would* (4a(4)). English also has **phrasal modals**, which are modal auxiliaries consisting of more than one word. They have meanings similar to those of one-word modals.

be able to (ability): We **were able to** find the original document.

have to (obligation): You **have to** report your test results.

Other common phrasal modals are *be going to, be supposed to, had better, need to,* and *used to.* Modal auxiliaries and phrasal modals can sometimes be combined. The modal precedes the phrasal modal.

I <u>**should**</u> **be able to** finish the project by Tuesday.

Both modal auxiliaries and phrasal modals indicate a variety of meanings, including obligation, permission, and probability. Modal auxiliaries have only two forms: the base form and the perfective form (base form + *have* + past participle). Most phrasal modals have more than two forms (*am able to, is able to, were able to, has been able to*). Only *had better* and *used to* have a single form. The following box shows the most common uses of modal verbs in academic writing.

USING MODAL VERBS

Modal Auxiliaries

Verb	Meaning	Example
can	Ability	New legislation **can** change tax rates.
could	Possibility	The announcement **could** cause unrest.
may	Possibility	Funding **may** be the problem.
must	Obligation	Judges **must** be neutral.
should	Obligation	Dissent **should** be acknowledged.
will	Certainty	A statistical analysis **will** be performed.
would	Prediction	All **would** benefit from fewer obligations.

Modal Auxiliaries with *Have* + Past Participle

Verb	Meaning	Example
might have	Conjecture	The accident **might have** caused the delay.
must have	Conjecture	The police **must have** known about the protest.
should have	Criticism	Monitors **should have** reported the incident.

Phrasal Modals in the Present Tense

Verb	Meaning	Example
be able to	Ability	They **are able** to respond quickly to emergencies.
have to	Obligation	The president **has to** attend the meeting.
need to	Necessity	A good summary **needs to** be objective.

Phrasal Modals in the Past Tense

Verb	Meaning	Example
was/were able to	Ability	They **were able to** finish on time.
had to	Obligation	The journalist **had to** divulge his sources.

EXERCISE 2

Fill in the blank with a modal auxiliary or a phrasal modal and describe the meaning it conveys.

1. Nations at war _____ follow the Geneva Conventions.
2. Everyone _____ be treated humanely.
3. In various wars, humanitarian groups _____ protect innocent victims.
4. Without humanitarian groups, many more people _____ lost their lives.
5. Critics of past wars state that more aid _____ been provided.

38c Prepositional verbs and phrasal verbs

A prepositional verb consists of a verb followed by a preposition; a phrasal verb consists of a verb followed by a particle.

(1) Prepositional verbs

Some verbs are typically followed by prepositions. Following are ten prepositional verbs that commonly occur in academic writing. Some are more often used in the active voice; others are more often used in the passive voice.

TEN PREPOSITIONAL VERBS COMMON IN ACADEMIC WRITING

Active Voice	Passive Voice
depend on	be applied to
lead to	be derived from
look at	be divided into
refer to	be known as
result in	be used in

(2) Phrasal verbs

A **phrasal verb** consists of a verb and a particle such as *up, out,* or *on*. A phrasal verb is often idiomatic, conveying a meaning that differs from the common meanings of the individual words. For example, the definitions that first come to mind for the words *blow* and *up* are not likely to help you understand the phrasal verb *blow up* when it means "to enlarge."

> She **blew up** the photograph so that she could see the faces better.

Phrasal verbs may have more than one meaning. *To blow up* means not only "to enlarge" but also "to inflate" or "to explode." A few phrasal verbs retain the common meanings of the verb and the particle.

> The protesters **hung up** a banner.

The verb and particle in most phrasal verbs may be separated by a short noun phrase (**1d(1)**).

> She **called** the meeting **off.**   OR   She **called off** the meeting.

If you use a pronoun with a phrasal verb, always place it between the verb and the particle.

> The student **turned** it **in** yesterday.

Some phrasal verbs are not separable, however.

> The group **went over** the proposal.
>
> I **came across** an interesting fact.

You should be able to find the definitions of phrasal verbs in a conventional dictionary; however, a specialized dictionary will also provide information about the separability of these verbs.

EXERCISE 3

Insert an appropriate preposition or particle after the verb in each sentence.

1. Overpopulation has brought _____ great changes on earth.
2. Deforestation often leads _____ extinctions.
3. High levels of carbon dioxide result _____ increased global temperatures.
4. Proposals for curbing emissions should be looked _____ closely.
5. Scientists have taken _____ the challenge of slowing the destruction.

38d Participles used as adjectives

Both present participles and past participles can be used as adjectives; however, they are not interchangeable. When you want to indicate an emotion, use a present participle with a noun referring to someone or something that is the cause of the emotion. In the phrase *the exciting tennis match,* the tennis match is the cause of the excitement. Use the past participle with a noun referring to someone who experiences an emotion. In the phrase *the excited crowd,* the crowd is experiencing the excitement.

EXERCISE 4

Choose the correct form of each participle.

1. My uncle is interesting/interested in most but not all sports.
2. He was exciting/excited by the World Cup matches in South Africa.
3. However, he did not like the annoying/annoyed sound of the vuvuzelas.
4. Soccer is his favorite sport; baseball he finds boring/bored.
5. He jokes that being a sports fan is a tiring/tired job.

39 Word Order

To help you understand and write sentences that are longer and more varied, this chapter discusses the conventional ordering of words in phrases and clauses.

39a Ordering adjectives

In English, two or three adjectives modifying the same noun are used in a particular order based on their meanings. The following list shows the usual order for adjectives of different types and gives examples of each type:

Evaluator	*fascinating, painful, content*
Size	*large, long, small, short*
Shape	*square, round, triangular*
Age	*young, old, aged, newborn, antique*
Color	*black, white, green, brown*
Origin	*Arabian, Cuban, Peruvian, Slavic*
Material	*silk, paper, pine, rubber*

We visited a **fascinating Italian** village. [evaluator, origin]
An **old black** dog stared at us. [age, color]

39b Placing adverbs of frequency

Adverbs of frequency (such as *always, never, sometimes,* and *often*) appear before one-word verbs.

He **rarely** goes to horror movies.

However, these adverbs appear after a form of *be* when it is the main verb.

Novels written by Stephen King <u>are</u> **always** popular.

When a sentence contains more than one verb in a verb phrase, the adverb of frequency is placed after the first auxiliary verb.

My friends <u>have</u> **never** <u>read</u> *The Shining*.

39c Placing adverbs and direct objects

An adverb may be placed after a verb when the verb has no direct object (**1c**).

They worked **efficiently**.

Revise any sentence that includes an adverb before a direct object.

I read ~~quickly~~ the letter ^quickly^. OR I ^quickly^ read ~~quickly~~ the letter.

39d Ordering words within clauses

The word order of embedded questions and adjectival clauses differs from the standard subject-verb-object order of clauses.

(1) Embedded questions
The word order of questions and embedded questions is not the same. Notice the difference in each of the following pairs of sentences:

Is the source reliable? [question]
 V   S

I do not know whether **the source is** reliable. [embedded question]
                         S   V

How **was the source evaluated?** [aux / s / v] [question]

He explained how **the source was evaluated.** [s / aux + v] [embedded question]

Does the author make a good argument? [aux / s / v] [question]

We should decide whether **the author makes** a good argument. [s / v] [embedded question]

In the question in each pair, the subject and the verb (or the auxiliary verb if there is one) are inverted; in the embedded question, they are not. The auxiliary verb *do* is not used in embedded questions.

If a question begins with an interrogative pronoun such as *who* or *what* as the subject, the order of the question and the embedded question are the same.

Who worked on the project? [s] [question]

They did not mention **who worked** on the project. [s] [embedded question]

(2) Adjectival clauses

If a relative pronoun is the subject of an adjectival clause (**1e(2)**), the word order of the clause is standard.

Twitter is based in San Francisco, California. [s / v]

Twitter, **which is based** in San Francisco, California, has users from around the world. [s / v]

If the relative pronoun is the object of the adjectival clause, no direct object follows the verb.

Tweets **that** protestors sent ~~them~~ to journalists were highly effective.

EXERCISE 1

Revise the word order of each sentence.

1. The Human Genome Project, which Francis Collins initiated it, turned into an international effort.

2. Prior to 1953, scientists did not know for certain was the structure of DNA a double helix.

3. The discovery of the double helix, which James D. Watson and Francis Crick described it in 1953, eventually led to the study of human genetics.

4. Without an understanding of gene sequences, scientists would not know how do people inherit traits.

5. No one can predict with certainty how will people in the future use this knowledge.

Glossary of Usage

By learning about usage in this glossary, you will increase your ability to use words effectively.

Agreement on usage occurs slowly–often after a period of debate. An asterisk (*) before an entry indicates that a new usage has been reported by dictionary editors. This usage, however, might not yet be accepted by everyone.

a lot of *A lot of* is conversational for *many, much,* or *a great deal of:* They do not have ~~a lot of~~ **much** time. *A lot* is sometimes misspelled as *alot.*

a while, awhile *A while* means "a period of time." It is often used with the prepositions *after, for,* and *in:* We rested for **a while.** *Awhile* means "a short time." It is not preceded by a preposition: We rested **awhile.**

accept, except The verb *accept* means "to receive": I **accept** your apology. The verb *except* means "to exclude": The policy was to have everyone wait in line, but mothers and small children were **excepted.** The preposition *except* means "other than": All **except** Joe will attend the conference.

advice, advise *Advice* is a noun: They asked their attorney for **advice.** *Advise* is a verb: The attorney **advised** us to save all relevant documents.

affect, effect *Affect* is a verb that means "to influence": The lobbyist's pleas did not **affect** the politician's decision. The noun *effect* means "a result": The **effect** of his decision on the staff's morale was positive and long lasting. When used as a verb, *effect* means "to produce" or "to cause": The activists believed that they could **effect** real political change.

all ready, already *All ready* means "completely prepared": The rooms are **all ready** for the conference. *Already* means "by or before the time specified": She has **already** taken her final exams.

* **all right** *All right* means "acceptable": The students asked whether it was **all right** to use dictionaries during the exam. *Alright* is not yet a generally accepted spelling of *all right,* although it is becoming more common in journalistic writing.

all together, altogether *All together* means "as a group": The cast reviewed the script **all together**. *Altogether* means "wholly, thoroughly": That game is **altogether** too difficult.

allude, elude *Allude* means "to refer to indirectly": The professor **alluded** to a medieval text. *Elude* means "to evade" or "to escape from": For the moment, his name **eludes** me.

allusion, illusion An *allusion* is a casual or indirect reference: The **allusion** was to Shakespeare's *Twelfth Night*. An *illusion* is a false idea or an unreal image: His idea of college is an **illusion**.

alot See **a lot of**.

already See **all ready, already**.

alright See **all right**.

altogether See **all together, altogether**.

* **among, between** To follow traditional usage, use *among* with three or more entities (a group): The snorklers swam **among** the fish. Use *between* when referring to only two entities: The rivalry **between** the two teams is intense. Current dictionaries also note the possibility of using *between* to refer to more than two entities, especially when these entities are considered distinct: We have strengthened the lines of communication **between** the various departments.

amount of, number of Use *amount of* before nouns that cannot be counted: The **amount of** rain that fell last year was insufficient. Use *number of* with nouns that can be counted: The **number of** students attending college has increased.

and/or This combination denotes three options: one, the other, or both: a parent **and/or** a teacher. These options can also be presented separately with *or:* The student's application should be signed by a parent, a teacher, **or** both.

* **angry at, angry with** Both *at* and *with* are commonly used after *angry,* although according to traditional guidelines, *with* should be used when a person is the cause of the anger: She was **angry with** me because I was late.

another, other, the other *Another* is followed by a singular noun: **another** book. *Other* is followed by a plural noun: **other** books. *The other* is followed by either a singular or a plural noun: **the other book, the other books.**

anymore, any more *Anymore* meaning "any longer" or "now" most frequently occurs in negative sentences: Sarah doesn't work here **anymore.** Its use in positive sentences is considered conversational; *now* is generally used instead: All he ever does ~~anymore~~ **now** is watch television. As two words, *any more* appears with *not* to mean "no more": We do not have **any more** time.

anyone, any one *Anyone* means "any person at all": We did not know **anyone.** *Any one* refers to one of a group: **Any one** of the options is better than the current situation.

* **anyplace, everyplace, someplace** These words are becoming increasingly common in academic writing. However, according to traditional usage rules, they should be replaced by *anywhere, everywhere,* and *somewhere.*

as Conversational when used after such verbs as *know, say,* and *see.* Use *that, if,* or *whether* instead: I do not know ~~as~~ **whether** my application is complete. Also considered conversational is the use of *as* instead of *who, which,* or *that:* Many of the performers ~~as~~ **who** have appeared on our program will be giving a concert this evening.

* **as, like** According to traditional usage, *as* begins either a phrase or a clause; *like* begins only a phrase: My brother drives too fast, just ~~like~~ **as** my father did. Current dictionaries note the informal use of *like* to begin clauses after verbs such as *look* and *sound.*

assure, ensure, insure *Assure* means "to state with confidence, alleviating any doubt": The flight attendant **assured** us that our flight would arrive on time. *Ensure* and *insure* are usually interchangeable to mean "make certain," but only *insure* means "to protect against loss": The editor **ensured** [OR **insured**] that the reporter's facts were accurate. Physicians must **insure** themselves against malpractice suits.

awhile   See **a while, awhile**.

bad   Unconventional as an adverb; use *badly* instead. The team played **badly**. However, the adjective *bad* is used after sensory verbs such as *feel, look,* and *smell:* I feel **bad** that I forgot to return your book yesterday.

being as, being that   Unconventional; use *because* instead. ~~Being as~~ Because the road was closed, traffic was diverted to another route.

beside, besides   According to traditional usage, these two words have different meanings. *Beside* means "next to": The president sat **beside** the prime minister. *Besides* means "in addition to" or "other than": She has written many articles **besides** those on political reform. Current dictionaries report that professional writers regularly use *beside* to convey this meaning, as long as there is no risk of ambiguity.

better, had better   *Better* is conversational. Use *had better* instead: We ~~better~~ had better finish the report by five o'clock.

between   See **among, between**.

can, may   *Can* refers to ability, and *may* refers to permission: You **can** [are able to] drive seventy miles an hour, but you **may** not [are not permitted to] exceed the speed limit. Current dictionaries report that in contemporary usage *can* and *may* are used interchangeably to denote possibility or permission, although *may* is used more frequently in formal contexts.

capital, capitol   *Capital* means either "a governing city" or "funds": The **capital** of Minnesota is St. Paul. An anonymous donor provided the **capital** for the project. As a modifier, *capital* means "chief" or "principal": This year's election is of **capital** importance. It may also refer to the death penalty: **Capital** punishment is legal in some states. A *capitol* is a statehouse; the *Capitol* is the U.S. congressional building in Washington, DC.

cite, site, sight   *Cite* means "to mention": Be sure to **cite** your sources. *Site* is a location: The president visited the **site** for the new library. As a verb, *site* also means "to situate": The builder sited the factory near the freeway. *Sight* means "to see": The crew **sighted** land. *Sight* also refers to a view: What an incredible **sight!**

climactic, climatic *Climactic* refers to a climax, or high point: The actors rehearsed the **climactic** scene. *Climatic* refers to the *climate:* Many environmentalists are worried about the recent **climatic** changes.

coarse, course *Coarse* refers to roughness: The jacket was made of **coarse** linen. *Course* refers to a route: Our **course** to the island was indirect. *Course* may also refer to a plan of study: I want to take a **course** in nutrition.

compare to, compare with *Compare to* means "to regard as similar," and *compare with* means "to examine for similarities and/or differences": She **compared** her mind **to** a dusty attic. The student **compared** the first draft **with** the second.

complement, complementary, compliment, complimentary *Complement* means "to complete" or "to balance": Their personalities **complement** each other. They have **complementary** personalities. *Compliment* means "to express praise": The professor **complimented** the students on their first drafts. Her remarks were **complimentary.** *Complimentary* may also mean "provided free of charge": We received **complimentary** tickets.

* **compose, comprise** *Compose* means "to make up": That collection **is composed** of medieval manuscripts. *Comprise* means "to consist of": The anthology **comprises** many famous essays. Dictionary editors have noted the increasing use of *comprise* in the passive voice to mean "to be composed of."

conscience, conscious, consciousness *Conscience* means "the sense of right and wrong": He examined his **conscience** before deciding whether to join the protest. *Conscious* means "awake": After an hour, the patient was fully **conscious.** After an hour, the patient regained **consciousness.** *Conscious* may also mean "aware": We were **conscious** of the possible consequences.

continual, continually, continuous, continuously *Continual* means "constantly recurring": **Continual** interruptions kept us from completing the project. Telephone calls **continually** interrupted us. *Continuous* means "uninterrupted": The job applicant had a record of ten years' **continuous** employment. The job applicant worked **continuously** from 2000 to 2009.

could of *Of* is often mistaken for the sound of the unstressed *have:* They **could of have** [OR might **have,** should **have,** would **have**] gone home.

couldn't care less *Couldn't care less* expresses complete lack of concern: She **couldn't care less** about her reputation. *Could care less* is considered unconventional in academic writing.

council, counsel A *council* is an advisory or decision-making group: The student **council** supported the new regulations. A *counsel* is a legal adviser: The defense **counsel** conferred with the judge. As a verb, *counsel* means "to give advice": She **counsels** people with eating disorders.

criteria, criterion *Criteria* is a plural noun meaning "a set of standards for judgment": The teachers explained the **criteria** for the assignment. The singular form is *criterion:* Their judgment was based on only one **criterion.**

* **data** *Data* is the plural form of *datum,* which means "piece of information" or "fact": When the **data are** complete, we will know the true cost. However, current dictionaries also note that *data* is frequently used as a mass entity (like the word *furniture*), appearing with a singular verb.

desert, dessert *Desert* can mean "a barren land": Gila monsters live in the **deserts** of the Southwest. As a verb, *desert* means "to leave": I thought my friends had **deserted** me. *Dessert* refers to something sweet eaten at the end of a meal: They ordered apple pie for **dessert.**

device, devise *Device* is a noun: She invented a **device** that measures extremely small quantities of liquid. *Devise* is a verb: We **devised** a plan for work distribution.

differ from, differ with *Differ from* means "to be different": A bull snake **differs from** a rattlesnake in a number of ways. *Differ with* means "to disagree": Senator Brown has **differed with** Senator Owen on several issues.

different from, different than *Different from* is generally used with nouns, pronouns, noun phrases, and noun clauses: This school was

different from most others. The school was **different from** what we had expected. *Different than* is used with adverbial clauses; *than* is the conjunction: We are no **different than** they are.

discreet, discrete *Discreet* means "showing good judgment or self-restraint": His friends complained openly, but his comments were quite **discreet**. *Discrete* means "distinct": The participants in the study came from three **discrete** groups.

disinterested, uninterested *Disinterested* means "impartial": A **disinterested** observer will give a fair opinion. *Uninterested* means "lacking interest": She was **uninterested** in the outcome of the game.

distinct, distinctive *Distinct* means "easily distinguishable or perceived": Each proposal has **distinct** advantages. *Distinctive* means "characteristic" or "serving to distinguish": We studied the **distinctive** features of hawks.

* **due to** Traditionally, *due to* was not synonymous with *because of*: ~~Due to~~ Because of holiday traffic, we arrived an hour late. However, dictionary editors now consider this usage of *due to* acceptable.

effect See **affect, effect**.

elicit, illicit *Elicit* means "to draw forth": He is **eliciting** contributions for a new playground. *Illicit* means "unlawful": The newspaper reported their **illicit** mishandling of public funds.

elude See **allude, elude**.

emigrate from, immigrate to *Emigrate* means "to leave one's own country": My ancestors **emigrated from** Ireland. *Immigrate* means "to arrive in a different country to settle": The Ulster Scots **immigrated to** the southern United States.

ensure See **assure, ensure, insure**.

especially, specially *Especially* emphasizes a characteristic or quality: Some people are **especially** sensitive to the sun. *Especially* also means "particularly": Wildflowers are abundant in this area, **especially** during May. *Specially* means "for a particular purpose": The classroom was **specially** designed for music students.

etc. Abbreviation of *et cetera*, meaning "and others of the same kind." Use only within parentheses: Be sure to bring appropriate camping gear (tent, sleeping bag, mess kit, **etc.**). Because *and* is part of the meaning of *etc.*, avoid using the combination *and etc.*

everyday, every day *Everyday* means "routine" or "ordinary": These are **everyday** problems. *Every day* means "each day": I read the newspaper **every day**.

everyone, every one *Everyone* means "all": **Everyone** should attend. *Every one* refers to each person or item in a group: **Every one** of you should attend.

everyplace See **anyplace, everyplace, someplace**.

except See **accept, except**.

explicit, implicit *Explicit* means "expressed clearly and directly": Given his **explicit** directions, we knew how to proceed. *Implicit* means "implied or expressed indirectly": I mistakenly understood his silence to be his **implicit** approval of the project.

farther, further Generally, *farther* refers to geographic distance: We will have to drive **farther** tomorrow. *Further* means "more": If you need **further** assistance, please let me know.

* **feel** Traditionally, *feel* was not synonymous with "think" or "believe": I ~~feel~~ **think** that more should be done to protect local habitat. Dictionary editors now consider this use of *feel* to be a standard alternative.

fewer, less *Fewer* occurs before nouns that can be counted: **fewer** technicians, **fewer** pencils. *Less* occurs before nouns that cannot be counted: **less** milk, **less** support. *Less than* may be used with measurements of time or distance: **less than** three months, **less than** twenty miles.

* **first, firstly; second, secondly** Many college instructors prefer the use of *first* and *second*. However, dictionary editors state that *firstly* and *secondly* are also well-established forms.

former, latter Used together, *former* refers to the first of two; *latter* to the second of two. John and Ian are both English. The **former** is from Manchester; the **latter** is from Birmingham.

further See **farther, further**.

get Considered conversational in many common expressions: The weather ~~got better~~ **improved** overnight. I did not know what he ~~was getting at~~ **meant**.

good, well *Good* is an adjective, not an adverb: He pitched ~~good~~ **well** last night. *Good* in the sense of "in good health" may be used interchangeably with *well:* I feel **good** [OR **well**] this morning.

had better See **better, had better**.

half *A half a* or *a half an* is unconventional; use *half a/an* or *a half:* You should be able to complete the questionnaire in **a half ~~an~~** hour.

hanged, hung *Hanged* means "put to death by hanging": The prisoner was **hanged** at dawn. For all other meanings, use *hung:* He **hung** the picture above his desk.

has got, have got Conversational; omit *got*: I **have** ~~got~~ a meeting tomorrow.

he/she, his/her As a solution to the problem of sexist language, these combinations are not universally accepted. Consider using *he or she* and *his or her*. See **12c**.

herself, himself, myself, yourself Unconventional as subjects in a sentence. Joe and ~~myself~~ **I** will lead the discussion. See **5a(3)**.

hopefully Conversational to mean "I hope": ~~Hopefully,~~ **I hope** the game will not be canceled.

hung See **hanged, hung**.

i.e. Abbreviation of *id est,* meaning "that is." Use only within parentheses: All participants in the study ran the same distance (**i.e.,** six kilometers). Otherwise, replace *i.e.* with the English equivalent, *that is:* Assistance was offered to those who would have difficulty boarding, ~~i.e.,~~ **that is,** the elderly, the disabled, and parents with small children. Do not confuse *i.e.* with *e.g.,* meaning "for example."

illicit See **elicit, illicit**.

illusion See **allusion, illusion**.

immigrate See **emigrate from, immigrate to**.

***impact** Though *impact* is commonly used as a verb in business writing, many college teachers still use it as a noun only: The new tax ~~impacts~~ **affects** everyone.

implicit See **explicit, implicit**.

imply, infer *Imply* means "suggest without actually stating": Though he never mentioned the statistics, he **implied** that they were questionable. *Infer* means "draw a conclusion based on evidence": Given the tone of his voice, I **inferred** that he found the work substandard.

in regards to   Unconventional; see **regard, regarding, regards.**

inside of, outside of   Drop *of* when unnecessary: Security guards stood **outside ~~of~~** the front door.

insure   See **assure, ensure, insure.**

irregardless   Unconventional; use *regardless* instead.

its, it's   *Its* is a possessive form: The committee forwarded **its** recommendation. *It's* is a contraction of *it is:* **It's** a beautiful day.

kind of a, sort of a   The word *a* is unnecessary: This **kind of ~~a~~** book sells well. *Kind of* and *sort of* are not conventionally used to mean "somewhat": The report was ~~**kind of**~~ **somewhat** difficult to read.

later, latter   *Later* means "after a specific time" or "a time after now": The concert ended **later** than we had expected. *Latter* refers to the second of two items: Of the two versions described, I prefer the **latter.**

lay, lie   *Lay* (*laid, laying*) means "put" or "place": He **laid** the book aside. *Lie* (*lay, lain, lying*) means "rest" or "recline": I had just **lain** down when the alarm went off. *Lay* takes an object (to **lay** something), while *lie* does not. These verbs may be confused because the present tense of *lay* and the past tense of *lie* are spelled the same way.

lead, led   As a noun, *lead* means "a kind of metal": The paint had **lead** in it. As a verb, *lead* means "to conduct": A guide will **lead** a tour of the ruins. *Led* is the past tense of the verb *lead:* He **led** the country from 1949 to 1960.

less, less than   See **fewer, less.**

lie   See **lay, lie.**

like   See **as, like.**

literally   Conversational when used to emphasize the meaning of another word: I was ~~literally~~ **nearly** frozen after I finished shoveling the sidewalk. *Literally* is conventionally used to indicate that an expression is not being used figuratively: My friend **literally** climbs the walls after work; his fellow rock climbers join him at the local gym.

lose, loose *Lose* is a verb: She does not **lose** her patience often. *Loose* is chiefly used as an adjective: A few of the tiles are **loose**.

lots, lots of Conversational for *many* or *much:* He has ~~lots of~~ many friends. We have ~~lots~~ much to do before the end of the quarter.

mankind Considered sexist because it excludes women: All ~~mankind~~ humanity will benefit from this new discovery.

may See **can, may**.

may of, might of See **could of**.

maybe, may be *Maybe* is an adverb: **Maybe** the negotiators will succeed this time. *May* and *be* are verbs: The rumor **may be** true.

* **media, medium** According to traditional definitions, *media* is a plural word: The **media** have sometimes created the news in addition to reporting it. The singular form is *medium:* The newspaper is one **medium** that people seem to trust. Dictionary editors note the frequent use of *media* as a collective noun taking a singular verb, but this usage is still considered conversational.

might could Conversational for "might be able to": The director **might** ~~could~~ be able to review your application next week.

most Unconventional to mean "almost": We watch the news ~~most~~ almost every day.

myself See **herself, himself, myself, yourself**.

nothing like, nowhere near Unconventional; use *not nearly* instead: Her new book is ~~nowhere near~~ not nearly as mysterious as her previous novel.

number of When the expression *a number of* is used, the reference is plural: **A number of** positions **are** open. When *the number of* is used, the reference is singular: **The number of** possibilities **is** limited. See also **amount of, number of**.

off of Conversational; omit *of:* He walked **off** ~~of~~ the field.

on account of Conversational; use *because of:* The singer canceled her engagement ~~on account of~~ because of a sore throat.

on the other hand Use *however* instead or make sure that the sentence or independent clause beginning with this transitional phrase is preceded by one starting with *on the one hand.*

other See **another, other, the other**.

Glossary of Usage

passed, past *Passed* is the past tense of the verb *pass:* Deb **passed** the other runners right before the finish line. *Past* means "beyond a time or location": We walked **past** the high school.

per In ordinary contexts, use *a* or *an:* You should drink at least six glasses of water ~~per~~ a day.

percent, percentage *Percent* (also spelled *per cent*) is used with a specific number: **Sixty percent** of the students attended the ceremony. *Percentage* refers to an unspecified portion: The **percentage** of students attending college has increased in recent years.

perspective, prospective *Perspective* means "point of view": We discussed the issue from various **perspectives.** *Prospective* means "likely to become": **Prospective** journalists interviewed the editor.

phenomena, phenomenon *Phenomena* is the plural form of *phenomenon:* Natural **phenomena** were given scientific explanations.

plus *Plus* joins nouns or noun phrases to make a sentence seem like an equation: Her endless curiosity **plus** her boundless energy makes her the perfect camp counselor. Note that a singular form of the verb is required (e.g., **makes**). *Plus* is not used to join clauses: I telephoned ~~plus~~ and I sent flowers.

precede, proceed To *precede* is to "go ahead of": A moment of silence **preceded** the applause. To *proceed* is to "go forward": After stopping for a short rest, we **proceeded** to our destination.

prejudice, prejudiced *Prejudice* is a noun: They were unaware of their **prejudice.** *Prejudiced* is an adjective: She accused me of being **prejudiced.**

pretty *Pretty* means "attractive," not "rather" or "fairly": We were ~~pretty~~ fairly tired after cooking all day.

principal, principle As a noun, *principal* means "chief official": The **principal** greeted the students every day. It also means "capital": The loan's **principal** was still quite high. As an adjective, *principal* means "main": Tourism is the country's **principal** source of income. The noun *principle* refers to a rule, standard, or belief: She explained the three **principles** supporting the theory.

proceed See **precede, proceed.**

prospective See **perspective, prospective.**

quotation, quote In academic writing, *quotation*, rather than *quote*, refers to a repeated or copied sentence or passage: She began her speech with a ~~quote~~ **quotation** from *Othello*. *Quote* expresses an action: My friend sometimes **quotes** lines from television commercials.

raise, rise *Raise* (*raised, raising*) means "to lift or cause to move upward, to bring up or increase": Retailers **raised** prices. *Rise* (*rose, risen, rising*) means "to get up" or "to ascend": The cost of living **rose** sharply. *Raise* takes an object (to **raise** something); *rise* does not.

real, really *Really* rather than *real* is used to mean "very": He is from a ~~real~~ **really** small town. To ensure this word's effectiveness, use it sparingly.

** **reason why** Traditionally, this combination was considered redundant: No one explained **the reason** ~~why~~ the negotiations failed. [OR No one explained ~~the reason~~ **why** the negotiations failed.] However, dictionary editors report its use by highly regarded writers.

regard, regarding, regards These forms are used in the following expressions: *in regard to, with regard to, as regards,* and *regarding* [NOT *in regards to, with regards to,* or *as regarding*].

** **relation, relationship** According to traditional definitions, *relation* is used to link abstractions: We studied the **relation** between language and social change. *Relationship* is used to link people: The **relationship** between the two friends grew strong. However, dictionary editors now label as standard the use of *relationship* to connect abstractions.

respectfully, respectively *Respectfully* means "showing respect": The children learned to treat one another **respectfully**. *Respectively* means "in the order designated": We discussed the issue with the chair, the dean, and the provost, **respectively**.

rise See **raise, rise**.

should of See **could of**.

sight See **cite, site, sight**.

sit, set *Sit* means "to be seated": Jonathan **sat** in the front row. *Set* means "to place something": The research assistant **set** the chemicals on the counter. *Set* takes an object (to **set** something); *sit* does not.

site See **cite, site, sight**.

so Instead of using *so* to mean "very," find a precise modifier: She was ~~so~~ **intensely** focused on her career. See 7g.

someplace See **anyplace, everyplace, someplace**.

sometime, sometimes, some time *Sometime* means "at an unspecified time": They will meet **sometime** next month. *Sometimes* means "at times": **Sometimes** laws are unfair. *Some time* means "a span of time": They agreed to allow **some time** to pass before voting on the measure.

sort of a See **kind of a, sort of a**.

specially See **especially, specially**.

stationary, stationery *Stationary* means "in a fixed position": Traffic was **stationary** for an hour. *Stationery* means "writing paper and envelopes": The director ordered new department **stationery**.

supposed to, used to Be sure to include the frequently unsounded *d* at the end of the verb form: We are **suppose**d **to** leave at 9:30 a.m. We **use**d **to** leave earlier.

than, then *Than* is used in comparisons: The tape recorder is smaller **than** the radio. *Then* refers to a time sequence: Go straight ahead for three blocks; **then** turn left.

their, there, they're *Their* is the possessive form of *they:* They will give **their** presentation tomorrow. *There* refers to location: I lived **there** for six years. *There* is also used as an expletive (see 14a(3)): **There** is no explanation for the phenomenon. *They're* is a contraction of *they are:* **They're** leaving in the morning.

theirself, theirselves Unconventional; use *themselves*. The students finished the project by ~~theirself~~ **themselves**.

then See **than, then**.

to, too, two *To* is an infinitive marker: She wanted **to** become an actress. *To* is also used as a preposition, usually indicating direction: They walked **to** the memorial. *Too* means either "also" or "excessively": I voted for her **too**. They are **too** busy this year. *Two* is a number: She studied abroad for **two** years.

toward, towards Although both are acceptable, *toward* is preferred in American English.

try and Conversational for *try to:* The staff will **try ~~and~~ to** finish the project by Friday.

uninterested See **disinterested, uninterested.**

* **unique** Traditionally, *unique* meant "one of a kind" and thus was not preceded by a qualifier such as *more, most, quite,* or *very:* Her prose style is ~~quite~~ **unique.** However, dictionary editors note that *unique* is also widely used to mean "extraordinary."

use, utilize In most contexts, *use* is preferred to *utilize:* We ~~utilized~~ **used** a special dye in the experiment. However, *utilize* may suggest an effort to employ something for a purpose: We discussed how to **utilize** the resources we had been given.

used to See **supposed to, used to.**

very To ensure this word's effectiveness, use it sparingly. Whenever possible, choose a stronger word: She was ~~very satisfied~~ **delighted** with her new digital camera.

ways Conversational when referring to distance; use *way* instead: It's a long ~~ways~~ **way** from home.

well See **good, well.**

where . . . at, where . . . to Conversational; omit *at* and *to:* **Where is the library ~~at~~? Where are you moving ~~to~~?**

with regards to Unconventional; see **regard, regarding, regards.**

would of See **could of.**

your, you're *Your* is a possessive form: Let's meet in **your** office. *You're* is a contraction of *you are:* **You're** gaining strength.

yourself See **herself, himself, myself, yourself.**

Credits

This page constitutes an extension of the copyright page. We have made every effort to trace the ownership of all copyrighted material and to secure permission from copyright holders. In the event of any question arising as to the use of any material, we will be pleased to make the necessary corrections in future printings. Thanks are due to the following authors, publishers, and agents for permission to use the material indicated.

Text

p. 296 (Fig. 33.1): Page from *American Literary History* 20: 1–2 (Spring/Summer 2008), by permission of Oxford University Press.

pp. 300–301 (Figs. 33.2 and 33.3): Skin: a natural history by Nina Jablonsky. Copyright 2006 by UNIVERSITY OF CALIFORNIA PRESS - BOOKS. Reproduced with permission of UNIVERSITY OF CALIFORNIA PRESS - BOOKS in the format Textbook via Copyright Clearance Center.

p. 344 (Fig. 34.1): Thomas and Woods (2003) Working with People with Learning Disabilities, Jessica Kingsley Publishers, London and Philadelphia. Reproduced with kind permission of Jessica Kingsley Publishers.

p. 349 (Fig. 34.2): Excerpt from "Tricksters and the Marketing of Breakfast Cereals" by Thomas Green, *The Journal of Popular Culture*, Vol. 40, No 1, January 24, 2007, p. 49. Reprinted by permission of John Wiley through Rightslink.

p. 351 (Fig. 34.3): "Children's Eyewitness Reports After Exposure to Misinformation From Parents" by Debra Ann Poole and D. Stephen Lindsay, *Journal of Experimental Psychology: Applied*, Vol. 7, No 1, p. 27. Copyright © 2001 by the American Psychological Association. Reproduced with permission.

Photos and Illustrations

p. 220 (Fig. 27.3): Courtesy of Canon USA, Inc. © 2005 Canon USA, Inc.

p. 249: © Danny Daniels/PhotoLibrary.

p. 269 (Fig. 32.1): © Michael & Patricia Fogden/Corbis.

p. 310 (Fig. 33.4): © The Art Institute of Chicago.

p. 313 (Fig. 33.5): Copyright © 2005 ProQuest.

p. 360: © Tim Graham/Getty Images.

p. 362: © Eric Anthony Photography/Monsoon Images/PhotoLibrary.

p. 364: © Color-Blind Images/Blend Images/Corbis.

p. 394 (left): © The Trustees of the National Museums of Scotland; **(right):** Courtesy of the Silver Trust, London.

Index

Numbers and letters in color refer to chapters and sections in the handbook; other numbers refer to pages.

a, an, **1a**: 5
    with abbreviations, acronyms, or numbers, **23d**: 194
    with count nouns, **37b**: 400, **37c**: 402
    omission of, from name of periodical, **33b**: 295
a lot of, 425
a while, awhile, 425
abbreviation(s), **23**: 191
    in academic and professional writing, **23c**: 192
    for addresses in correspondence, **23b**: 192
    in APA documentation style, **34a**: 337, **34b**: 344, 345, 346, 354
    in CSE documentation style, **36a**: 388, 389
    indefinite articles with, **23d**: 194
    for Latin expressions, **23c**: 193
    in MLA documentation style, **33a**: 283, 285, 286, **33b**: 302, 306, 312, 315, 316
    parentheses around, **19e**: 169, 170
    for parts of speech, **1a**: 2
    periods with, **19a**: 166
    plurals of, **17c**: 158–159
    postal, **23b**: 192
    with proper names, **23a**: 191
    for state names, **23b**: 192, **35a**: 371, **36a**: 389
    for time periods and zones, **23c**: 192–193
    for *United States,* **23c**: 193

absolute claim, **28d**: 223
absolute modifiers, **6b**: 80
absolute phrase, **1d**: 20
    commas with, **15d**: 144
    as sentence fragment, **2b**: 26
abstract
    in APA-style paper, **34c**: 356, 358
    in CSE-style paper, **36b**: 392, 393
    MLA documentation of, **33b**: 314
abstract nouns, **1a**: 3
abstract word, definition of, **13a**: 128
Academic Info, **30d**: 253
academic publishers, **31b**: 261
academic writing. *See also* essay(s); research paper(s)
    abbreviations acceptable in, **23c**: 192–193
accept, except, 425
access date, **30d**: 254, **32b**: 265, **33b**: 309, 310, 318, **35a**: 377, **36a**: 390
accuracy
    in paraphrases, **32d**: 272–273
    of quotations, **32d**: 270
acronyms, **23**: 191
    indefinite articles with, **23e**: 194
    parentheses around, **19e**: 169–170
    spelling out first usage of, **23d**: 193
action, calling for, **28e**: 224
action verbs, **1a**: 2–3, **1c**: 12
active voice, **4d**: 47, 48
Ad*Access, **30e**: 255

Index

address(es)
  abbreviations in, **23b**: 192
  commas in, **15e**: 146
  numerals in, **23f**: 195
  return, **29a**: 237, 239
Adflip, **30e**: 255
adjectival clause(s), **1e**: 22, **5a**: 58–60, **6a**: 78, **8b**: 98
  as nonessential modifier, set off by commas, **1e**: 22, **15d**: 143
  word order in, **39d**: 422–423
adjective(s), **1a**: 4
  abbreviation for *United States* as, **23c**: 193
  versus adverbs, **6a**: 75–77
  beginning sentence with, **10f**: 111, **11b**: 115
  comparative and superlative forms of, **6b**: 79–80
  as complements, **1c**: 13
  determiners with, **37d**: 403
  ordering of, **39a**: 420
  participles as, **6a**: 76
  pronouns as, **5a**: 57
adverb(s), **1a**: 5–6
  versus adjectives, **6a**: 75–77
  beginning sentence with, **11b**: 115
  comparative and superlative forms of, **6b**: 79–80, **37d**: 403–404
  conjunctive, **1a**: 9–10
  of frequency, **6d**: 83, **39b**: 420–421
  of manner, **6a**: 76
  placement of, **39b**: 420–421, **39c**: 421
  relative, **1e**: 22
adverbial clause(s), **1e**: 22–23, **6a**: 78
  comma use with, **15d**: 143
adverbial conjunctions, **1a**: 9
advertisement(s)
  MLA documentation style for, **33b**: 309, 319
  on Web sites, **30e**: 255
Advertising World, **30e**: 255

advice, advise, 425
affect, effect, 425
African American, use of, **12c**: 124
afterword, MLA documentation style for, **33b**: 302–303
age, referring to, **12c**: 125
agreement
  of pronoun and antecedent, **5c**: 66–68
  of subject and verb, **4f**: 51–56
aircraft names, italics for, **22b**: 189
all ready, already, 426
all right, 426
all together, altogether, 426
allude, elude, 426
allusion, illusion, 426
alot. See a lot of
already. See all ready, already
alright. See all right
altogether. See all together, altogether
a.m., p.m., **23c**: 193
American Indian, use of, **12c**: 125
American Psychological Association (APA), **34**: 337. *See also* APA style
American Reference Books Annual (*ARBA*), **30b**: 251
among, between, 426
amount of, number of, 426
ampersand, in APA documentation, **34a**: 338, **34b**: 345
an. See a, an
and, as conjunction, **1b**: 11–12, **4f**: 52
and/or, 426
angle brackets, **19f**: 171, **33b**: 309, 310
angry at, angry with, 427
annotated bibliography, **32c**: 267
anonymous work
  APA style for citation of, **34a**: 339
  MLA style for citation and documentation of, **33a**: 285, **33b**: 302
another, other, the other, 427

Index

antecedent(s), **1a**: 4
   agreement of pronoun with, **5c**: 66–68
   collective noun as, **5c**: 68
   indefinite pronoun as, **5a**: 60
   of relative pronoun in adjectival clause, **4f**: 53, **5a**: 58–60
anthology
   CMS documentation style for, **35a**: 374
   MLA documentation style for, **33b**: 303–304
anymore, any more, 427
anyone, any one, 427
anyplace, everyplace, someplace, 427
APA style, **34**: 337
   abbreviations in, **34a**: 337, **34b**: 345
   for abstract, **34c**: 356, 358
   for body of paper, **34c**: 356, 359
   capitalization in, **21b**: 185, **21c**: 186
   for documentation of articles, **34b**: 347–350, 352
   for documentation of books, **34b**: 344–347, 353
   for documentation of electronic or online sources, **34b**: 350–355
   for documentation of films and television programs, **34b**: 355
   for in-text citations, **34a**: 337–340
   italics in, **34b**: 344, 347, 348
   for reference list, **34b**: 340–341, **34c**: 365
   sample paper in, **34c**: 357–365
   for spaces with punctuation marks, **19**: 166
   spelling out of numbers in, **23e**: 194
   for title page of paper, **34c**: 356, 357
apostrophe
   forming plurals with, **17c**: 158–159
   indicating ownership and other relationships, **17a**: 154–158
   marking omissions of letters or numbers, **17b**: 158

appeals, rhetorical, **28f**: 226–227
application, letters of, **29d**: 245–246
appositive(s), **1d**: 19
   nonessential, set off by commas, **1d**: 19, **15d**: 143–144
   as sentence fragment, **2b**: 26
appositive pronouns, **5b**: 63–64
arguable statement, **28b**: 222
argument, **28**: 221
   arrangement of, **28g**: 227–228
   claim for, **28d**: 223–224
   evidence for, **28e**: 224–226
   fact and opinion in, **28c**: 223
   purpose of, **28a**: 221–222
   rhetorical appeals in, **28f**: 226–227
   sample student, **28h**: 228–235
   topics for, **28b**: 222
argumentative writing, **24c**: 201
arrangement
   of argument, **28g**: 227–228
   of ideas, **25c**: 206–207
art
   MLA documentation style for, **33b**: 318–319, 321
   Web sites for, **30e**: 255
Artchive, The, **30e**: 255
articles (part of speech), **1a**: 5, **5c**: 67, **23d**: 194, **37a–e**: 398–405
articles (publications)
   APA documentation style for, **34b**: 347–350, 352
   CMS documentation style for, **35a**: 376–379
   CSE documentation style for, **36a**: 390, 391, 392
   evaluating, **31b**: 261–262
   finding, **30c**: 252
   MLA documentation style for, **33b**: 295–298, 305, 310–311
as, 427
as, like, 427
Asian American, use of, **12c**: 124

Index

Ask, **30d**: 253
assure, ensure, insure, 427
asterisks, in keyword search, **30b**: 250
attachments, to e-mail messages, **29b**: 242
attributive tags, **32d**: 268–269
    comma use with, **15f**: 146, **18c**: 163
    to divide quotations, **3c**: 33
audience(s), **24a**: 199, **24c**: 201–202
    purpose of argument and, **28a**: 221–222
    for research paper, **30a**: 249
    rhetorical appeals to, **28f**: 226–227
author(s)
    APA citation style for, **34a**: 337, 338–339
    APA documentation style for, **34b**: 343–345, 347–349
    CMS documentation style for, **35a**: 368, 370–373
    credibility of, **24a**: 199–200, **31a**: 259–261
    CSE documentation style for, **36a**: 385, 388, 389, 392
    MLA citation style for, **33a**: 281, 282–284
    MLA documentation style for, **33b**: 299–302, 307, 308, 311–312
    reasoning of, **32f**: 277
    sources for information about, **31a**: 259
    world view of, **31a**: 260–261
author-date system, **34**: 337
authorship, in business writing, **29**: 236
auxiliary verb(s), **1a**: 2, **4a**: 37–38, **38b**: 414–417
    do as, **4a**: 37
    in verb phrases, **1d**: 15
awhile. See *a while, awhile*
axes, of line graph, **27b**: 218

background, in argument, **28g**: 228
bad, 428
Balay, Robert, **30b**: 251

bar charts, **27b**: 218
base form, of verb, **4a**: 34, 35–36, **38a**: 406, 407
be, **4a**: 37, **4d**: 47
    forms of, **4a**: 35
    illogical equation with, **7d**: 90–91
be able to, **38b**: 415
be going to, **38a**: 408
being as, being that, 428
beside, besides, 428
better, had better, 428
between. See *among, between*
Bible. See sacred texts
bibliography. *See also* reference list; works-cited list
    abbreviations in, **23c**: 192
    annotated, **32c**: 267
    CMS style for, **35a**: 366, 368, **35b**: 379, 383
    for paper in the humanities, **35b**: 379, 383
    working, **32c**: 267–268
bills, congressional, MLA-style documentation of, **33b**: 316
Bing, **30d**: 253
Black (or *black*), use of, **12c**: 124
block format, for letter, **29a**: 237
block quotation, **32d**: 270, **33a**: 289
blog
    APA documentation of posting to, **34b**: 353
    MLA documentation of posting to, **33b**: 316
body
    of APA-style paper, **34c**: 356, 359–364
    of business letter, **29a**: 238, 239
    of business memo, **29b**: 240, 241
    of historical research paper, **35b**: 379–381
book(s)
    APA documentation style for, **34b**: 343–347, 353

CMS documentation style for, **35a**: 370–375
CSE documentation style for, **36a**: 388–389, 390, 392
evaluating, **31b**: 261
finding, **30b**: 250–251
MLA documentation style for, **33a**: 280, **33b**: 299–306, 311–312
numerals for pages and divisions in, **23f**: 195
book publishers, **31b**: 261
book reviews
    APA documentation style for, **34b**: 350
    for assessing author's credibility, **31a**: 260–261
    MLA documentation style for, **33b**: 299
Boolean operators, **30b**: 250
both . . . and, **1a**: 9
brackets. *See* angle brackets; square brackets
bridges, capitalization of names of, **21a**: 183
brochure(s), APA documentation style for, **34b**: 354
building names, capitalization of, **21a**: 183–184
bulletin, MLA documentation style for, **33b**: 307
business letters, **29a**: 237–239
    colon use in, **16b**: 152
business memos, **29b**: 240–242
business writing, **29**: 236. *See also specific types*
    conventions of language and organization in, **29**: 236–237

call number, **30b**: 251
can, may, 428
capital, capitol, 428
capitalization
    of company names, **21a**: 183–184
    of computer keys, menu items, and icons, **21d**: 187
    of days of week, **21a**: 183
    of first word of sentence, **21c**: 185–187
    following a colon, **21c**: 186
    of geographical features, **21a**: 183–184
    of government agencies, **21a**: 183–184
    of historical documents, periods, events, movements, and styles, **21a**: 183–184
    of holidays, **21a**: 183–184
    of military terms, **21a**: 183–184
    of months, **21a**: 183–184
    of names of bridges, buildings, and monuments, **21a**: 183–184
    of names of ethnic or cultural groups and languages, **21a**: 183
    proofreading for, **26c**: 213
    of proper names, **21a**: 183–184
    of religions, their adherents, holy days, titles of holy books, and words denoting the Supreme Being, **21a**: 183–184
    of specific persons or things, **21a**: 183–184
    of titles accompanying proper names, **21a**: 183–184
    of titles and subtitles, **21b**: 184–185, **35a**: 370, **36a**: 388
capitol. See capital, capitol
Carey, Ken, **2c**: 27
cartoon, MLA documentation style for, **33b**: 308, 319
case
    legal, MLA documentation of, **33b**: 307, 317
    of pronouns, **5b**: 61–66
catalog, online, **30b**: 250–251
CD, MLA documentation style for, **33b**: 322

Index

CD-ROM, MLA documentation style for, **33b**: 321–322
chapter of book
    APA documentation style for, **34b**: 353
    CSE documentation style for, **36a**: 389, 392
chart(s), **27a**: 217–218
    MLA documentation style for, **33b**: 308, 319
checklist, in survey question, **30e**: 257
Chicano/Chicana, use of, **12c**: 124
Chicago Manual of Style, The, **21c**: 186, **35**: 366. *See also* CMS style
choppy sentences, revision of, **1d**: 17, **11a**: 113–114
citation(s). *See* in-text citations
citation-name system, of CSE, **36a**: 384, 386, 388
citation-sequence system, of CSE, **36a**: 384, 385, 386, 388–391
cite, site, sight, 428–429
city
    of publication, **33b**: 298, 299, **34b**: 343, **35a**: 370, 371, **36a**: 389
    and state, comma separating, **15e**: 145
claim, of argument, **28d**: 223–224, **28e**: 224–226
classical arrangement, **28g**: 227, 228
clause(s), **1e**: 20–23. *See also* adjectival clause(s); adverbial clause(s); dependent clause(s); independent clause(s)
    comma following introductory dependent, **15b**: 139
    comma linking independent, **15a**: 138–139
    elliptical, **1e**: 23, **5b**: 65, **6e**: 85
    essential versus nonessential, **5a**: 59
    including *that* before, **7f**: 94
    integrating, **3b**: 32
    linking of, **3b**: 31, 32, **8a**: 97–98, **8b**: 98–99
    as modifiers, **6a**: 78–79
    noun, **1e**: 21, **4f**: 56, **7d**: 92
    parallel, **9a**: 103, **9b**: 104
    separating with period, **3b**: 30–31
cliché, **13b**: 129–130
climactic, climatic, 429
climactic order, **10c**: 109
clip art, Web sites for, **30e**: 255
closing, of business letter, **29a**: 238, 239
CMS style
    for bibliography, **35a**: 366, 368, **35b**: 379, 383
    for capitalization of titles, **35a**: 370
    for capitalization with colon, **21c**: 186
    for documentation of articles, **35a**: 376–379
    for documentation of books, **35a**: 370–375
    for documentation of interview, **35a**: 379
    for documentation of videocassette or DVD, **35a**: 379
    general documentation guidelines for, **35a**: 366–368
    notes in, **35a**: 366, 367–368
    sample paper in, **35b**: 379–383
coarse, course, 429
coherence, of paragraphs, **26a**: 209–212
collective noun(s), **1a**: 3
    agreement of verbs with, **4f**: 54
    as antecedent, **5c**: 68
collocations, **13c**: 130–131
    choosing right preposition in, **13c**: 131
colloquial words, **12b**: 121
colon
    in business correspondence, **16b**: 152
    capitalization following, **21c**: 186

Index

directing attention to explanation, summary, or quotation, **16b**: 151
to emphasize words, **10a**: 108
to join clauses, **3b**: 30–31
quotation marks with, **18c**: 164
separating chapter and verse, **16b**: 152, **33a**: 285–286
separating title and subtitle, **16b**: 152
separating volume and page numbers, **33a**: 289
signaling list that follows, **16b**: 152
comic strip, MLA documentation style for, **33b**: 308, 319
comma(s)
in APA documentation style, **34a**: 338
before coordinating conjunction linking independent clauses, **1a**: 9, **3b**: 30, **15a**: 138–139
with direct quotations accompanied by attributive tags, **15f**: 146
following transitional words, **16a**: 150
with geographical names and items in dates and addresses, **15e**: 145–146
between independent clauses, **3**: 29
with interjection, **1a**: 10
after introductory clauses, phrases, or words, **15b**: 139–140
in MLA in-text citations, **33a**: 282, 289
with nonessential elements, **1d**: 19, **15d**: 142–145
with numerals, **23f**: 196
quotation marks with, **18c**: 163–164
semicolon separating elements that contain, **16a**: 150
separating coordinate adjectives, **15c**: 141–142
separating elements in series, **15c**: 141–142
unnecessary or misplaced, **15g**: 147–148
comma fault, **3**: 29

comma splice(s), **3**: 29
recognizing, **3a**: 29–30
revising, **3b**: 30–33
command, for variety of sentences, **11c**: 117
commercial publishers, **31b**: 261
common ground, in argumentative writing, **28a**: 221–222, **28f**: 226
common knowledge, **32e**: 274
common nouns, **1a**: 3
determiners with, **37b**: 399–402
company names, capitalization of, **21a**: 183–184
comparative form, of adjective or adverb, **6b**: 79–80, **37d**: 403–404
comparatives, double, **6b**: 80
compare to, compare with, 429
comparisons, effective, **6b**: 79–80
complement(s), **1c**: 12–13
mismatch of, with verb, **7d**: 90–92
noun phrases as, **1d**: 14
with verbs for attribution, **7d**: 92
complement, complementary, compliment, complimentary, 429
compose, comprise, 429
compound noun, apostrophe use with, **17a**: 157
compound objects, **5b**: 63
compound predicate, **1b**: 11
avoiding comma between elements of, **15g**: 147
compound subject, **1b**: 11, **5b**: 61
comprise. See compose, comprise
computer, organizing notes with, **32b**: 265, 266
computer keys, capitalization of, **21d**: 187
concession, **28f**: 226, **28g**: 227
conciseness
in business writing, **29**: 236, **29b**: 241
deleting *there are* and *it is* for, **14b**: 135
deleting unnecessary words for, **14a**: 134

Index

conciseness *(cont.)*
  elliptical constructions for, **14b**: 135
  redundancy and wordiness and, **14a**: 133–134
  replacing wordy expressions for, **14a**: 134
  using relative pronouns and, **14a**: 133
conclusion, of argument, **28g**: 227, 228
concrete nouns, **1a**: 3
concrete word, definition of, **13a**: 128
confirmation, in argument, **28h**: 228
congressional document, MLA documentation style for, **33b**: 316
conjunction(s), **1a**: 8–10, **8b**: 99, **8c**: 100. *See also* coordinating conjunctions; correlative conjunctions; subordinating conjunctions
  adverbial, **1a**: 9–10
  combining short sentences with, **11a**: 113–114
conjunctive adverbs, **1a**: 9–10
connotation, **13a**: 127
conscience, conscious, consciousness, 429
consistency, in verb tenses, **4c**: 44–46
Constitution, MLA documentation style for, **33a**: 286–287, **33b**: 307
context, **24a**: 199, **24d**: 203
continual, continually, continuous, continuously, 429–430
contractions, versus possessive forms, **17a**: 156, **20b**: 177
contrasted elements, set off by commas, **15e**: 145
conversational words, **12b**: 121
coordinate adjectives, **15c**: 141–142
  comma separating, **15c**: 141–142
coordinating conjunctions, **1a**: 8, **8b**: 99
  avoiding comma following, **15g**: 147
  to combine sentences, **11a**: 113–114
  comma before, **15a**: 138–139
  joining independent clauses, **3b**: 30
  joining parallel elements, **9a**: 103
coordination, **8b**: 98–99
  avoiding faulty or excessive, **8c**: 100–101
  effective use of, **8b**: 98–99
copyright
  date, **33b**: 300
  of images, **30d**: 254–255
corporate author
  APA documentation style for, **34b**: 345
  CSE documentation style for, **36a**: 389, 392
  MLA documentation style for, **33a**: 284, **33b**: 302
correlative conjunctions (correlatives), **1a**: 9
  parallelism and, **9b**: 106
could of, 430
couldn't care less, 430
council, counsel, 430
Council of Science Editors (CSE), **36**: 384. *See also* CSE style
counsel. See council, counsel
count noun(s), **1a**: 3
  determiners with, **37b**: 399–400
course. See coarse, course
coverage, of research source, **32f**: 276
credentials, of authors, **31a**: 259
credibility
  and argumentative writing, **28e**: 225
  of authors, **31a**: 259–261
  of publishers, **31b**: 261–262
  of research paper, **32a**: 264
criteria, criterion, 430
Cronin, Sarah, **34c**: 357
CSE style, **36**: 384
  citation-name system of, **36a**: 384, 386, 388
  citation-sequence system of, **36a**: 384, 385, 386, 388–391

for documentation of articles, **36a**: 390, 391, 392
for documentation of books, **36a**: 388–389, 390, 392
for documentation of electronic sources, **36a**: 390–391
for end references list, **36a**: 386, 392, **36b**: 392, 395–396
for in-text references, **36a**: 385–386
name-year system of, **36a**: 384–385, **36b**: 392
sample paper in, **36b**: 392–396
cultural groups, capitalization of, **21a**: 183
cumulative sentence, **10b**: 108–109
currency, of sources, **32f**: 276

dangling modifier(s), **6e**: 84–85
dash
  to emphasize words, **10a**: 108
  following introductory list or series, **19d**: 168
  marking break in normal flow of sentence, **19d**: 168
  quotation marks with, **18c**: 164
  setting off nonessential element for emphasis or clarity, **19d**: 168
data, 430
database, electronic, **30c**: 252
  CMS documentation style for work from, **35a**: 377
  CSE documentation style for work from, **36a**: 391
  MLA documentation style for work from, **33b**: 312–314, 322
date. *See also* access date; publication date
  comma separating day and, **15e**: 145
  cultural conventions for writing, **23f**: 195
  numerals versus words for, **23f**: 195
days of week, capitalization of, **21a**: 183
decimals, using numerals for, **23f**: 195

definite article, **1a**: 5
definition(s)
  for exactness, **13d**: 131–132
  formal, **13d**: 132
  indefinite article in, **1a**: 5
  mismatches in, **7d**: 91
Delaney, Joseph F., **29c**: 243
demonstrative pronouns (demonstratives), **5a**: 60, **37a–c**: 398–401
denotation, **13a**: 127
dependent clause(s), **1e**: 21, **8a**: 97–98
  for revising comma splice, **3b**: 31
  as sentence fragments, **2c**: 27
description, spatial order and, **26a**: 211
desert, dessert, 430
detail(s)
  developing paragraph with, **25d**: 207–208
  for sentence unity, **7a**: 88–89
determiners
  and adjectives, **37d**: 403–404
  and count nouns, **37b**: 399–400
  and noncount nouns, **37c**: 400–402
  and proper nouns, **37a**: 398–399
device, devise, 430
dialogue, enclosing in quotation marks, **18a**: 161
diction, editing for, **26b**: 212
dictionaries
  MLA documentation style for entry in, **33b**: 306
  specialized, **30b**: 251
Didion, Joan, **10e**: 110
differ from, differ with, 430
different from, different than, 430–431
digital object identifier (DOI), **34b**: 350, 351, 352
digital sources, MLA documentation style for, **33b**: 321–322
direct address. *See* vocative
direct object(s), **1c**: 12
  placement of adverbs and, **39c**: 421

Index

direct quotation(s), **32d**: 269–270.
See also quotation(s)
directness, in business writing, **29**: 236
directories, subject, **30d**: 253
disability, referring to, **12c**: 125
discreet, discrete, 431
discussion group or forum. *See* online discussion group(s)
discussion section, in research report, **36b**: 392
disinterested, uninterested, 431
dissertation, MLA documentation style for, **33b**: 308
distinct, distinctive, 431
diverse audience, **24c**: 202
diverse views, argument and, **28f**: 226
divided quotations, **3c**: 33
do, **4a**: 38, **38b**: 415
documentation of sources. *See also* APA style; CMS style; CSE style; MLA style
   abbreviations in, **23c**: 192
   with paraphrase, **32e**: 274
   with quotation, **32e**: 275
DOI, **34b**: 350–352, **35a**: 376–378
domain, **31c**: 262
Dorfman, Ariel, **11c**: 116
double negatives, **6c**: 81
draft, sample of final, **26c**: 213–216
drafting, **25a**: 204
   of well-developed paragraphs, **25d**: 207–208
due to, 431
DVD
   CMS documentation style for, **35a**: 379
   MLA documentation style for, **33b**: 322

EBSCO, **30c**: 252
   MLA documentation style for article from, **33b**: 312, 313

-ed form of verb, **4a**: 34
edited work
   APA documentation style for selection from, **34b**: 347
   MLA documentation style for selection from, **33b**: 304
editing, **25a**: 204, **26a**: 209, **26b**: 212
edition of book
   APA documentation style for, **34b**: 346
   CMS documentation style for, **35a**: 373
   MLA documentation style for, **33b**: 302
editor(s)
   APA documentation style for, **34b**: 345
   CMS documentation style for, **35a**: 372
   CSE documentation style for, **36a**: 389, 392
   MLA documentation style for, **33b**: 302
editorial(s), MLA documentation style for, **33b**: 299, 311
effect. See affect, effect
either . . . or, **1a**: 9
electronic database, **30c**: 252, **33b**: 312–314, 322
electronic sources
   APA documentation style for, **34b**: 350–355
   CMS documentation style for, **35a**: 376–378
   CSE documentation style for, **36a**: 390–391
   MLA documentation style for, **33a**: 287, **33b**: 309–319
electronic texts. *See* e-mail; Web documents
elicit, illicit, 431
Eliot, T. S., **19g**: 173

Index

ellipsis points
 for omission within quoted passage, **19g**: 171–173, **32d**: 270, **33a**: 289
 for reflective pause or hesitation, **19g**: 173
 to show sentence intentionally left incomplete, **19g**: 173
elliptical clause(s), **1e**: 23, **6e**: 85
elliptical constructions, **5b**: 65
elude. See allude, elude
em dash. *See* dash
e-mail
 as form of business writing, **29b**: 240–242
 multiple audiences and, **24c**: 202
embedded questions, **39d**: 421–422
emigrate from, immigrate to, 431
emotional appeals, **28f**: 226–227
emphasis
 climactic order and, **10c**: 109
 cumulative and periodic sentences and, **10b**: 108–109
 dash for, **10a**: 108, **19d**: 168
 exclamation point for, **19c**: 167
 inverting word order for, **10e**: 110–111
 italics for, **22b**: 189
 parallelism for, **9**: 103, **9c**: 105
 placing words for, **10a**: 108
 repeating words for, **10d**: 109–110
 short sentences for, **10f**: 111
 voice and, **4d**: 48
emphatic order, **26a**: 211
encyclopedia(s)
 APA documentation style for entry in, **34b**: 354
 specialized, **30b**: 251
end references list, in CSE style, **36a**: 386, 392, **36b**: 392, 395–396
endnotes, CMS style for, **35a**: 366, 367–368, **35b**: 382
ensure. See assure, ensure, insure
-*er* suffix, **6b**: 79–80, **37d**: 403–404

Erdrich, Louise, **13a**: 128
ERIC, **30c**: 252
 MLA documentation style for article from, **33b**: 312, 313
especially, specially, 431
essay(s). *See also* writing
 arranging or outlining ideas in, **25c**: 206–207
 developing paragraphs for, **25d**: 207–208
 editing of, **26b**: 212–213
 focusing topic of, **25b**: 205–206
 proofreading of, **26b**: 212–213
 revision of, **26a**: 209–212
 sample final draft of, **26c**: 213–216
 selecting subjects for, **25a**: 204
 thesis of, **25b**: 205–206
-*est* suffix, **6b**: 79–80, **37d**: 403–404
et al., **23c**: 193, **33a**: 283, **33b**: 311–312, **34a**: 338–339, **34b**: 345, **35a**: 372
etc., **23c**: 193, 431–432
ethical appeals, **28f**: 226
ethnic groups
 capitalization of, **21a**: 183
 terms for, **12c**: 124–125
ethos, **28f**: 226
euphemisms, definition of, **13c**: 130
European American, use of, **12c**: 124
evaluation
 of authors' credibility, **31a**: 259–261
 of online and print sources, **31c**: 262, **31d**: 262, 263
 of publishers' credibility, **31b**: 261–262
evaluation claim, **28d**: 224
Evans, Walker, **11c**: 117
events, capitalization of, **21a**: 183, 184
everyday, every day, 432
everyone, every one, 432
everyplace. See anyplace, everyplace, someplace

Index

evidence, for argument, **28e**: 224–226, **28f**: 226
exactness
    clear definitions for, **13d**: 131–132
    figurative language and, **13a**: 128–129
examples, as supporting evidence, **28e**: 225
except. See accept, except
exclamation point, **19c**: 167–168
    with interjection, **1a**: 10
    quotation marks with, **18c**: 164–165
exclamatory sentence, for variety, **11c**: 117
exigence, **24a**: 198
    and research question, **30a**: 248
experts, as source for research, **30e**: 256
explanation, colon directing attention to, **16b**: 151
expletive
    it as, **14b**: 135
    overuse of, **14b**: 135
    there as, **4f**: 53, **14b**: 135
explicit, implicit, 432
expository writing, **24c**: 201, **26a**: 211
expressive writing, **24c**: 201

fact(s)
    distinguishing from opinion, **28c**: 223
    as evidence, **28e**: 225
farther, further, 432
faulty predication, **7d**: 90
FedWorld, **30d**: 254
feel, 432
fewer, less, 432
field research, **30e**: 255–258
figurative language, **13a**: 128–129
figures, **27b**: 219. *See also* graphics
figures of speech, **13a**: 128–129
film
    APA documentation style for, **34b**: 355
    MLA documentation style for, **33b**: 318, 320, 322

film review, MLA documentation style for, **33b**: 299
final draft, **26c**: 213–216
first, firstly; second, secondly, 432
first mention of noun, indefinite article with, **1a**: 5
first person, **5b**: 61
FirstGov, **30d**: 254
focused questions, **30e**: 256
focusing topic for essay, **25b**: 205–206
footnotes, CMS style for, **35a**: 366, 367
foreign words, italics for, **22b**: 189
foreword, MLA documentation style for, **33b**: 302–303
form, parallel structure through repetition of, **9b**: 104–105
formal definition, **13d**: 132
formatting, of business documents, **29**: 237, **29a**: 237, **29b**: 240, **29c**: 242–244, **29d**: 245
former, latter, 432
forum. *See* online discussion group(s)
fractional numbers, hyphens in, **20e**: 181
fragment. *See* sentence fragment(s)
freewriting, **25a**: 204
frequency, adverbs of, **6d**: 83
full note form, CMS style for, **35a**: 366, 367
functional résumé, **29c**: 242
further. See farther, further
fused sentence(s), **3**: 29
    recognizing, **3a**: 29–30
    revising, **3b**: 30–32
future perfect progressive tense, **4b**: 44, **38a**: 413–414
future perfect tense, **4b**: 43, **38a**: 411
future progressive tense, **4b**: 42, **38a**: 410
future tense(s), **4b**: 40–44

Gadsby, Patricia, **19g**: 171, 172
gender, usage and, **12c**: 122–124
general words, **13a**: 128

Index

geographical areas, referring to, **12c**: 125–126

geographical features, capitalization of, **21a**: 183, 184

geographical names, commas with, **15e**: 145

gerund(s), verbs followed by, **1d**: 18

gerund phrase, **1d**: 15, 16
    apostrophe use with, **17a**: 157–158

get, 432

Gladwell, Malcolm, **26a**: 210

good, well, **6a**: 77, 433

Google, **30d**: 253, **31a**: 260

Gorman, James, **4c**: 45–46

government agencies, capitalization of, **21a**: 183, 184

government document or publication
    APA documentation style for, **34b**: 346
    CMS documentation style for, **35a**: 374
    MLA documentation style for, **33b**: 306–307, 316, 317

grammar checker, **1e**: 24

graphics, **27a**: 217
    in research papers, **32d**: 269

graphs, **27a**: 217–218

group author, APA documentation style for, **34b**: 345

Guide to Reference Books (Balay), **30b**: 251

had better. See better, had better

half, 433

hanged, hung, 433

has got, have got, 433

Haslett, Adam, **10d**: 109

have, **4a**: 38

have to, **4a**: 39, **38b**: 415

he, generic, **12c**: 123, 433

heading(s), of business memo, **29b**: 240, 241

hearings, congressional, MLA documentation style for, **33b**: 316

helping verbs, **1a**: 2. *See also* auxiliary verb(s)

herself, himself, myself, yourself, 433

Hester, Nicole, **35b**: 379

his or her, **5c**: 67, 433

Hispanic, use of, **12c**: 125

historical documents, **21a**: 183, 184, **22b**: 189

historical present (tense), **4b**: 41

holidays, capitalization of, **21a**: 183, 184

homophones, proofreading for, **26c**: 213

hopefully, 433

however, **1a**: 10

humanities, writing in, **35**: 366
    sample of, **35b**: 379–383

Humiston, Paul K., **4c**: 44–45

hung. See hanged, hung

hyphen
    to clarify meaning, **20e**: 181
    linking two or more words that form compound, **20e**: 181
    in MLA documentation style, **33a**: 281, 289
    in numbers, fractions, and units of measure, **20e**: 181–182

Ibid., **35a**: 367

Icon Browser, **30e**: 255

icon names, capitalization of, **21d**: 187

identification, numerals for, **23f**: 195

idiom(s), **13c**: 130–131

i.e., **23d**: 193, 433

illicit. See elicit, illicit

illness, referring to, **12c**: 125

illusion. See allusion, illusion

image(s)
    from Internet sources, **30d**: 254–255
    MLA documentation style for, **33b**: 308–309, 318–319, 321

immigrate to. See emigrate from, immigrate to
impact, 433
imperative mood, **4e**: 49
implicit. See explicit, implicit
imply, infer, 433–434
in regards to. See regard, regarding, regards
in-text citations, **32e**: 275
    APA style for, **34a**: 337–340
    CMS style for, **35a**: 366
    CSE style for, **36a**: 385–386
    MLA style for, **33a**: 280–290
inclusive language, **12c**: 122–126
indefinite articles, **1a**: 5
    with abbreviations, acronyms, or numbers, **23e**: 194
indefinite pronoun(s), **5a**: 60, **5c**: 67
    agreement errors with, **4f**: 53–54
independent clause(s), **1e**: 20–21
    capitalization of, following a colon, **21c**: 186
    colon following, **16b**: 151
    in fused sentence, **3**: 29
    joined by coordinating conjunction, **1a**: 8, **15a**: 138–139
    linked by conjunctive adverbs, **1a**: 9–10
    punctuation with, **1a**: 10, **3b**: 30–31, **16a**: 149
index cards, **32b**: 266
indicative mood, **4e**: 49
indirect object(s), **1c**: 12
indirect question, **19b**: 167
indirect source
    APA documentation style for, **34b**: 340
    CMS documentation style for, **35a**: 375
    MLA citation style for, **33a**: 285
infer. See imply, infer

infinitive(s)
    pronouns with, **5b**: 65
    split, **1d**: 17–18
    verbs followed by, **1d**: 18
infinitive marker *to*, **1d**: 17
    repeated for parallel structure, **9b**: 104
infinitive phrase(s), **1d**: 17–18
    as modifiers, **6a**: 78
InfoTrac College Edition, **30c**: 252
    MLA documentation style for article from, **33b**: 312, 314
-ing ending, **1d**: 15–17
-ing form, of verb, **4a**: 34
initials, of authors, **33a**: 283, **35a**: 376, **36a**: 388
inside of, outside of, 434
institution names, capitalization of, **21a**: 183
institutional review boards (IRBs), **30e**: 257
insure. See assure, ensure, insure
integration
    of clauses, **3b**: 32
    of source material, **32d**: 268–273
intended audience, **24c**: 202
intensifier(s), adverbs as, **1a**: 6
intensive pronoun(s), **5a**: 58
interjections, **1a**: 10
Internet Public Library, **30d**: 253
interrogative pronouns, **5a**: 60
interview(s)
    CMS documentation style for, **35a**: 379
    MLA documentation style for, **33b**: 318, 320
    as research source, **30e**: 256
introduction
    of argument, **28h**: 228
    of book, MLA documentation style for, **33b**: 302–303

of historical research paper, **35b**: 380–381
to questionnaire, **30e**: 257
of research report, **36b**: 392, 394
introductory clause, phrase, or word, comma following, **15b**: 139–140
introductory list, dash following, **19d**: 168
introductory series, dash following, **19d**: 168
inverted word order
  agreement errors and, **4f**: 52–53
  for emphasis, **10e**: 110–111
  in questions, **39d**: 422
IRBs, **30e**: 257
irregardless, 434
irregular verbs, **4a**: 35–36
is because/reason, mismatch of, **7d**: 91
issue number(s), **33b**: 297, **35a**: 376, **36a**: 390
it, **5d**: 70
  as expletive, **5d**: 71, **14a**: 135
italics
  for aircraft names, **22b**: 189
  for emphasis, **22b**: 189
  for foreign words, **22b**: 189
  for legal cases, **22b**: 189
  for satellite names, **22b**: 189
  for ship names, **22b**: 189
  for spacecraft names, **22b**: 189
  for submarine names, **22b**: 189
  for titles of works, **22a**: 188–189, **34b**: 347, **35a**: 370
  for words, letters, or figures referred to as such, **22b**: 190
its, it's, 434

jargon, **12c**: 122
Jensen, Heather, **4d**: 48
journal(s), **33b**: 295
  APA documentation style for articles from, **34b**: 347–349, 352
  CMS documentation style for articles from, **35a**: 376–377
  CSE documentation style for articles from, **36a**: 390, 391, 392
  MLA documentation style for articles from, **33b**: 295–298, 304, 310–311
  scholarly, **30c**: 252, **31b**: 261
Jr., **23a**: 191
JSTOR, **30c**: 252, **33b**: 312, 314

Kakutani, Michiko, **10d**: 109
keyword search, **30b**: 250
Kidder, Tracy, **18a**: 161
kind of a, sort of a, 434
King, Martin Luther, Jr., **9c**: 105
Kingsolver, Barbara, **25d**: 208

Lakoff, Robin, **19e**: 169
language(s)
  capitalization of names of, **21a**: 183
  inclusive, **12c**: 122–126
later, latter, 434
Latin American, use of, **12c**: 124
Latin expressions
  abbreviation of, **23d**: 193
  italics for, **22b**: 189
Latino/Latina, use of, **12c**: 125
law case. *See* legal case(s)
lay, lie, 434
lead, led, 434
least, **6b**: 79, **37d**: 403–404
lecture, MLA documentation style for, **33b**: 319–320
lecture notes, APA documentation style for, **34b**: 353
legal case(s)
  italics for, **22b**: 189
  MLA documentation style for, **33b**: 307, 317
less, **6b**: 79, **37d**: 403–404

less, less than. See fewer, less
letter
   of application, **29d**: 245–246
   business, **29a**: 237–239
   to editor, documentation of, **34b**: 350
   of inquiry, **29a**: 238–239
   published, documentation of, **33b**: 308, **35a**: 375
LexisNexis, **30c**: 252
   MLA documentation style for article from, **33b**: 312, 314
Librarian's Index to the Internet, **30d**: 253
library, and research, **30b**: 250–251, **30c**: 252
lie. See lay, lie
like. See as, like
line drawings, **27b**: 219
line graphs, **27a**: 217–218
linking verbs, **1a**: 2
   with subject complements, **1c**: 13, **6a**: 77
list
   colon signaling, **16b**: 152
   dash following introductory, **19d**: 168
   parentheses around numbers or letters in, **19f**: 170
listserv, **30e**: 258
literally, 434
literary present (tense), **4b**: 41
live performances, MLA documentation style for, **33b**: 319–320
logic, in comparisons, **6b**: 79–80
logical appeals, **28f**: 226
logical order, **26a**: 211–212
logos, **28f**: 226
lose, loose, 435
lots, lots of, 435
lowercase letters, in APA documentation style, **34a**: 340, **34b**: 341

-ly ending, **6a**: 76
Lycos, **30d**: 253, **31a**: 260

magazine(s), **30c**: 252, **33b**: 295
   APA documentation style for articles from, **34b**: 349, 352
   CMS documentation style for articles from, **35a**: 376, 378
   CSE documentation style for articles from, **36a**: 390, 391, 392
   evaluating, **31b**: 261–262
   MLA documentation style for articles from, **33b**: 295–299, 311
main clause, **1e**: 20. *See also* independent clause(s)
main idea, revising and, **26a**: 209–210, 211
man/mankind, as sexist usage, **12c**: 123, 435
manner, adverbs of, **6a**: 76
manuals. *See* style manuals
map, MLA documentation style for, **33b**: 308
Marx, Patricia, **26a**: 210
may. See can, may
may of, might of. See could of
maybe, may be, 435
McKibben, Bill, **1a**: 8
meaning, reading for, **24d**: 203
measurement words, agreement of verbs with, **4f**: 54
media, **4f**: 55
media, medium, 435
medium
   as part of context, **24d**: 203
   of publication, **33b**: 297, 309, 312–313, 315
memos, **29b**: 241–243
   colon use in, **16b**: 152
menu items, computer, capitalization of, **21d**: 187
message, in rhetorical situation, **24a**: 199

Index

metaphor(s), **7b**: 89, **13a**: 128, 129
method section, in research report, **36b**: 392
Mexican American, use of, **12c**: 124
might could, 435
military terms, capitalization of, **21a**: 183, 184
misplaced modifiers, **6d**: 82
mixed construction, **7c**: 89
mixed metaphor(s), **7b**: 89
MLA Handbook for Writers of Research Papers, **17a**: 155, **33**: 280
MLA style, **33**: 280
    abbreviations in, **33a**: 283, 285, 286, **33b**: 305, 306, 312, 315, 316
    for block quotations, **33a**: 288–289
    capitalization in, **16b**: 151, **21c**: 185
    for citations of poetry, drama, and sacred texts, **16b**: 152, **33a**: 285–286
    for documentation of advertisements, **33b**: 309, 319
    for documentation of art, **33b**: 318–319, 321
    for documentation of articles, **33b**: 295–299, 305, 310–311
    for documentation of books, **33b**: 299–306, 311–312
    for documentation of bulletin, **33b**: 307–308
    for documentation of cartoon or comic strip, **33b**: 308, 319
    for documentation of dictionary entry, **33b**: 306
    for documentation of digital sources, **33b**: 321–322
    for documentation of encyclopedia entry, **33b**: 316
    for documentation of government publication, **33b**: 306–307, 316, 317
    for documentation of images, **33b**: 308–309, 318–319, 321
    for documentation of legal case, **33b**: 307, 317
    for documentation of live and recorded performances, **33b**: 317–318, 319–320, 322
    for documentation of map or chart, **33b**: 308–309, 319
    for documentation of online source, **33b**: 309–319
    for documentation of pamphlet, **33b**: 307–308
    for documentation of public law, **33b**: 307, 317
    for documentation of published dissertation, **33b**: 308
    for documentation of published letter, **33b**: 308
    for documentation of republished book, **33b**: 304–305
    for documentation of sacred text, **33b**: 306, 317
    for documentation of translated book, **33b**: 304
    for in-text citations, **33a**: 280–290
    italics in, **22b**: 189
    for numbered notes, **33a**: 281
    for punctuation in citations and quotations, **33a**: 288–290
    for quotation marks, **18c**: 163–164
    sample student paper in, **28h**: 229–235, **33c**: 323–336
    for spaces following punctuation marks, **19**: 166
    spelling out of numbers in, **23e**: 194
    for title page of paper, **33c**: 323
    for works-cited list, **33a**: 280–281, **33b**: 290
modal auxiliaries, **4a**: 38, **38b**: 415–416

Modern Language Association (MLA), **33**: 280. *See also* MLA style
modifier(s), **6**: 75. *See also* adjective(s); adverb(s)
  absolute, **6b**: 80
  commas with nonessential elements used as, **15d**: 143
  comparative and superlative forms of, **6b**: 79–80
  as double negatives, **6c**: 81
  infinitive phrases as, **1d**: 17, **6a**: 78
  nouns as, **6a**: 77–78
  placement of, **6d**: 82–84, **6e**: 84–85
  prepositional phrases as, **1d**: 19, **6a**: 78
  recognizing, **6a**: 75–78
  verbal phrases as, **1d**: 16
monetary amounts, words versus numerals for, **23f**: 195
months, capitalization of, **21a**: 183–184
monument names, capitalization of, **21a**: 183
mood, **4e**: 49–51
more, **6b**: 79, 80, **37d**: 403–404
most, **6b**: 79, 80, **37d**: 403–404, 435
motion picture. *See* film
multiple audiences, **24c**: 202
multiple-choice questions, **30e**: 257
multivolume work
  APA documentation style for, **34b**: 346
  CMS documentation style for, **35a**: 373
  MLA documentation style for, **33a**: 284–285, **33b**: 305
musical work, MLA documentation style for, **33b**: 317–318, 322
must, **4a**: 39
myself. *See* herself, himself, myself, yourself

n. pag., **33b**: 311
name-year system, for CSE documentation, **36a**: 384–385, **36b**: 392, 395–396
names. *See* proper names
narration, **26a**: 211
Native American/Native People, use of, **12c**: 124–125
n.d., **33b**: 315
near, as logical operator, **30b**: 250
negation, **6c**: 81
neither . . . nor, **1a**: 9, **4f**: 52
never, **15e**: 145
New York Public Library Picture Collection Online, **30d**: 255
newsgroup, MLA documentation style for posting to, **33b**: 316
newspaper(s), **30c**: 252, **33b**: 295
  APA documentation style for article from, **34b**: 349, 350, 352
  CMS documentation style for article from, **35a**: 378
  CSE documentation style for article from, **36a**: 390, 391, 392
  evaluating, **31b**: 261–262
  MLA documentation style for article from, **33b**: 295–299, 311
  use of italics for, **22a**: 188, 189
noncount noun(s), **1a**: 3, **1d**: 14
  determiners with, **37c**: 400–402
none, agreement with, **4f**: 54
nonessential elements, **15d**: 142
  set off by commas, **1d**: 19, **15d**: 142–145
  set off by dash or pair of dashes, **19d**: 168
nonracist language, **12c**: 124–125
nonrestrictive element(s), **15d**: 142. *See also* nonessential element(s)
nonsexist language, **12c**: 122–124
nonspecific references, **37b**: 400, **37e**: 404–405
nor
  joining antecedents, **5c**: 67
  joining subjects, **4f**: 52

Index

not, as logical operator, **30b**: 250
not only . . . but also, **1a**: 9, **9d**: 106, **15e**: 145
notes
in MLA-style paper, **33a**: 281, **33c**: 334
for research paper, **32b**: 265–266
nothing like, nowhere near, 435
noun(s), **1a**: 3. *See also specific types*
agreement of singular and plural in same sentence, **4f**: 55
apostrophe use with, **17a**: 154–158
as complements, **1c**: 12, 13
determiners with, **37a–c**: 398–402
formation of plural of, **20c**: 179–180
gerund phrases as, **1d**: 15
infinitive phrases as, **1d**: 17
as modifiers, **6a**: 77–78
-s ending to, **4f**: 55
as subject of sentence, **1b**: 11
verbal phrases as, **1d**: 15
noun clause, **1e**: 21
beginning with *what,* and verb agreement, **4f**: 56
following verb for attribution, **7d**: 92
noun phrase, **1d**: 14
N.p./n.p., **33b**: 315, **34b**: 353
number, agreement in, **1d**: 14, **5c**: 66–68
number of, 435
numbers. *See also* issue number(s); page number(s); volume number(s)
in addresses, **23f**: 195
call, **30b**: 251
colons in, **16b**: 152
to express decimals and percentages, **23f**: 195
hyphens in, **20e**: 181–182
for identification, **23f**: 195
indefinite articles with, **23d**: 194
in MLA-style citations of poems, plays, and sacred texts, **33a**: 285–286
for monetary amounts, **23f**: 195
of paragraphs or sections in MLA-style citations, **33a**: 287
parentheses around, **19f**: 170
to refer to pages and divisions of books and plays, **23f**: 195
referred to as such, **17c**: 158, **22b**: 189
superscript, **33a**: 281, **35a**: 366, 367, **36a**: 385, 386
words versus, **23e**: 194

object(s)
dependent clause as, **1e**: 21
direct and indirect, **1c**: 12
of preposition, **1d**: 14, 19
pronouns as, **5b**: 61–62
object complement, **1c**: 13
objective case, **5b**: 62–63
off of, 435
omission
apostrophe marking, **17b**: 158
ellipsis points to mark, **19g**: 171–173
on account of, 435
on the other hand, 435
online catalog, **30b**: 250–251
online discussion group(s), **30e**: 256
MLA documentation style for posting to, **33b**: 315
online sources, **30d**: 253–254
APA documentation style for, **34b**: 350–355
CMS documentation style for, **35a**: 376–377
CSE documentation style for, **36a**: 390–391, 392
evaluating, **31d**: 262
of information about authors, **31a**: 260–261
MLA documentation style for, **33b**: 309–319
open questions, **30e**: 256, 257, 258

Index

operators, logical (or Boolean), **30b**: 250
opinion, distinguishing from fact, **28c**: 223
or
    joining antecedents, **5c**: 67
    joining subjects, **4f**: 52
    as logical operator, **30b**: 250
organization
    as author, in CSE style, **36a**: 389, 392
    of data in tables, **27a**: 217
    of notes, **32b**: 265–267
    of paragraphs, **26a**: 211–212
organizations' names, capitalization of, **21a**: 183
other. See another, other, the other
outline, for essay, **25c**: 206–207
ownership, apostrophe indicating, **17a**: 154–158

page numbers
    APA style for, **34a**: 337, 338
    CMS style for, **35a**: 366, 367, 374
    CSE style for, **36a**: 390, 392
    MLA style for, **33a**: 280–281, **33b**: 297, 303, 305, 312, 313
pagination, of journal, **34b**: 348
paintings, MLA documentation style for, **33b**: 318, 321
Palmer, Parker, **11c**: 117
pamphlet, MLA documentation style for, **33b**: 307
paragraph(s)
    coherence of, **26a**: 209, 211–212
    in dialogue, **18a**: 161
    drafting of, **25d**: 207–208
    examples for development of, **25d**: 208
    numbers of, in MLA-style citations, **33a**: 287
    revising of, **26a**: 209–212
    unity of, **26a**: 209, 210–211
parallelism, **9**: 103
    breaking from, **9c**: 105
    correlative conjunctions and, **9d**: 106
    to link sentences, **9c**: 105
    recognizing parallel elements, **9a**: 103
    through repetition of form, **9b**: 104
    through repetition of words, **9b**: 104
paraphrase(s)
    creating, **32d**: 270–273
    documentation with, **32e**: 274–275
    versus summary, **32d**: 273
parentheses
    around acronyms and abbreviations, **19e**: 169–170
    in APA documentation style, **34b**: 354
    with MLA-style citations, **33a**: 280–290
    for numbers or letters in list, **19f**: 170
    to set off information, **19e**: 169
parenthetical citations. *See* in-text citations
parenthetical element, set off by commas, **15d**: 144
parenthetical sentence, capitalization of first word of, **21c**: 186
participial phrase(s), **1d**: 16–17
    in absolute phrase, **1e**: 20
    as modifiers, **6a**: 78–79
    as nonessential modifier set off by commas, **15d**: 143
participle(s). *See also* past participle(s), present participle(s)
    as adjectives, **6a**: 76, **38d**: 419
    beginning sentence with, **10f**: 111
particle, **4a**: 37
parts of speech, **1a**: 2–11. *See also* adjective(s); adverb(s); conjunction(s); noun(s); preposition(s); pronoun(s); verb(s)
passed, past, 436
passive voice, **4d**: 47–48
    to avoid *his or her*, **5c**: 67
    of perfect subjunctive, **4e**: 49–50
    of prepositional verbs, **38c**: 417
past form, of verb, **4a**: 34, 35–36

Index

past participle(s), **4a**: 34, 35–36
    as adjectives, **6a**: 76, **38d**: 419
    in participial phrase, **1d**: 16–17
    in passive voice, **4d**: 47
past perfect progressive tense, **4c**: 44, **38a**: 413
past perfect tense, **4b**: 43, **38a**: 411
past progressive tense, **4b**: 41–42, **38a**: 409
past subjunctive mood, **4e**: 49
past tense(s), **4b**: 40–44
pathos (emotional appeal), **28f**: 226
per, 436
percent, percentage, 436
percentages, using numerals for, **23f**: 195
perfect progressive tenses, **4b**: 40, 43–44, **38a**: 412–414
perfect subjunctive mood, **4e**: 49
perfect tenses, **4b**: 40, 42–43, **38a**: 410–412
performance, MLA documentation style for, **33b**: 319
period (historical), capitalization of, **21a**: 183
period (punctuation mark)
    in abbreviations, **19a**: 166
    in biblical citations, **33a**: 285–286
    in divided quotations, **3c**: 33
    at end of sentence, **19a**: 166
    with interjection, **1a**: 10
    with MLA-style citations, **33a**: 289–290
    with numerals, **23f**: 196
    quotation marks with, **18c**: 163–164
    to separate act, scene, and line numbers in MLA-style citations, **33a**: 285–286, 290
    to separate clauses, **3b**: 30–31
periodic sentence, **10d**: 109
periodicals, **30c**: 252. *See also* journal(s); magazine(s); newspaper(s)
    evaluating, **31b**: 261–262
permission, to use image, **30e**: 255
person, **5b**: 61

personal communication, APA documentation style for, **34a**: 340, **34b**: 354
personal pronoun(s), **1a**: 4, **5a**: 57
perspective, prospective, 436
persuasion, emphatic order and, **26a**: 211
phenomena, phenomenon, 436
photocopies, taking notes on, **32b**: 265
photographs, **27b**: 218–220
    MLA documentation for, **33b**: 319, 321
    Web sites for, **30e**: 255
phrasal modals, **4a**: 39, **38b**: 415–416
phrasal prepositions, **1a**: 7–8
phrasal verb, **4a**: 37, **38c**: 417, 418
phrase(s), **1d**: 14. *See also* absolute phrase(s); participial phrase(s); prepositional phrase(s); transitional words or phrases
    appositive, **1d**: 19
    comma following introductory, **15b**: 139
    comma separating series of, **15c**: 141
    as modifiers, **6a**: 78
    noun, **1d**: 14, 19
    parallel, **9a**: 103
    as sentence fragments, **2b**: 25–26
    between subject and verb, **4f**: 52
    verb, **1d**: 15
    verbal, **1d**: 15–16
pie charts, **27a**: 217–218
Pinter, Rachel, **34c**: 357
plagiarism, **32d**: 271, **32e**: 274–275
planning, of essay, **25**: 204
play(s)
    MLA documentation style for, **33a**: 285–286, **33b**: 319
    pages and divisions in, **23f**: 195
plural. *See also* number, agreement in
    forming with apostrophes, **17c**: 158–159
    spelling of, **20c**: 179–180

plural verb forms, **4f**: 51
plus, 436
p.m. See a.m., p.m.
poetry
    MLA citation style for, **33a**: 285–286
    quotations from, **18b**: 162, **19g**: 173, **19h**: 173
point(s) of view, argument and, **28b**: 222, **28f**: 226
policy claim, **28e**: 224
popular magazines, **30c**: 252
positive form, of adjective or adverb, **6b**: 79
possessive case, **5a**: 58, **5b**: 63
    apostrophe for, **17a**: 154–155
possessive forms, versus contractions, **17a**: 156, **20b**: 177
possessive pronouns (possessives), **5a**: 58, **5c**: 66, **37a**: 398, **37b**: 399
    confusion of with contractions, **17a**: 156, **20b**: 177
    no apostrophe with, **17a**: 155
postal abbreviations, **23b**: 192
posting date, **30d**: 254, **32b**: 265
precede, proceed, 436
preciseness. *See* exactness
predicate, **1b**: 11. *See also* compound predicate
predicate adjective, beginning sentence with, **11b**: 115
predication, faulty, **7d**: 90
preface, MLA documentation style for, **33b**: 302–303
prefix, spelling of words with, **20c**: 178
prejudice, prejudiced, 436
preliminary bibliography. *See* working bibliography
preposition(s), **1a**: 7–8, **6a**: 78
    in collocations, **13d**: 131
    objects of, **1d**: 14, **5b**: 62
    phrasal, **1a**: 7
    repeating for parallel structure, **9b**: 104

prepositional phrase(s), **6a**: 78
    in absolute phrase, **1e**: 20
    comma following introductory, **15b**: 139
    following indefinite pronoun, **4f**: 54
    as modifiers, **6a**: 78
    with passive voice, **4d**: 47
    as sentence fragment, **2b**: 26
prepositional verb, **4a**: 37, **38c**: 417
present participle(s), **1d**: 17, **5b**: 65
    as adjectives, **6a**: 76, **38d**: 419
    in participial phrase, **1d**: 16, 17
present perfect progressive tense, **4b**: 43, **38a**: 412–413
present perfect tense, **4b**: 42–43, **38a**: 410–411
present progressive tense, **4b**: 41–42, **38a**: 408–409
present subjunctive mood, **4e**: 49
present tense(s), **4b**: 40–44
presentation, MLA documentation style for, **33b**: 319–320
pretty, 436
previewing a text, **24a**: 199–200
prewriting, **25a**: 204
primary audience, **24c**: 202
primary sources, **30a**: 249–250
principal, principle, 436
printouts, for taking notes, **32b**: 265
proceed. See precede, proceed
progressive tenses, **4b**: 41–42, 43–44, **38a**: 408–410
Project MUSE, **33b**: 312, 314
pronoun(s), **1a**: 4, **5a**: 57. *See also specific types*
    as adjectives, **5a**: 57
    agreement with antecedent of, **5c**: 66–68
    in appositives, **5b**: 63
    cases of, **5b**: 61–65
    clear references of, **5d**: 69–71
    as complements, **1c**: 13

first-person, **5b**: 61
as objects, **5b**: 62–63, 64–65
with phrasal verb, **38c**: 418
point of view and, **5b**: 61
replacing gerund phrases, **1d**: 15
second-person, **5b**: 61
as subject of sentence, **1b**: 11, **5b**: 61–62
types of, **5a**: 57–60
pronunciation, misspelling and, **20a**: 176–177
proof, in argument, **28h**: 228
proofreading, **26**: 209, **26b**: 212–213
proper names
abbreviations with, **23a**: 191
capitalization of, **21a**: 183–184
proper nouns, **1a**: 3, **21a**: 183
determiners with, **37a**: 398–399
proposition, **28h**: 228. *See also* claim, of argument
ProQuest, MLA documentation style for article from, **33b**: 312, 314
prospective. See perspective, prospective
protocol, in URL, **33b**: 309
PsycInfo, **30c**: 252
public domain, images in, **30d**: 255
public law, MLA documentation style for, **33b**: 307, 317
publication data
APA documentation style for, **34b**: 343, 345, 346
CMS documentation style for, **35a**: 370, 371
CSE documentation style for, **36a**: 388, 389, 390
MLA documentation style for, **33b**: 297, 300, 309, 312–313, 315
publication date
APA documentation style for, **34a**: 337, 338, 339–340, **34b**: 347
CMS documentation style for, **35a**: 370

CSE documentation style for, **36a**: 386, 388, 390, 392
MLA documentation style for, **33b**: 297, 309, 315
Publication Manual of the American Psychological Association, **34**: 337
published dissertation, MLA documentation style for, **33b**: 308
published letter, MLA documentation style for, **33b**: 308
publisher(s)
in APA documentation style, **34b**: 343, 345
in CMS documentation style, **35a**: 370
credibility of, **31b**: 261–262
in MLA documentation style, **33b**: 315
Puerto Rican, use of, **12c**: 125
punctuation
apostrophe as, **17a–c**: 154–159
colon as, **16b**: 151–152
comma as, **15a–g**: 138–148
dash as, **19d**: 168–169
ellipsis points as, **19g**: 171–173
exclamation point as, **19c**: 167–168
with MLA-style citations, **33a**: 289–290
parentheses as, **19e**: 169–170
period as, **19a**: 166
proofreading for, **26c**: 213
question mark as, **19b**: 167
quotation marks as, **18a–c**: 160–165
semicolon as, **16a**: 149–150
slash as, **19h**: 173
spaces with, **19**: 166
square brackets as, **19f**: 170–171
purpose (rhetorical), **24a**: 199, 200
of argument, **28**: 221, **28a**: 221–222
of business writing, **29a**: 237
of research paper, **30a**: 249

Index

qualifier(s), adverbs as, **1a**: 6
quantifiers, **37a**: 398, **37b**: 400, **37c**: 402
question(s)
    and argument, **28b**: 222
    capitalization of abbreviated, **21d**: 187
    interrogative pronouns in, **5a**: 60
    for interviews, **30e**: 256
    research, **30a**: 248
    rhetorical, **11c**: 116
    for survey, **30e**: 256–258
    for variety, **11c**: 116
    word order in, **39d**: 421–422
question mark
    with quotation marks, **18c**: 164–165, **33a**: 290
    use of, **19b**: 167
questionnaire, **30e**: 256–258
quotation(s)
    APA style for, **34a**: 337
    attributive tags set off by commas in, **15f**: 146
    block, **32d**: 270, **33a**: 288–289
    capitalization of first word of, **21c**: 185
    colon directing attention to, **16b**: 151
    divided, **3c**: 33
    ellipsis points to mark omission in, **19g**: 171–173
    quotation marks for, **18a**: 160–161
    in research papers, **32d**: 269, **32e**: 275
    square brackets for additions or alterations to, **19g**: 170–171
quotation, quote, 437
quotation marks
    with commas and periods, **18c**: 163–164
    for dialogue, **18a**: 161
    for direct quotations, **18a**: 160–161, **32d**: 270, **32e**: 275
    with question mark, exclamation point, or dash, **18c**: 164, **33a**: 290
    with semicolons and colons, **18c**: 164
    for short excerpts of poetry, **18b**: 162
    single, for quotations within quotations, **18a**: 161
    thoughts enclosed in, **18a**: 162
    for titles of short works, **18b**: 162–163, **35a**: 374

race, referring to, **12c**: 124–125
radio program, MLA documentation style for, **33b**: 318, 320–321
raise, rise, 437
ranking scale, in survey question, **30e**: 257
reading, **24**: 198, **24a**: 199–200
real, really, 437
reason/is because, mismatch of, **7d**: 91
reason why, 437
reasoning, examining author's, **32f**: 277
reasons, in argument, **28e**: 224–226, **28g**: 227
redundancy, **14a**: 133
reference book(s), **30b**: 250, 251
    APA documentation style for selection from, **34b**: 347
reference list
    APA style for, **34b**: 340–341, 343–355
    CSE style for, **36a**: 386, 392, **36b**: 392, 395–396
reflexive pronoun(s), **5a**: 58
refutation, **28f**: 226, **28g**: 227–228
regard, regarding, regards, 437
regionalisms, in academic writing, **12b**: 121
regular verbs, **4a**: 34
relation, relationship, 437
relative adverb, **1e**: 22
relative clause, **1e**: 22. *See also* adjectival clause(s)
relative pronoun(s), **5a**: 58–60, **5d**: 69
    to combine short sentences, **11a**: 113
    connection of, with verb, **7d**: 91–92
    deleting unnecessary, **14b**: 135
    in dependent clause, **1e**: 22, **8b**: 98

Index

match of, with antecedent, **4f**: 53
omission of, **1e**: 22
redundant, **14a**: 133
relevance, of sources, **31d**: 262–263
reliability
of information (evidence), **28d**: 223
of periodicals, **31b**: 261–262
of research findings, **32f**: 276–277
religion(s)
capitalization of, **21a**: 183
referring to, **12c**: 122
repetition
for emphasis, **10d**: 109
for parallelism, **9b**: 104–105
reports, congressional, MLA documentation style for, **33b**: 316
reprinted works, MLA documentation style for, **33b**: 304
republished book, MLA documentation style for, **33b**: 304
research, **30**: 248
field, **30e**: 255–258
library resources for, **30b**: 250–251, **30c**: 252
online sources for, **30d**: 253–255
rhetorical situation and, **30a**: 248–250
research paper
in APA style, **34c**: 355–365
in CMS style, **35b**: 379–383
in CSE style, **36b**: 392–396
rhetorical situation and, **32a**: 264
research question(s), **30a**: 248
resolution, congressional, MLA documentation style for, **33b**: 316
resources, of rhetorical situation, **24a**: 199
respect, in writing about differences, **12c**: 125–126
respectfully, respectively, 437
response, to sources, **32f**: 276–277
restrictive clause, **15d**: 143
results section, of research report, **36b**: 392

résumés, **29c**: 243–245
return address, **29a**: 237, 239
review, MLA documentation style for, **33b**: 299
revision, **25a**: 204, **26**: 209
of choppy sentences, **1d**: 17, **11a**: 113–114
of comma splices and fused sentences, **3b**: 30–32
of double negatives, **6c**: 81
of misplaced modifiers, **6d**: 83, **6e**: 85
of mixed metaphors, **7c**: 89
of sentence fragments, **2b**: 26, **2c**: 27
for unified and coherent paragraphs, **26a**: 209–212
rhetoric, **1**: 2
definition of, **24a**: 198
rhetorical appeal(s), **28f**: 226–227
rhetorical purpose. *See* purpose (rhetorical)
rhetorical question(s), **11c**: 116
rhetorical situation, **24a**: 198–200
adverb use and, **1a**: 6
gerund phrases and, **1d**: 16
noun choice and, **1a**: 3
and parallelism, **9c**: 105
research and, **30a**: 248–250
of research paper, **32a**: 264
sentence fragments and, **2c**: 27
and short sentences, **11a**: 114
usage and, **1**: 2
and use of commas and conjunctions in a series, **15c**: 141
and use of commas, dashes, and colons, **19e**: 169
and use of dashes and parentheses, **19f**: 170
and use of images, **30d**: 254–255
verb choice and, **1a**: 3
rise. See raise, rise
root words, **20c**: 178
run-on sentence, **3**: 29. *See also* fused sentence(s)

running head, in APA-style paper, **34c**: 356, 357

-s ending, **4f**: 55
-s form, of verbs, **4a**: 34, **38a**: 406
sacred texts, **22b**: 189
    MLA documentation style for, **16b**: 152, **33a**: 285–286, 290, **33b**: 306, 317
satellite names, italics for, **22b**: 189
scholarly books, **30b**: 250
scholarly journals, **30c**: 252, **31b**: 261
Scientific Style and Format: The CSE Manual for Authors, Editors, and Publishers, **36**: 384
scriptural references. *See* sacred texts
search, in online catalog, **30b**: 250–251
search engines (search tools), **30d**: 253, **31a**: 260
second person, **5f**: 73
second-person pronouns, **5f**: 73–74
secondary audience, **24c**: 202
secondary source(s), **30a**: 250. *See also* indirect source(s)
section, of newspaper, in MLA documentation style, **33b**: 298
section numbers, in MLA-style citations, **33a**: 287
Seitz, Anna, **28h**: 228, 229
semicolon
    in APA-style citations, **34a**: 339
    between independent clauses, **1a**: 10, **3b**: 30, **16a**: 149
    in CSE-style citations, **36a**: 385, 390
    in MLA-style citations, **33a**: 284
    quotation marks with, **18c**: 164
    separating elements that contain commas, **16a**: 150
senior citizens, use of, **12c**: 125
sensory verbs, **1c**: 13
sentence(s). *See also specific types*
    capitalization in, **21c**: 185–187
    combining, **1d**: 17, **8b**: 98, **11a**: 113–114
    conjunctions and conjunctive adverbs in, **1a**: 8
    cumulative and periodic, **10b**: 108–109
    editing of, **26b**: 212
    ending with preposition, **1a**: 7
    intentionally incomplete, **19h**: 173
    parallelism and, **9a**: 103, **9c**: 105
    period at end of, **19a**: 166
    relating parts of, **7d**: 90–92
    run-on, **3**: 29
    short, **10f**: 111, **11a**: 113–114
    subjects and predicates of, **1b**: 11–12
sentence fragment(s), **2**: 25
    dependent clauses as, **2a**: 25, **2c**: 27
    phrases as, **2b**: 25–26
    recognizing, **2a**: 25
sentence structure, and paraphrasing, **32d**: 271–273
series
    book in, MLA documentation style for, **33b**: 306
    comma separating elements in, **15c**: 141–142
    dash following, **19d**: 168
sexist language, **5c**: 67, **12c**: 122–124
sexual orientation, referring to, **12c**: 126
ship names, italics for, **22b**: 189
short note form, in CMS style, **35a**: 366, 367–368, **35b**: 382
should of. See could of
Shreeve, James, **7c**: 89
sight. See cite, site, sight
signature, on business letter, **29a**: 238, 239
Silko, Leslie Marmon, **10a**: 108
simile, **13a**: 128–129
simple future tense, **4b**: 41, **38a**: 408
simple past tense, **4b**: 41, **38a**: 407
simple predicate, **1b**: 11

simple present tense, **4b**: 40–41, **38a**: 406–407
simple sentences, combining, **11a**: 113–114
simple subject, **1b**: 11
simple tenses, **4b**: 40–41
singular number, **5c**: 67
singular verb forms, **4f**: 51
singular words, ending in *-s*, **4f**: 55
sit, set, 437
site. See cite, site, sight
slang, **12b**: 121
slash, **19h**: 173
   in URL, **33b**: 309
Smithsonian Images, **30d**: 255
so, 438
social sciences, samples of writing in, **34c**: 357–365
Solnit, Rebecca, **10a**: 108
someplace. See anyplace, everyplace, someplace
sometime, sometimes, some time, 438
sort of a. See kind of a, sort of a
sound recording, MLA documentation style for, **33b**: 317–318, 322
sources. *See also* documentation of sources; electronic sources; online sources; primary sources; secondary sources
   articles as, **30c**: 252
   books as, **30b**: 250–251
   coverage of, **32f**: 276
   evaluation of, **31a**: 259–261, **31b**: 261–262, **31c**: 262
   field research as, **30e**: 255–258
   indirect, **33a**: 285, **34b**: 340
   integrating into writing, **32d**: 268–273
   questionnaires as, **30e**: 256–258
   relevance and timeliness of, **31d**: 262, **32f**: 276
   reliability of, **32f**: 276–277
   responding to, **32f**: 276–277
   U.S. government documents as, **30d**: 254
spacecraft names, italics for, **22b**: 189
spatial order, **26a**: 211
specialized audience, **24c**: 202
specialized dictionaries, **30b**: 251
specialized reference books, **30b**: 251
specially. See especially, specially
specific references, **37b**: 399, **37c**: 401, **37e**: 404–405
specific word, definition of, **13a**: 128
speech, MLA documentation style for, **33b**: 318, 319–320
spell checker, **20**: 176
   and proofreading, **26c**: 213
spelling
   confusion of *ei* and *ie* in, **20d**: 180
   of homophones, **20b**: 177
   hyphens in, **20e**: 181–182
   of numbers, **23e**: 194–195
   of plural nouns, **20c**: 179–180
   prefixes and, **20c**: 178
   pronunciation and, **20a**: 176–177
   proofreading for, **26b**: 213
   spell checkers and, **20**: 176
   suffixes and, **20c**: 178–179
   of words from Latin or Greek, **20c**: 180
sponsors, of Web sites, **31c**: 262, **33b**: 309, 312, 315, **34b**: 354
square brackets, **19f**: 170–171, **21c**: 185, **32d**: 270, **33b**: 290, **34c**: 355, **36a**: 391
squinting modifier, **6d**: 83
Sr., **23a**: 191
state name
   in addresses, **23c**: 192
   in APA documentation style, **34b**: 344
   in CMS documentation style, **35a**: 371
statement, arguable, **28b**: 222
stationary, stationery, 438

statistics, as supporting evidence, **28e**: 225
style, clarity in, **12a**: 120–121
style manuals
    for writing in the arts and humanities, **33**: 280, **35**: 366
    for writing in the sciences, **36**: 384
    for writing in the social sciences, **34**: 337
subject (of essay), focusing into specific topic, **25b**: 205–206
subject (of sentence), **1b**: 11
    avoiding comma between verb and, **15g**: 147
    mismatch of, with verb, **7d**: 90
    noun phrase as, **1d**: 14
    pronoun as, **5b**: 61–62
    verb agreement with, **4f**: 51–56
subject complement, **1c**: 13, **4f**: 55
subject directories, **30d**: 253
subjective case, **5b**: 61–62, 63
subjunctive mood, **4e**: 49–50
submarine names, italics for, **22b**: 189
subordinating conjunction(s), **1a**: 9, **8a**: 97–98, **8b**: 99, **8c**: 100–101
    to combine short sentences, **11a**: 113
    introducing dependent clause, **1a**: 9
subordination, **8a**: 97
    avoiding faulty or excessive, **8c**: 100–101
    effective use of, **8a**: 97–98
subscription database, MLA documentation style for work from, **33b**: 312–314
subsequent mention, definite article and, **1a**: 5, **37e**: 405
substantiation claim, **28d**: 223–224
subtitles, capitalization of, **21b**: 184–185, **35a**: 370, **36a**: 389
suffix(es)
    of adjectives, **6a**: 75
    spelling and, **20c**: 178–179
    of URL, **31c**: 262

summary
    colon directing attention to, **16b**: 151
    of source material, **32d**: 273
superlative forms, of adjectives and adverbs, **6b**: 79–80, **37d**: 403–404
superlatives, double, **6b**: 80
superscript numbers, **33a**: 281, **35a**: 366, 367, **36a**: 385, 386
supposed to, used to, 438
Supreme Being, words denoting, capitalization of, **21a**: 183, 184
surveys, questions for, **30e**: 256–258
Suslin, Marianne, **33c**: 324
synonyms, as appositives, **13d**: 132

tables, **27a**: 217–218
tags, attributive. *See* attributive tags
take. See bring, take
Tebbe, Michelle, **36b**: 392, 393
technical words, audience and, **12c**: 122
television program
    APA documentation style for, **34b**: 355
    MLA documentation style for, **33b**: 318, 320–321
tense(s), **4b**: 40–44, **38a**: 406–414
    consistency of, **4c**: 44–46
    in writing about historical events or literary works, **4b**: 41
testimony, as supporting evidence, **28e**: 225
than, then, 438
that, omitting, **1e**: 21, **5a**: 59–60
that, which, who, **5a**: 58–60
the, **1a**: 5
    with adjectives, **37d**: 403
    with count nouns, **37b**: 399
    omission of, from name of periodical, **33b**: 295
    with proper nouns, **37a**: 398–399
their, there, they're, 438
theirself, theirselves, 438

then. *See* than, then
there, as expletive, **4f**: 53
   deleting, **14b**: 135
thesis, **25b**: 205
   for argument, **28b**: 222
   assessing, **25b**: 205
thesis statement, **25b**: 205
   developing, **25b**: 205–206
   placement of, **28g**: 227, 228
third person, **5b**: 61
third-person pronouns, **5b**: 61
thoughts, enclosed in quotation marks, **18b**: 162
three-em dash, **35a**: 368
time designations, abbreviation of, **23c**: 192–193
time periods, abbreviations of, **23c**: 192–193
time zones, abbreviations of, **23c**: 192–193
timeliness, of sources, **31d**: 262–263, **32f**: 276
title(s)
   of address, abbreviation of, **23a**: 191
   APA documentation style for, **34b**: 343–344
   capitalization of, **21a**: 183, 184, **21b**: 184–185
   CMS documentation style for, **35a**: 370, 374
   colon separating subtitle and, **16b**: 152
   CSE documentation style for, **36a**: 388, 389
   italics for, **22a**: 188–189
   MLA documentation style for, **33b**: 295
   previewing and, **24a**: 199
   quotation marks with, **18b**: 162–163
   set off by commas, **15d**: 144
   singular verb with, **4f**: 55

title page
   for APA-style paper, **34c**: 356, 357
   of book, **33b**: 300, **34b**: 344
   for CSE-style paper, **36b**: 393
   for MLA-style paper, **33c**: 323
to, as infinitive marker, **1d**: 17, **9b**: 104
to, too, two, 438
tone, and sentence fragments, **2c**: 27
topic
   for argument, **28b**: 222
   assessing, **25b**: 205
   focusing of, **25b**: 205–206
topic sentence, **26a**: 209
   to express main idea, **26a**: 209–210
   and paragraph unity, **26a**: 210–211
toward, towards, 438
trade books, **30b**: 250, **31b**: 261
trade magazines, **30c**: 252
transitional words or phrases, **24a**: 200
   beginning sentence with, **11b**: 115
   commas following, **15b**: 140, **16a**: 149
   to link independent clauses, **3b**: 32
   set off by commas, **15d**: 144
translated book
   APA documentation style for, **34b**: 346
   CMS documentation style for, **35a**: 373
   MLA documentation style for, **33b**: 304
try and, 439

uniform resource locator. *See* URL(s)
uninterested. See disinterested, uninterested
unique, 439
unique noun, definite article with, **1a**: 5
United States, abbreviation for, **23d**: 193
unity, of paragraphs, **26a**: 209, 210, 211
university presses, **31b**: 261
unsigned article, MLA documentation style for, **33b**: 298

URL(s), **30d**: 253, **31c**: 262, **33b**: 309–310, **34b**: 350, 352, **35a**: 377, 378, **36a**: 390
    angle brackets in, **19f**: 171, **33b**: 309, 310
U.S. Constitution, MLA documentation style for, **33a**: 286–287, **33b**: 307
U.S. Courts, **30d**: 254
U.S. Government, as source of public information, **30d**: 254
U.S. Government Printing Office, **30d**: 254
U.S. Postal Service, abbreviations of, **23b**: 192
usage, 397. *See also* word choice
    conciseness in, **14a–b**: 133–136
    exactness in, **13a–d**: 127–132
    rhetorical situation and, **1**: 2
use, utilize, 439
used to. See supposed to, used to

values, and argument, **28b**: 222, **28e**: 224
variety, in sentences, **11**: 113
    length and form and, **11a**: 113–114
    openings and, **11b**: 115–116
    type of sentence and, **11c**: 116–117
verb(s), **1a**: 3. *See also* action verb(s); auxiliary verb(s); linking verb(s); tense(s)
    agreement of subject with, **4f**: 51–56
    for attribution and their complements, **7d**: 92
    in attributive tags, **32d**: 269
    avoiding comma between subject and, **15g**: 147
    consistency in tenses of, **4c**: 44–46
    followed by gerunds and/or infinitives, **1d**: 18
    forms of, **4a**: 34–39, **38**: 406
    irregular, **4a**: 35–36
    mismatch of, with complement, **7d**: 91–92
    mismatch of, with subject, **7d**: 90
    mood and, **4e**: 49–51
    not used in progressive form, **4b**: 42
    phrasal, **4a**: 37, **38c**: 417, 418
    prepositional, **38c**: 417
    regular, **4a**: 34
    taking indirect objects, **1c**: 12
    tenses of, **4b**: 40–44, **38a**: 406–414
    voice and, **4d**: 47–48
verb phrase, **1d**: 15
verbal, **1d**: 15
verbal phrase(s), **1d**: 15–18
    as sentence fragment, **2b**: 26
    and variety in sentences, **11b**: 115
very, 439
video, online, MLA documentation style for, **33b**: 318
videocassette, CMS documentation style for, **35a**: 379
visual art. *See* art
visual elements, **27**: 217
    in combination with text, **27a–b**: 217–220
vocative, **15b**: 140
voice, **4d**: 47–48
volume number(s), **33a**: 284–285, **33b**: 296–297, **35a**: 373, 376, **36a**: 390

Walker, Alice, **13b**: 129, **25d**: 207–208
ways, 439
Web address. *See* URL(s)
Web Gallery of Art, **30e**: 255
Web log. *See* blog
Web site(s)
    APA documentation style for, **34b**: 353–354
    CSE documentation style for, **36a**: 391
    evaluation of, **31c**: 262
    MLA documentation style for, **33b**: 309–310, 311–312, 315
    sponsors of, **31c**: 262, **33b**: 309, 311, 315, **34b**: 354

Index

WebClipz, **30e**: 255
well. See good, well
what, in noun clause, and verb agreement, **4f**: 56
where, 439
where . . . at, where . . . to, 439
which. See also that, which, who
    beginning dependent clause, **8a**: 98
    versus *that,* **5a**: 59
White (or *white*), use of, **12c**: 124
who, whom, **5a**: 60, **5b**: 64–65
who, whose, whom, **5a**: 58–60
whoever, whomever, **5b**: 64–65
wire service article, MLA documentation style for, **33b**: 298
with regards to. See regard, regarding, regards
word choice, **12b**: 121–122, **13a**: 127–129, **32d**: 271
word order
    inverted, **4f**: 52–53, **10e**: 110–111
    in noun combinations, **6a**: 78
    in phrases and clauses, **39a–d**: 420–423
word processor. *See* grammar checker; spell checker
wordiness, **5d**: 71, **14a**: 133–135
words
    comma separating series of, **15c**: 141
    versus numerals, **23e**: 194–195
    placing for emphasis, **10a**: 108
    referred to as such, **22c**: 190
    repeating for emphasis, **10d**: 109–110
    repeating for parallelism, **9b**: 104
    useless, **14a**: 134
wordy expressions, replacements for, **14a**: 135
working bibliography, **32c**: 267–268
works-cited list, **33a**: 280–281, **33b**: 290–291
    sample student, **28h**: 235, **33c**: 335–336
world view, of author, **31a**: 260
would of. See could of
writer, in rhetorical situation, **24a**: 198
writing
    argumentative, **24c**: 201
    choosing subjects for, **25a**: 204
    expository, **24c**: 201
    expressive, **24c**: 201
    rhetorically, **24a**: 198–199
writing process, **25**: 204
    stages of, **25a**: 204
WWW Virtual Library, **30d**: 253

-y, changing to *i,* **20c**: 178
Yahoo, **30d**: 253
Yamamoto, Hisaye, **13b**: 129
year of publication, in APA-style citations, **34a**: 337, 340
yes-or-no questions, **30e**: 257
you, addressing reader as, **5f**: 74
your, you're, 439
yourself. See herself, himself, myself, yourself

SPECIAL TOPICS FOR MULTILINGUAL WRITERS

Chapter 1 Sentence Essentials
Article Usage 5
Number Agreement in Noun Phrases 14
Verbs Followed by Gerunds and/or Infinitives 18

Chapter 4 Verbs
Omission of Forms of Be in Other Languages 37
Phrasal Verbs 37
Phrasal Modals 39
Verbs Not Used in the Progressive Form 42

Chapter 5 Pronouns
Noun or Pronoun as Subject 62
Possessive Pronouns 66

Chapter 6 Modifiers
Noun Modifiers 78
Negation in Other Languages 81
Adverbs of Frequency 83

Chapter 8 Subordination and Coordination
Choosing Conjunctions 99

Chapter 10 Emphasis
Inverting Word Order 111

Chapter 14 Conciseness
Using Relative Pronouns 133

Chapter 19 The Period and Other Punctuation Marks
Indirect Questions 167

Chapter 23 Abbreviations, Acronyms, and Numbers
Using Articles with Abbreviations, Acronyms, or Numbers 194
Commas and Periods with Numerals 196

Chapter 37 Determiners, Nouns, and Adjectives 398

Chapter 38 Verbs and Verb Forms 406

Chapter 39 Word Order 420

CHECKLISTS

Assessing an Author's Credentials 259
Assessing a Topic 205
Creating a Questionnaire 258
Determining an Author's World View 260
Editing 212
Establishing Relevancy and Timeliness 263
Proofreading 213
Sources That Should Be Cited 275
Using Direct Quotations 270